The Life of
Muhammad

صلى الله عليه وسلم

his life based on the earliest sources

Tahia Al-Ismail

Ta-Ha Publishers Ltd.
1, Wynne Road, London, SW9 OBD.

D1321980

©1988 Ta Ha Publishers Ltd.

Reprinted: 1993, 1995, 2002, 2004

Published by:
Ta-Ha Publishers Ltd.
1 Wynne Road
London SW9 0BB
Website: http://www.taha.co.uk
Email: sales@taha.co.uk

British Library Cataloguing in Publication Data

Al-Ismail, Tahia
Life of Muhammad : his life based on the earliest source
    1. Islam, Muhammad (Prophet) - Biographies
    I. Title
    297' .63

ISBN: 0 90746-164-6

Printed in England by
Deluxe Printers Ltd.
245-a Acton Lane, Park Royal,
London NW10 7NR

In the name of Allah, most gracious and merciful!

CONTENTS

Chapter Fourteen

Chapter Fifteen

Chapter Sixteen

Chapter Seventeen

Chapter Eighteen

Notes:-

Please always invoke the following after their names are mentioned:

1. Sallalaho Alaihe Wasallam ﷺ (peace and blessings of Allah be upon him) when Prophet Muhammad's ﷺ name is mentioned.

2. Alaihis Salam عليه السلام (peace be upon him) when a Prophet's name is mentioned.

3. Radi Allaho a'nho'o رضى الله عنه (may Allah be pleased with him) when the name of any of the Companions of the Prophet Muhammad's ﷺ name is mentioned.

PREFACE

Before approaching the wonderfully exciting life of the Prophet Muhammadﷺ, may Allah bless him and grant him peace, and the account of his overwhelmingly successful struggle to fulfill against heavy odds the mission with which he was entrusted by his Lord, which was to establish the best possible human situation which has ever existed on the face of the earth, it is necessary to have an overview of the nature of prophethood and human history in general.

It is essential to see the story of Muhammadﷺ, upon him be peace and blessings, and his community not as an isolated historical event but in the context of the whole of history. If we do not do this, then a vital part of its significance will be missed and we are in danger of misunderstanding the nature of what happened during those few years which were scant in number, yet vast in effect.

To start with it is necessary to jettison the commonly held modern superstition that we have now reached the summit of a slow and laborious process of evolution during the course of which the human creature somehow emerged out of a remote bestial past into a savage prehuman and then into the supposedly "advanced", "civilized" creature of this time. As with many superstitions of this kind, quite the reverse is true.

It is true that the surface of the earth was made ready to receive the human being and that this happened in several quite clearly defined stages. What is not true is that human beings evolved out of other animal forms. The early accounts are true, the later ones fabricated. The human creature was created complete and perfect and with a totally different function to anything else in existence. Everything else was created to fulfill a limited defined role in creation in unconscious submission to the complex network of laws that governed its existence. The human being on the other hand, by virtue of faculties not present in any other creature, has the capacity to comprehend existence and therefore by extension worship the Creator of the universe. Human beings were created to recognise and worship their Creator and Lord. That is why we are here. Everything else was created to make this possible.

However it is in the nature of things that human beings are prone to lose sight of their true nature and fall prey to a short-sighted absorption in the world that surrounds them, becoming in the process virtually indistinguishable from animals and occasionally considerably worse. But because Allah is inexhaustibly merciful and desires the best for His creatures, human history was punctuated by the expression of that mercy in the form of Messengers and Prophets from Allah to His human creatures. These were men inspired directly by Allah Himself to recall their fellow men to the Truth, reminding them that worship of Allah is the cornerstone of their existence, and restoring the harmonious and just social situation which is the inevitable outcome when human beings live in tune with their real nature.

Not one human community was left without guidance and the stories of those who brought and rebrought this guidance from their Lord - a guidance which was in each case essentially the same but which varied in certain respects according to the particular time and place - follow a largely predictable pattern. They appear in communities which had either not previously received revealed guidance or who had received it in the past and then neglected it and fallen into decadence. Their call to their fellows was largely ignored and frequently ridiculed since they affirmed the power of Allah which is invisible against the power structure of their society which was all that was manifest to their people. In the face of continual opposition, frequently accompanied by physical persecution, they persevered in their task of delivering Allah's message that there is no god except Him and that justice and harmony in human society are only possible when this is recognised and put into practice, following the example of the Messenger and those who were sent before him. After a time they usually succeeded in gathering around them a larger or smaller group of followers, often from among the poor and oppressed in their society. Finally in the face of the continuing obduracy of those who opposed them, they were inspired to deliver warnings of the inevitable destruction of those who stand against the power of Allah. This was generally to little avail with the result that that society was wiped out with the exception of the Messenger and his band of followers who survived to form the basis of a new community. In its turn, this new community expanded and flourished under the guidance of the Messenger and his immediate successors until it in its turn went the way of the previous communities into decline and decadence. Then once more another Prophet would be sent and the story repeat itself again. This cycle of renewal, growth and decay occurring in conjunction with the ap-pearance of envoys from Allah mirroring as it does all natural processes, is the true picture of human history. There is no steady unbroken line of "evolution", "progress" or advancement as the modern myth makers would have us believe. Rather there have been a great number of these human cycles, some simple and unpretentious, others of unbelievable complexity and sophistication, stretching right back to he very, beginning of the human story.

The number of those sent by Allah in the course of the span of human history to bring His guidance and reimbue human communities with justice and moral parameters is certainly very great and reckoned by some traditional authorities to be 124,000. It is obviously beyond the scope of this or any work to ennumerate all of them, but it would be useful to look briefly at those who form, as it were, the landmarks of human history as we know it. This will enable us to see the story of the Prophet Muhammadﷺ in the perspective to which it belongs. These pivotal human beings around whom the whole human story revolves are Adam, Nuh (Noah), Ibrahim (Abraham), Musa (Moses), 'Isa (Jesus) and Muhammadﷺ, peace be upon all of them.

Adam was at once the first man and the first prophet and the progenitor of the whole human race. His story contains and prefigures the story of his descendants, and the Christian view of what happened completely misses the point. There was no original sin. The story of Adam is the story of the unfolding of the human creature. The important part of Adam's story is not his fall from the Garden. The important part of his story is his regaining the Mercy of Allah by means of the faculty of language and knowledge of the "Names" with which his Lord had endowed him. The fall was the necessary manifestation of the fraility of human nature, the process of veiling which must necessarily take place if guidance is to be gained. In this lies the whole secret and indeed the whole point of human existence.

Nuh (Noah) marks the end of the first people, the ancients, and at the same time his story demonstrates in an archetypal way the prophetic pattern referred to above. He called his people to the truth for nine and a half centuries and was ignored and mocked by them. In the end his guidance took the physical form of the ark and he was literally entrusted with the reintroduction of human life, and animal life for that matter, to the surface of the earth. The people of his time were totally destroyed by the Flood while he and his family and those who followed him by virtue of the guidance he received from his Lord floated free and began literally all over again.

Ibrahim (Abraham) also plays a vital part in the human story. The people of his time had once more become completely engrossed in and blinded by material existence until there was no one left practising pure worship of Allah. He was chosen by Allah and inspired directly by Him with a true understanding of the nature of the universe until he gained certain knowledge of the One God who is the Creator and Sustainer of everything in existence. He was the one chosen by Allah to bring back to the earth the knowledge of the Unity of Allah and he is the father both literally and metaphorically of all surviving true religious traditions. Literally because many of those who upheld and defended this unitarian belief, including both 'Isa and Muhammadﷺ, were his direct descendants, and metaphorically because all teachings containing the unitarian doctrine stem from his reaffirmation of Allah's unity.

The story of Musa (Moses) is again of immense significance for us as people of this time. In his confrontation with the monolithic power structure of Pharaonic Egypt there are many vital lessons for us, since the system which confronts us today is based on exactly the same principles. Much insight into our own situation can be gained from examining the details of the encounter between Musa and Fir'awn (Pharaoh). The second half of Musa's story deals with his relationship with his people, the Banu Isra'il. In the picture of these people which emerges from this story lies the key to the situation existing in the world today. The Jews' excessive love of this world, epitomised by their making of the Golden Calf and their desire for what they had left in Egypt, has stayed with them through-out their chequered history, and their tireless search for power in the world is largely responsible for the political and economic landscape of our time. It could be said that Musa marks the beginning of the modern and final age.

'Isa (Jesus) was the last of the prophets sent to the Banu Isra'il. He sealed the prophetic descent from Ibrahim in that line. His real function was to revive and purify the teaching of Musa among the Banu Isra'il but as we know, Paul, who never met the Prophet, invented the religon of Christianity based on certain personal visionary experiences. After this already perverted version of the prophethood of 'Isa had been subjected to Greek philosophical principles and Roman pragmatism, both heavily tinged with outright paganism, and had then been further compromised by unscrupulous powerbrokers, it was far removed from its original purity. It was nevertheless, despite the perversion and many changes, based on the prophetic model and because of this tenuous relationship was able to support the civilisation which grew up under the name of Christendom. At the same time because of the fundamental changes that were made to the original teaching, such as the attribution of divinity to 'Isa and the absorption of the trinitarian thesis from Greek philosophy, Christendom proved powerless in the face of the onslaught of rational materialism in the guise of humanism. Its total collapse, egged on at every stage by Jewish influence desiring power and revenge, has led to the moral and social distintegration we find ourselves in today. From the story of the Prophet 'Isa we can clearly see how the prophetic inspiration forms the basis of social renewal and how at the same time it becomes corrupted and in need of rejuvenation.

The final renewal of the prophetic tradition was the function of the last Prophet and Messenger Muhammad☀, and it is in this perspective of constantly renewed Divine guidance that we must view the story of Muhammad's☀ life. It was not an isolated event but rather the culmination of a lengthy series of constantly renewed Divine Revelations. The finality of the Prophethood of Muhammad☀ makes it, of course, relevant to us in a way that is not the case in any of the previous revelations, since by virtue of its lastness it contains the final instructions from the Creator to His creatures. Because of this, Allah has ensured that it has remained accessible to us in every detail both as regards the actual revealed Book, the Noble Qur'an, and as regards the implementation of the revelation in the life of Muhammad☀ and His Companions. For this reason study of this extraordinary story is absolutely necessary for all who want to know their place in human history and to know what a human being really is and how to become one.

INTRODUCTION

1. A SYNOPSIS OF THE HISTORY OF THE SEMITES

Between the giant continents of Asia and Africa lies the Arab Peninsula. Its inhabitants call it 'the Island of the Arabs' because it is separated from the rest of the world on all sides by natural barriers. In the west it is separated from Africa by the Red Sea, in the east it is separated by the Persian Gulf and the Gulf of Oman from the Asian mainland, in the south it is surrounded by the Gulf of Aden and the Indian Ocean, while in the north lies that most impenetrable of barriers, vast tracts of desert.

In pre-historic times the land was green and its mountain peaks were snow- capped, but with the receding of the Ice Age the land began to grow drier and drier and could no longer sustain all its people, so they emigrated from, it, in wave after wave, to more fertile climates. The first wave emigrated to Egypt through Bab al-Mandab around 4500 BC, mixed with the Hamitic population of that land and gave us the Ancient Egyptians of history. The second wave emigrated around 4000 BC to the land between the two rivers, now modern Iraq, where they found the Akkadians: They lived under Akkadian rule for some time and then formed a kingdom of their own, the kingdom of Babylon. Famous among the Babylonian kings was Hammurabi who had his laws engraved on a monument of stone.

The third wave to appear, though in fact closely akin to the Babylonians, were the Assyrians. They made their mark on history later than the Babylonians and created a military state in which science, medicine, astronomy, and mathematics flourished, as well as art and literature.

The fourth wave to emigrate were the people the Greeks called the Phoenicians. They started out around 2000 BC and were the tradesmen and mariners of the ancient world. They built great commercial cities like Sayda, Tyre, and Sidon. These mariners established colonies all along their trade routes, the most famous among them being the civilization of Carthage. They were the first people to write phonetically and carried their writing everywhere they traded in the ancient world. They taught it to the Greeks who in turn transmitted it to the Romans. Actually, the oldest phonetic writing yet found is a script found in Sinai in the North Arabian tongue; it is considered the link between the Ancient Egyptian hieroglyphics and the writing of the Phoenicians and dates from 1850 BC.

There were also other waves of emigrants such as the Aramites who settled near Babylon and established the Chaldean civilization around 2000 BC. In the south emigrants settled in Abyssinia and established the old Abyssinian Kingdom, and there were also the Hebrews who settled in Palestine.

All these people are called Semites. The word Semite is derived from Sam (or Shem), the son of Noah. It has no ethnic origin and is a term used for a group of languages found to have certain characteristics in common and to be derived from the same mother tongue or proto-language. These languages are divided into the northern and southern Semitic tongues. The southern tongues are further divided into North Arabian and South Arabian. North Arabian was the language of the people of Makka and is the tongue that has superseded other Arabian dialects to become known as Classical Arabic, the language honoured by the Qur'an. South Arabian was the language of the southern peninsular civilizations (Yemen and the lands around it) and the Abyssinian civilization.

We shall not record the wars, triumphs, and defeats of those who left the peninsula, although they were the oldest civilizations in history, because our main concern is those who remained behind. Geographically the Arabian Peninsula may be divided into two parts: north and south. Separating these two broad divisions are vast deserts, difficult to penetrate. The people of the north have remained nomadic, for the poor environment of the north does not encourage settled civilization, but forces the inhabitants to be constantly on the move in search of water and pasture. Those of the south were able to establish a succession of advanced civilizations whose ruins of citadels, dams, monuments, and palaces twenty stories high, bear witness to the prosperity and ability of the people who erected them. It was a purely Arab phenomenon with no external influences and had its own laws, codes, constitution, and customs. They had the knowledge and ability to control the heavy rainfall of those parts and store the water by means of dams, barrages, and reservoirs.

These southern Arabs had trade relations with Syria, Iraq, and Egypt. Their caravans crossed the desert bringing spices, incense, gum, and myrrh from India and returned carrying the goods that these lands produced. The first important South Arabian kingdom was that of the Mainians around 1200 BC. It controlled the trade routes and built caravanserais along these routes for their use.

The Mainians were succeeded by the Sabaeans who continued the on-flow of Arab culture and who inherited the trade routes of the Maanians along with their civilization. It was one of the queens of this kingdom, the Queen of Saba (Sheba), who went to visit Solomon. Several causes contributed to the weakening and final ruin of the Sabaean civilization; among them were their luxurious life-style and the neglect of their dams and barrages after they had grown wealthy from trade. In 270 BC Ptolemy the Second built a fleet that could ply the Red Sea which prior to this had been considered unnavigable. This contributed to their decline, since they had previously monopolized trade in the area. Their barrages had been neglected for some time and, when the Dam of Marib broke, the land was flooded and became mostly wasteland, forcing the people to emigrate northwards. Some went to the north of the peninsula in the vicinity of Madina, while others moved right up to the borders of Syria and Iraq where they formed new kingdoms.

The Sabaeans deified the heavenly bodies and worshipped a trinity. The moon, which they called Wudd, was their greatest god; the sun was its consort; and a son born of this union, one of the stars, possibly Venus or Jupiter, was the third. It was the Sabaeans, penetrating into the north via their trade routes who introduced the worship of the stars to the Arabs of the north.

During the first century after Christ, Judaism, then Christianity made their appearance in the land and vied for supremacy over it. This conflict brought in the two great powers that dominated the world at that time, the Roman and the Persian Empires. The Himyarite king of Yemen sought the assistance of the Persian Chosroes against his Abyssinian enemies who had overrun his land. In consequence, Yemen remained under Persian influence until the arrival of Islam in the country.

In the north two Arab states emerged. The first was Petra, a city state built by the Nabataeans out of solid rock. This civilization flourished from 300 BC to 106 CE when the Jewish uprising caused the Roman emperor Titus to destroy the city and annex the land to the Roman Empire.

Another Arab civilization arose soon after Petra's demise in the oasis of Palmyra. It was a trade centre like Petra, powerful and prosperous, and it took a neutral stance in the wars between the Romans and the Persians. It possessed fertile lands and clear, crystalline waters. In 42 BC, Mark antony tried to annex it but failed and when in 260 CE the Emperor Gallienus was captured by the Parthians who had invaded Syria, it was the Chieftain of Palmyra who rescued the Emperor, retrieved Syria, and followed the Parthians right up to their capital, Al-Madain.

In the protracted struggle between the Persians and the Romans, the Chieftain sided with the Romans and was granted the title of Dux Orientalis or Emperor of the East. He had power over Asia Minor, Egypt, Syria, and North Arabia. After the death of this Chief, his widow ruled on behalf of her son who was a minor. When the Romans saw her generals reach as far as Alexandria and Ankara, they revoked their treaty with this state, destroyed the city, and carried the proud Arab queen in chains to Rome. Her story has entered into Arabic verse and legend as the story of Al-Zawbae or in Latin Zenobia.

After the destruction of their civilization, the Nabataeans were merged among the Arab tribes of the north. The Arabs tended to build their cities further from the border and from the influence of foreign powers.

2. MAKKA AND THE KA'BA

About eighty kilometres from the coast in the eastern mountain chain, surrounded by mountains on all sides except for three narrow passes , stood Makka. It was on the caravan route of the tribes, but, having no water or plant life, was deserted except for an occasional passer-by. In this secluded place where not even a fly could live, Ibrahim was ordered to leave Hajar, his Egyptian wife and her young son, Isma'il, for in this valley where nothing could grow, Allah wanted men to go for the express purpose of worship and wanted the progeny of Ibrahim to cater to the needs of the worshipers.

When the provisions Ibrahim had left them ran out, Hajar looked around for a way of obtaining food and water, for her little son was beginning to suffer from thirst. She could find nothing at all,so she went back and forth, scanning the horizon, hurrying between two prominences called Al-Safa and Al-Marwa in order to see as far as possible. Back and forth she went seven times, and when she returned to her son to see how he fared,the child was kicking the earth with his foot, and from under his foot water gushed out.

Hajar remained with her son in this secluded valley surrounded by mountains. She began to give the passing tribes water in exchange for whatever she needed. The first tribe to be attracted to the waters of Zamzam were Banu Jurhum. Hajar allowed them to settle near her on condition that the water remained in her custody. When Isma'il grew up, he married a girl from this tribe.

On his travels, Ibrahim used to visit his son occasionally. On one of these visits, he was instructed to build a house of worship for Allah that would be a sanctuary for the worshipper, and so together Ibrahim and Isma'il built the first house for the worship of Allah on earth. They taught the people of those parts to worship one deity, Allah alone, unswervingly. To this day Muslims pray in the place where Ibrahim instructed the people at the Ka'ba, or the Ancient House, as it is called.

With the passage of the centuries, the Makkans grew rich and influential through trade. They began to live a life of luxury and neglected to draw out enough water from Zamzam (the name of Hajar's spring) to irrigate the land or attend to their stock. They also began to forget the teaching of Ibrahim and Isma'il and, when Zamzam started to dry up, they began to grow weaker. One of their great men, Al-Mudad ibn 'Amr of Jurhum, tried to warn them of the consequences but they would not listen to him. He knew that power would soon go out of their hands, so he took two gold statues in the form of gazelles and the money that was inside the Ka'ba, lowered them deep down into the well of Zamzam and covered it so that no one would know the place. Soon after he left Makka with the descendants of Isma'il.

The tribe of Khuza'a, who had vied with Banu Jurhum for the honour of guarding the Sacred House, ousted them out and took over. They passed on the honorary offices associated with the guardianship for generation after generation, and it is believed that they had a hand in introducing idol worship in Makka. The Sabaeans who were star worshippers also influenced the Makkans in this.

Power remained in the hands of the Khuza'a until the time of Qusayy ibn Kilab, the great great great great grandfather of the Prophet Muhammad⚜, may Allah bless him and grant him peace. He was known among his people for his good sense and judgment, and his trade prospered and his sons increased. The tribe of Quraysh, the descendants of Isma'il, rallied around him. The honorary offices of the Ka'ba were still in the hands of Khuza'a. Qusayy had married a girl from this tribe and before her father died he had entrusted the keys of the Ka'ba to her, but being a woman, she apologized and handed them to another man from her tribe called Abu Ghubshan. Abu Ghubshan was a man who liked to drink and one day, possibily when intoxicated, he sold the keys of the Ka'ba to Qusayy for a chalice of wine. When Khuza'a saw that the honorary offices of the Ka'ba had fallen into the hands of Qusayy, they decided to fight him for them, but all the Makkans, who held Qusayy in high esteem, rallied to him against Khuza'a and drove them out of Makka and made Qusayy their king. Then all the offices of catering to the pilgrims, held to be the greatest of honours, became Qusayy's by right.

He was the first to make hospitality to the pilgrims the duty of the Makkans. Thus he addressed his people: 'People of Quraysh, you are the neighbours of Allah and the people of His house and His holy precincts. The pilgrims are the guests of Allah, the visitors to His House. Of all guests they are the most worthy of your hospitality, so prepare food and drink for them on the days of pilgrimage until they leave the land.'

In those days when there were no hotels and few shops, the traveller relied solely on the hospitality of the people of the land. Hospitality to the stranger was one of the sacred duties, indeed the supreme duty, of the Arabs who lived in an environment where a man could perish from thirst and hunger if help was not forthcoming. After Qusayy, the honorary offices of catering to the pilgrims were divided among his sons, then their progeny. Hashim was the most capable of his brothers and, like his grandfather Qusayy, he called the Makkans to prepare food and drink for the pilgrims. He felt responsible for the people of Makka and in years of scarcity he used to feed and care for the needy. On a trip to Madina (then known as Yathrib) he met a striking woman who was managing her trade and taking charge of her dependants. He admired her greatly and asked for her hand in marriage. Knowing his position among his people, she accepted. Her name was Salma and she was from the tribe of Al-Khazraj. This union produced a child whose maternal uncles were Madinans and whose paternal uncles were Makkans; his name was Shayba.

3. 'ABDU'L-MUTTALIB

Hashim died on one of his trading trips to Gaza. His brother, Al-

Muttalib, became the head of the tribe. One day he thought of his little nephew living with his mother in Yathrib and decided that it was time that he should live with his father's people in Makka. So he went to Yathrib and brought the lad back with him to Makka. People, seeing him approaching with a young boy riding behind him, thought it was a new slave he had bought and called the lad, 'Abdu'l-Muttalib or slave of Al-Muttalib. When they learnt that this was his nephew, the son of Hashim, they still held to that first name, continuing to call him 'Abdu'l-Muttalib instead of Shayba.

Al-Muttalib wanted to give his nephew the money that belonged to Hashim, his father, but another uncle, Nawfal, had seized it and would not allow him to have it. When 'Abdu'l-Muttalib grew older, he called his uncles from Yathrib to his aid. Eighty horsemen came to Makka to assist their young cousin so that Nawfal was forced to deliver his father's money to him. 'Abdu'l-Muttalib inherited the positions that his father Hashim used to occupy, which were welcoming the pilgrims and giving them water. But finding water for the pilgrims was a task of great hardship for him as he had only one son to aid him and it needed many men to carry the water and bring it from distant places. All the Makkans remembered nostalgically the water source of Zamzam but 'Abdu'l-Muttalib thought of it as a cherished dream; it would make his task of providing the pilgrims with water so much easier. In his sleep he would dream over and over again of this well and of someone telling him to re-open it. He kept looking for it until at last he was inspired to search between two of the idols placed near the Ka'ba. There he dug and water gushed out. He kept on digging until the two golden gazelles, the money, and the swords of his ancestor Mudad were revealed.

Quraysh wanted him to share the treasure with them but he refused. Then re-considering, he offered to draw lots with them for it. The Makkans used to draw lots by writing their names on arrows, then casting them inside the Ka'ba in a particular place so that the decision would be that of their gods. According to this lottery, 'Abdu'l-Muttalib was to keep the swords, and the statues were to go to the Ka'ba. 'Abdu'l-Muttalib placed the gazelles at the door of the Ka'ba and he also placed the swords there as a decoration.

'Abdu'l-Muttalib was the immediate grandfather of Muhammad ﷺ. Thousands of years earlier, Ibrahim had prayed to Allah that He might provide for those of his descendants that remained in the desolate valley of Makka and to send them a

Messenger, from amongst themselves, to guide them to the straight way. Consequently, Muhammadﷺ used to say, 'I came in answer to the prayer of my grandfather Ibrahim.'

CHAPTER ONE

ON THE EVE OF ISLAM

Towards the middle of the sixth century CE the world had grown dark and ugly with superstitions which were clogging its spiritual life. Greed and tyranny had warped its moral being, and oppression had stifled the majority of its people. Peoples who had once been free and productive, the oldest civilizations in the world, the Assyrians, the Phoenicians, and the Egyptians, lay writhing under the paw of the Roman wolf, while the Babylonians, suffering from equally tyrannical Persian dominion, were only allowed a bare subsistence while all the wealth of their land, the fertile land between the two rivers, went to fill the coffers of the Persian emperors and their vassals. In the Roman Empire the privileged, who owned many slaves, were immensely rich and exempted from taxes while the native inhabitants of the lands they dominated had to carry all the burdens of taxation; they were overtaxed both financially and physically. In India people fared no better: there was a cruel caste system that divided people into four classes. The Brahmans had all the privileges and the untouchables all the sufferings and humiliations.

The Arabs whose land was situated between the Persian and the Roman empires, were in a deplorable state. Their border tribes were often under Persian or Roman rule and the whole land lived in fear of invasion by the Roman Empire or one of its powerful war lords. Their religion, after having been the purest monotheism, the religion of the patriarch Ibrahim, had been corrupted by generation after generation of associations with other peoples; with the Sabaeans who worshipped the stars, or the Persians who worshipped fire, as well as people who held other strange beliefs with which the world at that time was replete. They made offerings to stone idols and buried their daughters alive.

The Romans were Christians who considered themselves the masters of the world and wanted all the peoples under their dominion to follow their particular brand of Christianity. When the Copts of Egypt would not follow them but adhered to their own beliefs which differed slightly in dogma from the Romans, the Romans inflicted terrible punishments on them, cutting off their hands and feet and meting out slow death by melting them on candles because they would not give up their Monophysite Christianity.

Throughout history when man had forgotten the noble source of his inner life and looked greedily towards the world and its wealth, a messenger was sent by Allah to show him the way he had lost or remind him of the precepts he had forgotten or neglected. But for a long time no sign nor word from Allah had been heard. That age saw the lowest point that human thought and activities had so far descended to, the worst that man had ever become. Before this, messengers had come in regular succession, but for six hundred years no message had come from on high, no ray of hope or mercy touched the earth from the source of all hope and mercy. There was absolute silence.

In that cruel and corrupt age, women, children, and slaves had few rights in principle and even less in practice. They lived in pain and despair, day after day, until one day Allah took pity upon their plight and sent the greatest of all prophets, a messenger who used to pray, 'Thou art the Lord of the down-trodden and Thou art my Lord.'

A noble and glorious light permeated the heavens from east to west; from the confines of China to the shores of Morocco, from the Atlantic to the Pacific, an arc of light encompassed the world - a light that brought justice and knowledge to mankind, for it was a light that descended through the mercy of the Most Merciful. Allah tells His chosen prophet in the Qur'an, 'And We have not sent you except out of mercy to mankind.' But softly, let us begin the noble story from the beginning.

CHAPTER TWO

2.1 'Abdullah, the Prophet's Father'

Abdu'l-Muttalib had almost everything; he had health, wealth, and power and was respected by his tribe, but he had one source of sadness, he had only one son. At a time when the Arabs prided themselves on their numerous offspring, he had just one child and he needed many, many sons to help him in the noble office he had been entrusted with. This office was to provide the pilgrims who came to visit the Ka'ba every year with water to drink. It was an honorary office but it meant much to him. Over the honorary offices concerning the maintenance of the Ancient House and catering to its pilgrims so many struggles had taken place and so many pacts and covenants had been made. 'Abdu'l-Muttalib vowed that, if he should have ten sons and they all reached manhood, he would sacrifice one of them to the gods of the Ka'ba.

The years went by, 'Abdu'l-Muttalib became head of his tribe, revered and obeyed by all, and he had eleven sons. He realized that he should fulfill his vow to the gods of the Ka'ba but which of his dearly beloved sons should he sacrifice? All were dear to him, particularly 'Abdullah, the youngest, who had grown up to be a very fine young man, the handsomest that Quraysh could boast of. 'Abdu'l-Muttalib decided to draw lots for he could not part willingly with any of them. The name of 'Abdullah came out -'Abdullah, the youngest and the one closest to his heart. 'Abdu'l-Muttalib felt himself bound to fulfill his vow no matter how painful it would be to him, but all the people of Quraysh protested. Would he sacrifice a young man of such great promise, the pride and joy of Quraysh? 'Abdu'l-Muttalib did not know how to extricate himself from this terrible vow. Then some of the wise men in Makka counselled him to consult a renowned soothsayer in Al-Ta'if.

'Abdu'l-Muttalib went to see her with a group of the nobles of Makka. She asked them what the ransom of a man in their land was and they answered that it was ten camels. She told them to draw lots (these lots were drawn by the priests of their gods) between the name of 'Abdullah and ten camels. If the name of 'Abdullah came out again, they were to increase the number of camels each time by ten, until the gods were appeased.

In hope and fear 'Abdu'l-Muttalib returned to Makka. He went to the Ka'ba where they kept the arrows for drawing lots and asked to have lots drawn between 'Abdullah and ten camels. Ten times in succession did the name of 'Abdullah appear, and each time 'Abdu'l-Muttalib increased the number of camels by ten until they became a hundred camels. The tenth time the arrow of the camels appeared and not 'Abdullah's name. To make sure that the gods were truly appeased, 'Abdu'l-Muttalib drew lots three more times, and each time it was the camels' arrow that appeared. Thus he was satisfied that he was exonerated from his terrible vow and now he could keep his beloved young son.

When 'Abdullah reached twenty-four years old his father decided it was time for him to get married, so he chose for him Amina, the daughter of the chief of Banu Zuhra, a bride worthy of being the wife of the son of the Head of Quraysh and ruler of all Makka. After the wedding, 'Abdullah remained with his bride for three days in her father's house, according to the custom of the Arabs. Then he took her to his own home among the houses of Banu 'Abdu'l-Muttalib.

The Makkans built their houses according to their rank. The higher the rank, the closer the house was to the Ka'ba. The houses of Banu 'Abdu'l-Muttalib were the closest to the Ancient House for they were the most noble of Quraysh and gave precedence to no one. Those of lesser rank had houses further removed from the Ka'ba, while slaves and clients had houses still further off. People of ill repute had houses very far removed from the Ka'ba on the outskirts of the city.

'Abdullah did not remain long with his bride, but left to go on a trading expedition to Gaza in the north as most ambitious young men did. The Makkans lived chiefly by trade and had two annual journeys, one in the summer and another in the winter. The summer journey took their merchandise northwards to Al-Sham (modern Palestine, Syria, Lebanon, Jordan) and the winter journey took their merchandise southwards to the Yemen. Makka formed the meeting point between east and west, the link between the Roman empire and merchandise coming from India and China.

On his way back from the summer journey, 'Abdullah stopped at Yathrib (Madina) to visit his maternal uncles, Banu Najar. There he fell ill and the caravan had to leave without him. On its return to Makka, they reported his illness to his father who sent his elder brother, Al-Harith, to bring him back.

Arriving in Yathrib, Al-Harith found that 'Abdullah had died one month after the caravan had left and had been buried there. Al-Harith returned to bring the tragic news to his aged father and the waiting bride. Amina was with child, a child that would never see its father's face.

2.2 The Year of the Elephant

'Abdu'l-Muttalib had his private grief, but a general grief was soon to befall all Makka because from the south a great army was approaching it. It was led by Abraha, the Abyssinian, who with his troops had travelled hundreds of miles in order to pull down the Ancient House. Abraha had invaded Yemen and subjugated its fierce highland people to his rule. On this expedition, however, he was not interested in the land for it was mostly desert, but only in one spot, Makka, and one place, the Ka'ba.

The Ancient House of Ibrahim and Isma'il had great repute among the Arabs. They travelled hundreds of miles from remote parts of the peninsula to visit it. Simple and austere, it had a strange spiritual beauty that drew men towards it. The church Abraha had built at great cost, using the finest marble, gold, and ivory could not compete with it, therefore the Ancient House had to be pulled down.

When the Arabs heard of this, two tribes, together with volunteers from other tribes, tried to block his way but were defeated. Against Abraha's great army, his war elephants, and javelin throwers they did not stand a chance. Abraha travelled on towards Makka using an Arab captive as a guide.

As he approached Makka, the Makkans rose to fight for their beloved Ka'ba, the first house built on earth for the worship of Allah. But they soon learnt that they were no match for Abraha and his great host of trained soldiers with their war elephants.

Abraha sent a messenger to 'Abdu'l-Muttalib, the ruler of Makka, saying that he had not come to fight them but only to pull down the Ancient House. If they offered him no resistance, he would spare their lives. 'Abdu'l-Muttalib with a delegation of Makkans went to see Abraha, hoping that through negotiations they would be able to save the Ancient House.

Abraha, impressed by the dignity and distinguished air of 'Abdu'l-Muttalib, offered to return the latter's camels that his soldiers had taken, but he would not hear of his request that the

Ka'ba be spared. 'AbdulMuttalib and the delegation offered to give him one-third of the wealth of the Tihama region but Abraha refused. He had come from far richer lands and was not interested in taking money and returning; he had come to pull down the Ancient house. This House had a strange attraction to men and so long as it remained his church did not have a chance of stirring their hearts.

Exhausted and with a heavy heart, 'Abdu'l-Muttalib returned to tell the people of Makka that all was lost and to flee for their lives to the mountain heights. When questioned what would become of the Ancient House, he said, 'The Ka'ba has Allah[1] to protect it.'

After seeing the women and children conveyed to the safety of the mountains, 'Abdu'l-Muttalib took the men and went to pray by the Ancient House for the last time. They prayed with intense fervour, begging Allah to protect His House. 'Abdu'l-Muttalib kept clinging to the door of the Ka'ba and praying until the last moment.

Abraha directed his great lead elephant towards Makka. It would have been able to break down the walls of the Ka'ba in no time. The elephant walked until it reached the boundaries of the Sacred City and then stopped as if turned into stone. Abraha and his soldiers did all they could to make it move but it would not budge, so they directed it towards Al-Sham. The elephant now began to move so they directed it towards the Ka'ba again and again the elephant became like a granite boulder.

Suddenly in the sky there appeared birds in large numbers. Great flocks of birds covered the horizon like enormous black clouds. They swooped down upon Abraha and his men and kept pelting them with small sharp stones until many were stoned to death. Only a few were able to flee.

After the birds had done their work, Abraha and the remnants of his crushed army headed back towards Yemen where he died of shock and exhaustion.

Years later these holy verses from the Qur'an were to remind the Makkans, many of whom were old enough to remember, of the incident.

Have you not seen what your Lord did to the people of the elephant?

---

[1]. The name Allah had been used in the Arabic language long before the time of Muhammad☀, since the days of Ibrahim and Ismai'l who worshipped Allah alone. With the passage of time and the influence of other peoples the Arabs began to worship idols, but nominally they still admitted the existence of Allah, and said these were lesser gods.

Did He not make their cunning go astray?
And set upon them birds in great hordes
to pelt them with stones of hard mud,
making them like eaten-up leaves. (105:1-5)

They are both a warning that those who oppose Allah will come to grief and a reminder of the goodness of Allah to them in how He saved the Ancient House for them, when they stood unable to do anything.

After this miraculous incident the fame of the Ka'ba spread wider, its attraction increased, and the Arabs came from all parts of the peninsula to visit the Sacred House. The total rout of the army that had come to destroy it served only to enhance its sanctity. It was the year 570 CE, and of such tremendous importance to the Arabs that they called it 'The Year of the Elephant.'

2.3 The Birth of Muhammadﷺ

While people rejoiced at the great victory that Allah had bestowed on them, 'Abdu'l-Muttalib received some good news. Amina sent word that a grandson had been born to him. Great was the old man's joy when he came and took the child of his beloved son into his arms. He carried it straight to the Ka'ba and, after going around it seven times with the child, he said, 'Blessed child, I will call thee Muhammadﷺ. The birth of this child was ushered in by glory and triumph for the Ancient House, blessed is he!'

When his people asked him why he had named the child Muhammadﷺ, preferring it to the names of his forefathers, he said, 'Because I want him to be praised in the heavens of Allah above and on the earth of his people.' The name Muhammadﷺ means, 'He to whom praise is due.'

On the seventh day after Muhammadﷺ's birth his grandfather gave a great feast according to the custom of the Arabs.

2.4 The Wet-nurses

Now they waited for the wet-nurses to come down from the mountains for the air of Makka, cooped up in the middle of rocky mountains, was considered unhealthy for babies. It was the custom of Arab ladies of noble birth to give their babies to wet-nurses who lived in the envigorating desert air. Some of these tribes who lived in the desert were famous as wet-nurses, among them Banu Sa'd.

While waiting for their arrival, Amina gave the baby to

Thuwayba, a slave of Abu Jahl, Muhammad ﷺ's kinsman, to nurse. She nursed him only a few days, but he was very good to her all her life, and when she died, he asked about her son who had passed away before her.

The wet-nurses came; they were from Banu Sa'd and they selected the babies who had fathers and passed by the fatherless for they counted on being noticed and generously rewarded by the fathers. Muhammad ﷺ was left without a wet-nurse, but just as the tribe was about to leave, Halima, the daughter of Abu Dhu'ayb said to her husband, 'I hate to return with my companions without a child. I shall go and take that fatherless infant.'

'Yes, do so,' said her husband, 'perhaps Allah will cause him to be a blessing for us.'

Halima had not been given an infant at first because she was less well off than the rest. She relates that after she took Muhammad ﷺ everything seemed to prosper. Her goats increased in number and yielded more milk, her chickens grew fat and increased, and people used to tell their shepherds, 'See where Halima's sheep graze and let our sheep graze in the same pasture.'

2.5 Muhammad ﷺ in the Desert

One day, when Muhammad ﷺ was three years old, his foster brother went to Halima crying, 'Mother, mother, two men in white are holding my Qurayshi brother!'

Halima relates, 'I ran to him, and his foster father ran to him. We found him standing there looking pale. I asked him, "What is the matter, my son?" And he said, "Two men in white came and laid me on my back. They took out something from my inside and left."'

Halima and her husband did not know what to think, but the incident passed, and the child was well and rapidly grew bigger and stronger.

He remained in the desert, breathing the pure desert air, and learning the pure tongue of the desert Arabs until he was five years old. In later years, joking, he used to tell his friends, 'I am the purest Arab among you. I am a Qurayshi and I was nursed by Banu Sa'd.'

When Muhammad ﷺ was about five years old, Halima met some men from Abyssinia who seemed very much interested in the child and kept asking her questions about him. Then they said, 'This child will be an individual of great importance; we will take him to our country with us. We have heard about him before.' Halima could barely escape with Muhammad, then she returned him to his mother in Makka, judging that he would be safer there.

Halima and her people remained a happy memory to Muhammad. When he grew up, he used to shower her with gifts whenever she came to visit him. Once, after his marriage to Khadija, there was a year of scarcity in the mountains, so when Halima came to visit him she returned with camels carrying water and food, and forty head of sheep.

2.6 Return to Makka

When he was returned to Makka, his grandfather, now a venerable old man, supported him handsomely and lavished upon him love and care. This great old man used to have a couch placed for himself in the shade of the Ka'ba and all his sons used to come and sit on the ground around it as a sign of respect. But when Muhammad came, his grandfather made him sit on the couch beside him, patted him on the shoulder and showed him such marked affection that no one ever suggested that he ought to sit below with his uncles.

One day, when Muhammad was about six years old, his mother decided to take him with her to visit his father's uncles, Banu Najjar of Yathrib. She took Umm Ayman, the only slave his father had left, with them. When they arrived in Yathrib, she showed him where his father had been before them and where he was buried.

After a visit of one month in Yathrib, they mounted their camels and set out for Makka. On the way, in a village called Al-Abwa, Amina fell ill and died. She was buried there, a few miles away from where Muhammad's father was buried.

After his mother, the only parent he had known, was buried, Muhammad returned, a sad, small figure, with the slave Umm Ayman to Makka. This endeared him yet more to his aged grandfather, and made the great man, who showed no sign of affection for his grown sons, tender and loving in the treatment of this small, lonely figure, but, as if fate insisted on making bereavement and grief the little boy's portion, his grandfather died when he was eight years old. Muhammad was inconsolable, following his grandfather's bier sobbing all the way.

2.7 Under Abu Talib's Care

The death of 'Abdul-Muttalib was a blow to all Banu Hashim for none among his sons could take his place, none of Quraysh had his qualities of mind and character, his judgment, or his strength, and no man was held in such high esteem by the Arabs. Before his death 'Abdu'l-Muttalib had entrusted his son, Abu Talib, with the care of Muhammadﷺ. Abu Talib was not the eldest of his sons nor was he the wealthiest - Al-'Abbas being by far the richest. However, Abu Talib was the noblest in character, honoured and respected by all Quraysh.

Abu Talib began to like Muhammadﷺ and then to love him as if he were his own son, with a fierce loyalty, so that in later years, the years of trial and hardship, he stood firm like a mountain to protect Muhammadﷺ from the wrath of Quraysh. The boy had a most loving and lovable disposition, he was very kind-hearted, sensitive, and compassionate towards the suffering of others. He was good, so very good that he soon earned among his youthful companions the title of 'Al-Arvin' which means in Arabic 'the truthful, the sincere, the trustworthy', and he was worthy of this epithet which clung to him all his life, for Muhammadﷺ would never tell a lie. Even in very adverse circumstances, he would never speak anything but the truth.

2.8 Journey to Al-Sham

When Muhammadﷺ was around twelve years old, Abu Talib decided to go on a trading expedition to Al-Sham. He did not think of taking the young boy with him for the journey was long, the desert route rough, with little water and full of dangers. But Muhammadﷺ yearned to go with. his uncle whom he had grown to love as a father. Abu Talib hesitated but when he saw how the boy hated to be parted from him, he said, 'By Allah, I'll never leave you behind.'

On the way, approaching Al-Sham, the caravan of Quraysh passed by the cell of a Christian hermit, Bahira, who lived and worshipped in a secluded spot in the desert. It was not the first time that the caravans of Quraysh had passed by his cell. He had never taken any notice of them before, but this time he prepared food for them and insisted that they all partake of his food. He watched them, carefully scanning each face, then he cried, 'But I insisted that none of you refuse my hospitality.' They assured him that they were all present, but he repeated his words. They replied that they were all there except a little boy who was playing by the camels. Bahira sent them to bring him. When Muhammadﷺ appeared, the monk asked whose son he was.

18

'Mine,' said Abu Talib protectively.

'No, you are not telling the truth,' replied Bahira.

'Very well, my brother's child. His father has passed away,' said Abu Talib.

'Ah, this is as it should be,' said the monk, 'This boy should have no father.' Then he began to urge Muhammadﷺ to answer his questions.

'By Al-Lat and Al-'Uzza,' he began. These were the two famous idols of Quraysh.

Muhammadﷺ stopped him, saying, 'Ask what you will, but do not mention them to me. I loathe them.' This Bahira noted was also as it should be. He asked some more questions, then he saw that between the boy's shoulder-blades there was a birthmark which those who knew about such matters, recognized as the seal of prophethood. Bahira told his uncle that this child would be of very great importance in the years to come and advised him not to go further inland with him lest the Jews recognize in him the same marks he had recognized and harm the boy. Muhammadﷺ returned safely to Makka with Abu Talib and did not make any more journeys to Al-Sham.

CHAPTER THREE

3.1 Life with His Uncle

Muhammadﷺ continued to live with his uncle and to do the jobs that the young men of Makka used to do. When the Sacred Months arrived, the months when the Arabs did not fight and made the Pilgrimmage to the Ka'ba, he either remained with his uncle in Makka or visited the neighbouring fairs of 'Ukaz and Dhu'l-Majaz. In these fairs there were wares of all kinds for sale as well as declamations of poetry and oratory. The Arabs were poets by nature and poetry was in their blood. Whenever they felt great emotion they would speak in verse. They composed poems about everything: their history, their lineage, their clans, their loves, and their enemies. Verse was the language of their hearts. Each year there was a prize at the fair for the very best poems. They were hung on the walls for all to see and read and they became classics. Many critics consider this the golden age of Arabic poetry.

Muhammadﷺ listened, saw, admired but also criticised.

3.2 The Covenant of Redress (Al-Fudul)

It so happened that a man from one of the clans of Quraysh killed a man from the tribe of Hawazin out of jealousy, for the latter had acquired the job of guide to a caravan of Al-Mundhir which the man from Quraysh had coveted. The result was a war between Quraysh and Hawazin which lasted for four years. In this war Muhammadﷺ used to collect the arrows for his uncles to use again and perhaps, in the last year or so, he was old enough to take part in battle.

After this war Quraysh felt that it was their man who had been in the wrong and that, if they continued to support his claim, their prestige among the tribes would suffer and their unrivalled position as keepers of the Ancient House would be challenged. They were the keepers of the House of Allah and as such it was their duty, more than any other tribe, to be absolutely fair and impartial even against their own. They knew that had 'Abdu'l-Muttalib been alive this would not have happened. No man now held the position of high esteem and authority that 'Abdu'l-Muttalib had enjoyed, so they decided to make a covenant that would given them jointly the authority he had enjoyed. The different branches of Quraysh made a covenant together to be on the side of the wronged party until he obtained redress. Muhammadﷺ, young as he was, was delighted by this covenant. It was in accord with his upright nature and he used to remember it fondly, saying, 'It was a covenant I attended at the house of Jud'an and, if I had been called to fight to uphold it, I would have answered the call.'

3.3 The Life of Makka

War between the tribes did not take up more than a few days of every year. Between wars the Makkans had ample time to attend to trade, to amuse themselves, and enjoy life generally. They were fond of drink, women, poetry, and spending the warm summer nights in revelry. Muhammadﷺ, now on the threshold of manhood, cared for none of these pleasures of the night. He had a deep penetrating mind, an observant eye, and there was so much to see and hear in this world of marvels that afforded greater pleasure than drink and oblivion.

Like other Makkan youths he worked as a shepherd, tending the sheep of his people. Remembering this period of his life in later years, he used to say, 'Moses became a prophet while tending sheep and David became a prophet while tending sheep and I used to tend the sheep of my people at Al-Ajyad. Allah has made no man a prophet who was not a shepherd.' This job was in harmony with his meditative, incorruptible nature. He had the wide open spaces, the high mountains, the skies, all the majesty of creation to himself, away from the narrow streets of Makka, away from its narrower superstitions and futile worship of stones.

He relates that on two rare occasions he felt like going down to Makka to enjoy its gay night life. He left his sheep with a companion and descended towards Makka. The first time he saw a wedding procession and, being amused by it, stood to watch the wedding rites, then he felt drowsy and succumbed to sleep. On the second occasion, he heard strange and enthralling music as he was descending the mountain, so he sat to listen, fell asleep, and did not go down. So he remained elevated and unspoilt by the life of the city. He lived a life of observation and contemplation of the grandeur of creation, its exquisite harmony and variety.

3.4 Trade for Khadija

He had no ambition to earn more money or gain social status. He was tranquil, happy with his sheep. But his uncle who loved him dearly wanted more for him than tending sheep. Abu Talib had many children and was not well enough off to help his nephew. Nevertheless he wanted for Muhammad ﷺ the position in society that he felt was his due and so he was on the lookout for a suitable job for him.

One day he heard that Khadija, the daughter of Khuwaylid, wanted to hire a man from Quraysh to trade for her. Khadija was a very beautiful woman of intelligence and ability. She was extremely wealthy for she had inherited much money from her deceased husband. Many of the greatest of Quraysh had asked for her hand but she had refused them all, preferring to remain unattached and to attend to her trade and financial affairs.

When Abu Talib heard that she wanted someone to trade for her, he called his nephew and said, 'Nephew, I am not a wealthy man and times are hard for us. I have heard that Khadija has hired so-and-so for two bakras, but I won't accept that for you, would you like me to speak to her?'

'As you wish,' said Muhammad ﷺ.

So Abu Talib went to Khadija and said, 'Khadija, would you like to hire Muhammad ﷺ? You have hired so-and-so for two bakras, but we shan't accept less than four for Muhammad ﷺ.'

Always gracious, Khadija said, 'Had you asked this for a loathsome stranger I would have agreed, so how much more when you ask it for someone near and dear.'

Muhammad ﷺ's uncle returned and related to his nephew what had taken place, saying, 'This is provision that Allah has sent you.'

Muhammad ﷺ left with Maysara, Khadija's man, whom Abu Talib had charged to take good care of him. On route the caravan passed by the ancient ruins of Madian and Thamud, peoples who had rejected the message from Allah and in consequence had been destroyed. Muhammad ﷺ knew nothing of this as yet. They journeyed on to Al-Sham where he saw landscapes of luxurious vegetation and gushing rivers, very different from the austere and stark desert scenes.

Intelligent and honest, Muhammad ﷺ was able in his trade for Khadija to bring back more profit than those before him. His upright and modest nature earned him the liking and respect of Maysara. When the caravan reached the Al-Zahran Pass on its return journey towards Makka, Maysara said to Muhammad ﷺ, 'Muhammad ﷺ, go to Khadija ahead of us and tell what Allah has done for her at your hands, she will be most grateful.' So Muhammadﷺ rode alone and reached Makka towards noon. Khadija was standing on the balcony of her house. She recognized him as he approached on his camel and went down to receive him.

3.5 Marriage to Khadija

They sat in her house and Muhammadﷺ related the strange and beautiful things he had seen on this successful journey. Muhammadﷺ was twenty-three years old, very handsome, with dark, bright eyes, jet-black hair and beard, and long, thick lashes. His manner was refined, his speech elegant yet unaffected. He was neither too tall nor too short. He came from a long line of men who had been rulers of Makka, feared and respected. There was in his bearing that which inspired respect, and in his eyes that which made him obeyed in spite of his modesty.

Khadija was moved by his description of what he saw and what he had done for her and she soon realized that the emotion she felt was love - she who had spurned all the greats of the Quraysh! She confided in her friend, Nafisa, and Nafisa went to sound out Muhammadﷺ on the subject.

'Why don't you get married?' she asked.

'Because I do not have the means,' said Muhammadﷺ.

'Supposing you had the means, would you refuse beauty, ability, wealth, and honour?' asked Nafisa.

'But who could that be?' he said.

'Khadija,' Nafisa said.

Muhammadﷺ was rather surprised for he knew that Khadija had refused men of great importance. He liked Khadija, liked her very much, but marriage had not occurred to him. Now he gave his joyous consent. So a day was fixed when he came with his uncles to Khadija's house. Her people were also present and her uncle gave the bride away. Muhammadﷺ paid her a dowry of twenty bakras, according to the custom of the Arabs.

CHAPTER FOUR

4.1 Married Life

Here begins a new and happy chapter in the life of Muhammadﷺ. It is as if fate wanted to compensate him for the sad and lonely years he had spent in his childhood by giving him the best that Makka, perhaps the whole of Arabia, could offer. Khadija was a wonderful woman and he grew to love her as she loved him with a great and noble passion that lasted beyond the grave. Khadija became everything to him, wife, mother, sister, friend and companion. It was a happy and harmonious marriage. Muhammadﷺ, good-natured, refined, and considerate, and Khadija, intelligent, gracious, beautiful, and always looking up to him. They were well suited to each other. They had wealth, they had honour, they had a high position in society, but they had one source of sorrow - whenever Khadija bore a son he died. Muhammadﷺ so longed to have a son of his own, and Khadija also wanted a son, but one child after another passed away. Khadija feared that this was the wrath of the idols of the Ka'ba and used to sacrifice offerings to them. Muhammadﷺ, however loathed the idols of the Ka'ba and kept aloof from them.

They did, though, have four daughters. In an age that considered women inferior, and among a people who considered daughters a tribulation, Muhammadﷺ was a kind and affectionate father to them. He cared for their upbringing when they were little, and when they grew up. he was very careful in choosing husbands for them.

4.2 Social Life

Muhammadﷺ shared the life of his people and, without design on his part or theirs, he was growing more and more honoured and esteemed among them. His great goodness of heart was very engaging and he had a manliness that commanded respect and admiration.

At that time Quraysh were very much occupied by the Ka'ba, for a great flood had come down from the mountains and affected its foundations. They knew that they would have to rebuild it, but who would dare approach the sacred edifice? They all shied away in awe and fear. At last one of their leading men, Al-Walid ibn al-Mughira,

24

called upon the gods of the Ka'ba, then took a pick-axe and pulled down a part of the wall. People waited until the next day to see if anything would happen to him. When no evil befell him, they felt it was a sign that they had permission to rebuild it. So they all began to pull down the walls and carry them away. Each sub-tribe of Quraysh was in charge of pulling down a wall and then rebuilding it. Muhammadﷺ joined in the work. When they reached certain hard rock that the pick-axe would not cut into, they stopped and used that as the new foundation. They brought down blue granite from the mountains to build the walls. When the walls became as high as a man they decided that it was time to put the sacred Black Stone in its place before continuing the construction. But who among the tribes of Quraysh would have the honour of putting the stone in its place? Arguments began, then a dispute sprang up between them. The matter threatened to bring about a civil war for the clans swore solemn oaths and made covenants against each other.

When Abu Umayya of Banu Makhzum saw that matters were getting out of control, and being the oldest and wisest among them, he said, 'Wait, and let the first man who enters be the arbiter between you.' They waited in jealousy and hostility to see who would pass by. They saw Muhammadﷺ approach. Muhammadﷺ was of such upright nature, so frank and sincere that his tribe had called him 'the Truthful'. Now they all agreed to let him be the arbiter. 'The Truthful,' they said, 'We accept his arbitration.' They related their story to him, each from his own point of view. He could see the fire of hostility in their eyes. 'Bring me a cloak,' he said. When it was brought to him he placed the sacred Black Stone upon it, then he asked the head of each clan to carry one side of it so that they all shared the honour. They carried it to the place made for it, then Muhammadﷺ took it from the garment and put it in its place. Thus the threat of strife was averted.

The Quraysh continued to build the Ka'ba, making it eighteen cubits high, then they placed Hubal, their chief idol, in it together with all the precious things that were liable to be stolen. They made its door above the ground in such a way to let in whom they wanted and gave it a roof. Thus the Ancient House of Ibrahim and Isma'il was rebuilt.

4.3 Desire for Seclusion

At first Muhammadﷺ took over Khadija's trade. He was very

successful but he longed to be alone, to think, to reflect, to contemplate. Trade was only a duty to him and the substantial profit that he made was of no interest to him. Khadija, ever sympathetic and understanding, could perceive that his heart was not in it and so she relieved him from his duties in order to give him the leisure he longed for. At last he had the liberty to go up alone to the mountains to reflect and worship. In the heights of the mountain of Hira' there was a cave where he would go and spend the whole month of Ramadan every year.

This was not something peculiar to, Muhammad. It was an ancient custom of the Arabs, a custom they had practised since the days of Ibrahim when their religion, the religion of Ibrahim and Isma'il, was the pure worship of Allah alone. The years and the fraility of human memory and human nature had corrupted their religion, little by little, until it had become the base worship of stone idols, but, even so, they still retained some of the rites and customs of Ibrahim.

This custom suited Muhammad's reflective nature. Up in the cave of Hira' he would forget everything and think only of the Great Power that seemed to be guiding him to Itself, the Truth hidden behind the veils of material existence. He used to forget himself, to forget to eat and drink, and after such periods of worship and contemplation he used to return so thin that Khadija grew concerned about him.

4.4 The Revelation of the Qur'an

He longed to know the truth, the secret of this great universe, this vast creation, but all he could do was pray and wait for the Great Power that guided his heart to show Itself so that perhaps the truth would be revealed to him.

Muhammad was approaching forty years of age, of mature judgment and with a deep, penetrating mind. One day he began to have a strange vision, a vision that he saw clearly again and again. He felt this was the truth behind this gross world of matter. He prayed to know more and to perceive more. For six months he continued to have this vision of a reality beyond and greater than the material world; a vision of Allah, the Creator of everything and Ruler over everything. Again and again this vision of the truth appeared to him until he began to fear for his sanity. He confided in Khadija. Wise and perspicacious, she reassured him, saying that he was 'the

Truthful'. Allah would never visit him with insanity or let anything tamper with his being. She saw how truly good her husband was, and that such goodness would not be rewarded by insanity, but she had no suspicion that Allah was preparing His chosen Messenger for the great and terrible mission that awaited him.

Muhammadﷺ's dreams began to be an accurate picture of reality. Whatever he saw in a dream took place in real life when he woke up, so that he would realize that what he was experiencing was no madness, that the power that gave him these dreams had the ability to foretell and shape events.

One day, while asleep in the Cave of Hira, Muhammadﷺ saw an angel with a writ in his hand. The angel said, 'Read!'

'I cannot read,' said Muhammadﷺ.

The angel squeezed him in a constricting embrace, then let him go. 'Read,' he said again.

'I cannot read,' repeated Muhammadﷺ.

The angel squeezed him again, then let him go, saying, 'Read.'

In fear lest he be squeezed again, Muhammadﷺ said, 'What do I read?'

'Read in the name of your Lord who has created,
created man from a clot,
Read and your Lord is the Most Gracious,
Who has taught with the pen,
taught man what he did not know.' (96:1-5)

These were the first verses of the Qur'an to be sent down. Muhammadﷺ read them. They became engraved upon his heart and the angel left.

4.5 More About the Qur'an

Like most people at that time, Muhammadﷺ could not read. When he told the angel, 'I cannot read,' he was stating a fact. The Arabs loved poetry and often extemporized spontaneous verse, but Muhammadﷺ was no poet, he never composed spontaneous verse or wrote or read anything, therefore these verses were something very strange and precious to him. The very fine language together with their Origin made them a priceless treasure. Every verse that came down after that he memorized very, very carefully as something very precious that would be completely lost if he did not capture it then and there. This continued for some time until the holy verses descended assuring him that no word, no letter would be lost unless it was the will of Allah. He was admonished not to repeat immediately after Gabriel, as he used to do out of fear lest he forget, but to listen and he would be instructed in how to read the words of Allah and then on the background, meaning, and implications of the words. The holy verses say, 'We have sent down the Word, and We shall preserve it.' After this reassurance the Messenger began to relax and learn in an unhurried manner.

The Arabs are poets by instinct and that age was the golden age of their poetry, but the language of the Qur'an surpasses anything that the masters of poetry and oratory have produced in any age. It has the smooth rhythmic flow of verse, though it is not verse, and the stately majesty of the best prose, though it is not prose. The style is grand without being pompous, accurate and clear without being harsh or artificial. The Arabic language is an exceedingly fine language, but in the Qur'an it attains an excellence never reached before or since. It is not strange that those of literary bent find great joy in it while the spiritual are moved to tears, for, beyond its literary splendour, it has a nameless spiritual quality that affects people in different ways. It is said that 'Umar ibn Al-Khattab, who had towering rages, used to calm down immediately on hearing any verse of the Qur'an. Quraysh felt that in the Qur'an Muhammadﷺ had a weapon beyond anything they could produce and in envy and malice they accused him of being a 'magician of words' who took away people's senses by the sheer beauty of his utterances. Nothing could be further from the truth for the Qur'an appeals to the mind as well as the heart, moreover it urges man to think and reason to find out the truth.

4.6 Return to Khadija

Muhammadﷺ woke up terrified. What was this that he had experienced? Until then he had had visions that Allah was the One, who dominated all creation. But who was this reminding him of Him? Was he going insane? Was there a spirit in the cave? He ran out of the cave in terror and roamed the mountainside. Then he heard a voice calling him. He looked towards the sky. There upon the horizon he could see the same angel he had just seen in his dream. He was wide awake now but he could see the angel clearly. He looked away in horror but, wherever he looked, he could see the beautiful and awesome angel before him. The angel approached closer and closer to Muhammadﷺ, then he went back, finally he left.

In wild fear, Muhammadﷺ descended from the mountain towards

his house. During that time Khadija had sent someone with food to the Cave of Hira' but they could not find him. He went to her trembling with fear and wonder and said, 'Cover me up, cover me up,' for he felt cold all over. (It is said that contact with the supernatural, which is like a heavy charge of electricity, is extremely exhausting to the human frame.)

When he felt better he related to her what he had heard and seen, then he said, 'Khadija, what is the matter with me?'

Khadija's faith in her husband's basic sanity did not waver. She said, 'Be of good cheer, dear cousin, for by Him who has dominion over Khadija's soul, I do hope you are the prophet of this nation. Allah would never humiliate you. You are good to your-relatives, you are true of word, you aid the needy, you support the weak, and you respond to the call of the distressed.'

Muhammad ﷺ was reassured by her words, then peace in the form of a tranquil drowsiness overcame him and he went to sleep.

Khadija began to reflect upon what he had told her. When she saw that he slept peacefully, she decided to go and consult her cousin, Waraqa ibn Nawfal, whom she knew to be a man of knowledge. Many years earlier, Waraqa had rejected idol worship, studied religions, and become a Christian. He had translated parts of the Gospel into Arabic.

4.7 Waraqa ibn Nawfal

She went to him with Muhammad ﷺ's story. He listened pensively for a moment, then cried, 'Holy, Holy, Holy! By Him who has dominion over Waraqa's soul, if you would believe me, Khadija, he who has come to him is the Great Spirit who used to go to Moses. He is the prophet of this nation, so tell him to hold on steadfastly. He shall be belied, he shall be persecuted, he shall have to fight, and if I am alive then, Allah will see that I shall give a good account of myself.'

Khadija returned to find Muhammad ﷺ still asleep where he had been wrapped. Then suddenly he began to tremble in his sleep and sweat appeared over his forehead for in his sleep he saw the angel telling him:

> **You, wrapped in your garment,**
> **arise and warn,**
> **and say, 'My Lord is Greatest,'**
> **and your clothes purify,**

and the unclean forsake
Do not keep asking for more,
and with your Lord be patient. (74:1-7)

Muhammadﷺ got up. Khadija compassionately tried to get him to lie down again, but he said, 'No, Khadija, the time for sleep is over. Gabriel has ordered me to warn people and to call them to Allah. But whom shall I call? And who would respond to my call?'

Observant and perspicacious, Muhammadﷺ knew from the start that his mission would not be easy. Khadija tried to make the heavy responsibility laid upon him easier. She knew Muhammadﷺ well; she had been living with him for the last seventeen years. She had known him as a young man of three and twenty and had watched him grow into a mature man with a great, generous heart and steady judgment. He would never deceive anyone nor was he insane, and what kind of insanity was this that brought the truth to them in words of unparalleled majesty and beauty?

She announced her belief in Allah and in Muhammadﷺ as His Messenger. She was the first person on earth to believe in him, the first woman, and after Muhammadﷺ the first Muslim. The word Muslim means in Arabic, 'one who submits to Allah.'

CHAPTER FIVE

5.1. Religion in Makka before Islam

Nearly three thousand years before Muhammad☺ was born, the religion of the Arabs in Makka was the religion of their ancestor, Isma'il son of Ibrahim, who had settled in the Hijaz and married among them. It was the worship of Allah alone without deviation. It was clear and uncompromised, free from superstition and falsehood. It was Ibrahim and Isma'il who, by Allah's command, rebuilt the Ka'ba and made it a sanctuary for the worshipper. But three thousand years is a long time and the human mind and human memory are frail and corruptible. Gradually with the passage of time, they began to revere certain natural phenomena as aspects of Allah's power, then they began to consider them holy, then as entities worth worshipping in their own right. Superstition and falsehood began to accumulate around the core of the truth until little of it remained. The Sabaeans, with whom they had much contact and who worshipped the stars, influenced them in this. They began to worship certain meteoric stones as descended from heaven, then other natural phenomena as well. They reconciled these superstitions with their worship of Allah by saying that these were lesser gods and their intercessors with Allah. By the time Muhammad☺ came they had three hundred and sixty idols around the Ka'ba and the first house built for the worship of Allah on earth had become a place for idol worship. They paid Allah lip- service but it was the stones they worshipped and sacrificed offerings to.

Connected with these beliefs were all sorts of honorary offices, such as maintaining the Ka'ba and catering to its pilgrims, that only those of noble birth from the tribe of Quraysh could attain and inherit (from father to son). The Ka'ba was not only the centre of their religious and social life but also a symbol of their rank and prestige among all the tribes of Arabia. These tribes came every year from distant parts of the Arabian peninsula to pay homage to the gods of the Ka'ba during the Sacred Months. They also came to trade in Makka and the markets around it. They coupled business with religion and so the months they came to town were months of great economic prosperity among the Makkans. Since the Makkans had no natural resources and Makka and the surrounding lands were desert, trade was vital to them as their main source of income.

The Makkans profited by their religion economically and socially, and woe unto to any who would dare speak against their most sacred gods! No one had ever tried. The Christians and Jews in Makka were usually slaves of inferior status and were forbidden to speak of their religion in the Sacred Precincts, while their houses were on the outskirts of the city, far removed from the Sacred House.

5.2 The Communications Cease and Commence Again

Muhammadﷺ knew his people well. He knew what he was about to embark upon and he realized that his days of peace and esteem among them were over. From that moment onwards his life would be a dire struggle with all the forces of evil, a frank confrontation with all that was wicked, selfish, and corrupt in man. He would experience hostility, persecution, and rejection. Many would belie and many would fight him, but of what consequence was that in comparison with the secret of creation at last revealed? He had the courage and strength to persevere for the sake of the truth no matter what it cost. He was ready, he was eager, he was happy, but he did not know how to start. He waited for Gabriel to appear again to guide him, but no vision, no message nor any sign from Allah appeared. Abruptly all spiritual communication had ceased.

He waited in hope, then he waited in fear and anxiety. Why had the noble vision disappeared? Had he done something to drive it away? Had he been found unworthy? He began to worry and fret, he waited in sadness and despair. After he had seen so clearly, heard so certainly and unequivocally, where had the greatest hope gone? Was it irretrievably lost? Was he so detestable that Allah had forsaken him? Grief and a terrible sense of loss filled his heart. For six months there was absolute silence (some believe the period was longer, others shorter, but most commentators believe that it was around six months). For six months he heard nothing, saw nothing, after he used to hear and see things every day. Of what use was life if it did not contain the truth, the lofty ideal that he thought for a moment was within his grasp? Of what use was existence if it meant no more than living behind the opaque prison bars of the material world? Sick of the fake and superficial life of the Makkans, in sheer despair, he thought of throwing himself from a mountain height. Then at this moment of deepest despair, the angel Gabriel descended with the following verses:

By the full morn,
by the night when it grows still,
your Lord has not bid you farewell nor does He loathe you,
and for the eternal life you shall have better than the temporal,
And your Lord will give you to make you content.
Has He not found you fatherless and given you a home?
Has He not found you astray and guided you?
Has he not found you dependent and made you independent? (93:1-8)

These verses, in the resonant Qur'anic Arabic, are a masterpiece of literary excellence and psychological perspicacity. They begin by the dramatic contrast between light and dark, full morn and still night. The contrast of these two entities, so familiar to Muhammad鑻, were to make him understand two entities that he could not see. The morn represented the truth that had been revealed to him for a moment and then disappeared, while the night represented the six months of absolute silence. The reality of the spiritual experience came after silence as night follows day. He should not have panicked or thought that the day would never come. Silence would come again, as night followed day, but he should never be in terror of losing the truth, never again should he despair of the mercy of Allah, for it would surely come after despair as full morning came after deep darkness. This lesson, important to all Muslims was particularly pertinent to Muhammad鑻, the first Muslim, whose life was a sequence of very great darknesses followed by the most dazzling of triumphs.

The reappearance of the communication was a great joy to Muhammad鑻. He prayed and gave thanks again and again. The holy verses had reassured him that he was not detestable, that his Lord had not forsaken him. He would be guided and instructed again and his people were not doomed to be lost in dark superstition. The communications from Allah would continue and mankind would learn what they had never known.

He felt so relieved, so honoured, and yet so unworthy of this very great honour. Direct communication with the Most High was beyond the worth of any man but he would try to be worthy, he would work with all his heart and soul to please Allah, the Greatest, the Most Merciful, who had chosen him for this task of awesome responsibility, a terrible yet beloved vocation. So away with black ideas of suicide, away with doubts and despair. His life from now on would be dedicated to the service of his Lord.

One may wonder why the messages from heaven had stopped for six months after having clear and unequivocal. Perhaps the answer is found in the reaction of Muhammad☁ himself. At first he connected what he saw with insanity, He felt fear of the unknown. Therefore Allah, in His wisdom, was giving His Prophet time to reflect and get used to the idea, time to realize the greatness of the gift, the magnificence of the promise. Gradually from a terrifying vision that he fled from the mountainside to avoid, it became a strange but not terrifying idea, though full of grave responsibilities and dangers. Then when the vision stopped, he realized how dear this message was. It became something he cherished and for which waited eagerly. He wanted it so much; he felt his whole life was not worth living without it. The whole world was nothing in comparison with this great truth. This period of six months made him assess everything in the new light of the knowledge he had received, and realize that without this spiritual contact his life would mean nothing to him.

5.3 'Ali and Zayd

Living with Muhammad☁ and Khadija, apart from their daughters, were two little boys. The first was 'Ali, son of Abu Talib, Muhammad☁'s uncle. Muhammad☁ had never forgotten Abu Talib's kindness to him as a boy, so when he became independent and welloff, he decided to help out his uncle. He went to another uncle, Al'Abbas, and said to him (for Al'Abbas was very wealthy, but rather tightfisted) that this was a year of scarcity, and that Abu Talib had many children, so would Al'Abbas take one of them and Muhammad☁ take another? Al'Abbas could not refuse, and Muhammad☁ took 'Ali' to live to with him.

The other little boy was Zayd ibn AlHaritha. Zayd lost his way one day and some people kidnapped him, then sold him as a slave. Khadija bought him and gave him as a present to Muhammad☁. Muhammad☁ set him free and brought him up as his own son. When some years later, Zayd's father and uncle were at last able to find him, they offered to buy him back from Muhammad☁, and Muhammad☁ offered to give him to them free since he was their son. But the surprise came when Zayd, who although overjoyed to see his father and uncle, refused to leave Muhammad☁. To the little boy Muhammad☁ was the ideal of manhood and benevolence, and Zayd would not, even to return to his family, part from this beloved ideal.

5.4 'Ali Enters Islam

Now Allah taught His Messenger the rites of prayer, and Muhammadﷺ taught them to Khadija. One day, 'Ali, who was about ten years old, entered and found Muhammadﷺ and Khadija praying. He stood amazed. When they had finished, he asked, 'To whom do you prostrate yourselves?'

'We prostrate ourselves to Allah,' said Muhammadﷺ, 'who has made me a prophet and commanded me to call people to Him.'

Then he asked his cousin to enter into Islam and reject idol worship, and he read the Qur'an to him. 'Ali, who was of a poetic nature, sat enthralled, then he said to his cousin, 'Give me time to consult Abu Talib,' meaning his father.

He spent a turbulent night, then when morning came he went to Muhammadﷺ and Khadija and said, 'Allah has created me without consulting Abu Talib. What need have I to consult Abu Talib to worship Him?'

And from that time on he followed Muhammadﷺ unswervingly and grew up to be a wonderful man and a great Muslim leader whose words of wisdom and piety are studied by all Muslims and whose invincible sword fought for nearly half a century to uphold the truth.

A visitor to Makka at that time describes the following scene, 'I had business with Al-'Abbas, so I went to seek him by the Ka'ba. As I sat with him, a man of luminous complexion and great dignity entered. With him was a boy of pleasant aspect and a woman, dressed up as to cover her beauty. They went seven times round the Ka'ba, then they began to pray and prostrate themselves.' Whatever the man did, the boy who stood beside him did, and the woman who stood behind them did. I asked Al-'Abbas if this was something old that we did not know about or if it was some new form of worship, and he said, "This is my nephew, Muhammadﷺ, beside him is my nephew, 'Ali, and the woman is Khadija, daughter of Khuwaylid and wife to Muhammadﷺ; and they are the only people on earth who worship in this odd, new way.'

At first the Quraysh did not take what Muhammadﷺ did seriously, it was a curiosity and no more.

The next person to believe was Zayd ibn Al-Haritha. Zayd loved Muhammadﷺ, as all who knew him did, and had faith in him. Like 'Ali, Zayd grew up to be a fine young man, aiding and supporting

Muhammadﷺ, and a brave soldier.

5.5 Abu Bakr Enters Islam

The first man Muhammadﷺ approached on the subject of Islam was Abu Bakr ibn Abi Quhafa. Abu Bakr was a well-known merchant in a city where merchants were the ruling aristocracy. He came from the honourable tribe of Taym, a clan of Quraysh. He was thirty-eight years old, but he was already head of his tribe and had much power and influence in Quraysh as a whole. It is said that he was the man who knew most about the the genealogy of Quraysh and other Arab tribes, their descent and their connections.

He was rich, of pleasant features, and possessed a graceful, light frame. He was kind and debonair, affectionate to his family, and gracious and easy in his manner to both acquaintances and strangers. He was considered one of the leading intellects of Quraysh, a man of judgment who was often sought out for advice. Refined and sensitive, he cared little for the customs of Quraysh and even less for their religion. He neither participated in their night-time revelries nor sacrificed to their idols. He lived in the same district as Khadija and Muhammadﷺ, the place where many successful merchants lived. Muhammadﷺ and Abu Bakr knew and respected each other. If anyone could transcend the narrow vision of the Quraysh, it was Abu Bakr; nevertheless what Muhammadﷺ had to say was very strange and new. Abu Bakr listened carefully until he had finished, then he professed his belief in Allah and in Muhammadﷺ as His Messenger. He neither doubted nor hesitated for, to the pure of heart, truth proclaims its own truth. In later years Muhammadﷺ used to say, 'I have never approached a man who did not hesitate and feel a little reluctance at first except Abu Bakr. His faith was immediate without doubt or hesitation.' There sprang a warm friendship between the two men which grew and mellowed with the years into the noblest and greatest bond that friendship could offer. More than once did Abu Bakr risk his life to save Muhammadﷺ's.

5.6 The Nobles and the Common People of Makka

At first Muhammadﷺ used to sit with the few people who believed beside the Ka'ba teaching them the words of Allah. Many of them were clients and slaves who were considered of much lower rank than Quraysh. The dignitaries of Quraysh were willing to sit and amuse themselves by what Muhammadﷺ had to say, perhaps even to catch some gems of wisdom such as poets and bards repeated. They were as yet unaware of the gravity of the message or the power of the truth that was to pull down their whole social and economic system, and give them a new life-giving faith. Muhammadﷺ was one of them, but to sit in the same place with such common people was unthinkable to them, beneath their dignity, and an affront to their illustrious persons.

One day they asked Muhammadﷺ to disperse these people so that they could sit with him and hear what he had to say. Muhammadﷺ, though modest and kind-hearted, had been brought up in Qurayshi tradition, where people were clearly divided into masters and slaves. Also he wanted desperately to make the leaders of the Quraysh believe, for if they did, the whole of Makka would follow. He was about to acquiesce to their wishes when the following verses were revealed:

And do not drive away those who call
upon their Lord morning and evening, seeking His face.
You are not charged with anything of their account,
nor are they charged with anything of yours,
so that you drive them away and become of the wicked. (6:52)

These words were most shocking to the Arabs. The implications were very great. They implied that these common people had rights equal to Muhammadﷺ. If so, then they had rights equal to theirs!

The holy verses continue:

Thus have we tempted them with each other,
so that they say, 'Are those the ones Allah has favoured among us?'
Does not Allah know best who the thankful are? (6:53)

If the common people were given precedence in faith the nobles of Quraysh would say, 'Is it possible that they were able to grasp the truth before us? That Allah has preferred them to us?' It was a test for them that only the truly good could pass, that only the man free from arrogance and conceit would understand. Unfortunately many of them were not free of these traits and preferred their pomp and pride to the truth.

The rabble of Quraysh, at their masters' instigation, began to harass and disturb the Muslims during their prayers, so the Muslims sought privacy in the mountains. Whenever they wanted to pray they went off to the mountains. This lasted for three years until a young man, called Al-Arqam, who had entered into Islam and who had no one living with him except his aged father, offered to make his house a meeting place for them. The house was spacious enough for the purpose and Muhammadﷺ accepted. Now those who entered into Islam went to this house to swear allegiance to Allah and His Messenger.

Abu Bakr, who was very popular and well connected began to call people to Allah, disregarding the danger of what Quraysh might do to his person or to disrupt his trade. Many noble men from Quraysh entered into Islam through Abu Bakr, then went to Muhammadﷺ to declare their allegiance and learn more about religion. The number of Muslims began to grow steadily and the communications from Allah gradually taught them ideas and ideals far above anything their people or the world had ever known.

5.7 New Precepts

The Qur'an introduced the idea that all men, despite their wealth or position, were equal in the sight of Allah. This idea was completely alien to the Arabs who prided themselves on their lineage. Each tribe was careful to record the deeds of its heroes and ancestors and they extolled them in verse and prose. A man of unknown lineage was a nobody and had no place among them except as a slave. The Qur'an pointed out that it was not a matter of lineage, wealth, or children, the things they prided themselves upon, but the purity of the heart that Allah looked at. Even a foreigner would be approved by Allah if he was a righteous man. Race, nation, tribe, and sex were of no consequence. The holy verses say:

Mankind, We have created you male and female,
nations and clans to get acquainted.
To Allah the most honoured among you is the most, devout. (49:13)

Did these verses imply that their slaves could be their equals? And sex too was mentioned. Surely women were not to be compared with men! But in clear and majestic language the Qur'an continued to explain that all human beings were the descendants of Adam and Eve, their lineage was the same. Women were individuals and had clear, inalienable rights. A good woman was better than a bad man in the sight of Allah, and there was much more to shock the sensibilities of the leaders of the Quraysh. The fatherless, the widow, the slave, and all the downtrodden were discussed one by one and given rights and liberties. No one was forgotten.

The Qur'an introduced another concept that seemed to the Arabs cowardly and degrading - the idea of forgiveness and pardon was introduced. The Arabs had prided themselves in their ability in vendettas to pursue a debt of vengeance to the death. The Qur'an counselled tempering vengeance by mercy. To seek redress was a human right, according to the Qur'an, but to forgive was better, provided that one had the ability to attain redress and did not forgive out of weakness, but rather out of benevolence and understanding, and in the firm belief that all men were brethren and that one should forgive one's brethren if they had made a mistake.

As the precepts of the Qur'an unfolded, they began to divide the Makkans into two groups. The kind, the just, the idealistic were won over by these concepts and fought for them as the eternal truth, worth living by and worth dying for. The hard-hearted, the selfish, the narrow-minded, the arrogant began to fight them as a threat to their position in their society, their economic system, and their religion upon which their privileges and honour above other Arabs depended.

It was not everyone who was ready to make sacrifices for the downtrodden. It took a man with the innate sensitivity and goodness of Abu Bakr to feel his slave his equal and to accept the truth of this; it took a man with the deep sense of justice of 'Umar ibn Al-Khattab to grasp the righteousness of the idea and consider it fair, or someone with the generosity of 'Uthman ibn 'Affan to accept sacrificing his privileges for the sake of the downtrodden. Many did not want to become Muslims for the Qur'an stated that to be a Muslim meant to set slaves free as an act pleasing to Allah, to treat women with absolute fairness and tactful kindness, to care for orphans as if they were one's own children, and to give them their property as soon as they were old enough to manage it, to help the needy, to answer the call of the distressed, to be humble and reverential to one's aged parents, to be true in word, deed, and thought, and to pray to Allah five times a day.

To people who lived a life of luxury and idleness based on the service of their many slaves and dependants (the daughter of 'Abdu'l-Muttalib, one of Muhammadﷺ's aunts, gave forty of her slaves their freedom on one day), it was not a small thing to ask. To a people who thought it their right as men and masters to take the best of everything and give the weak - women, children, and slaves - whatever they would, it was indeed a sacrifice. To men whose highest pleasure was spending the night in drink, with slaves and poets extolling their greatness, their generosity, their lineage, or whatever they had done or said, it meant a totally new outlook, a very different concept of man and his relationship to his Creator. It was tantamount to starting a whole new life.

Islam decreed humility before one's Maker. Allah does not like the boastful, the vainglorious. It meant contemplation of His wondrous universe and the constant attempt to reflect and understand. The ability to think was a great gift bestowed by Allah, and it was man's duty to use it. Then above all, he was to do all the good he could, both actively by helping make the world a better place, and passively by controlling his own whims and desires.

In exchange Allah promised paradise to those who made the effort and worshipped Him alone. What Muhammadﷺ was asking of them was to shun the three hundred and sixty idols around the Ka'ba, those idols whom their fathers and forefathers had worshipped for generation after generation. What he asked was not little, indeed it was much; but the reward also was not little, it was beyond anything that man could achieve for himself.

From the dark heart of Makka, the noble, the good, the generous were being picked one by one and added to Muhammadﷺ's little group. The influential men of Makka looked on in wonder, then in alarm, then in fear. They felt the earth was being pulled from under their feet and they did not like it.

5.8 Stumbling Blocks

Before Islam their religion had been a token-sacrifice of a goat or a camel to their idols and then doing whatever they pleased. Islam made moral and spiritual demands that they were unwilling to accept. Moreover it introduced two concepts that their materialistic minds found very difficult to conceive. These two concepts were resurrection and the idea of reward and punishment. How could they be brought back to life after they had become dust? They found the idea impossible to accept. The Holy Qur'an tried to help them by pointing out how the earth seems dead but is revived as soon as water falls upon it, and that the creation of the heavens and earth is more difficult than the creation of man, so that He who created them and man for the first time would find no difficulty in creating them a second time. Indeed, it would be easier.

They took alarm at the description of the Day of Judgment and how people would be taken to account for everything they had done on earth. Their religion was very much of this world and the idea that this world was only an introduction to the Next World they found very strange. The idea of Hell (Jahannam) and the punishment of the wicked was something they feared and at the same time refused to believe in.

'If it is true that we shall be resurrected again,' they said to the Messenger, 'then bring back our fathers, if you are truthful.' They could not perceive that if they had the material proof they demanded, where would the test of faith be?

CHAPTER SIX

6.1 Proclaiming Religion to Kin

For three years Muhammadﷺ called people to Allah in secret, addressing those he knew to be men of mature thought and vision. Then after three years, Allah commanded His Messenger to proclaim His religion openly to all his family. Muhammadﷺ invited his relations to an evening meal and began to speak to them of Allah, but Abu Lahab, Muhammadﷺ's uncle, rose in fury and called everyone to leave.

Muhammadﷺ tried again. He invited them for a midday meal and after they had eaten, he said, 'I know of no man among the Arabs who has brought his people better than what I bring you. I bring you the best in this world and in the eternal world, so who will support me in this mission?'

They turned away and started to leave, when 'Ali, who was still a boy, spoke, 'I will support you, Messenger of Allah, I will be at war against those who fight you.' Banu Hashim (Muhammadﷺ and 'Ali's clan) smiled derisively and looked from Abu Talib to his son. Some laughed outloud but little did they know that, only a few years later, 'Ali was to become a formidable warrior of surpassing courage and prowess, whose very name struck terror in their hearts and whose words of piety and wisdom have been cherished by Muslims ever since.

Muhammadﷺ had brought them something alien to their culture, destructive to their religion, opposed to their economic and social interests, and they were not going to accept it. Whether it was the truth or not made little difference to them. It was enough that it demanded sacrifices from them and that it was against their whims, desires, and privileges.

6.2 Hamza Enters Islam

One day Abu Jahl (literally 'Father of Ignorance), who was one of the most strident enemies of the new religion, and also one of the most eminent men of Quraysh, was exceedingly abusive to Muhammadﷺ, injuring and insulting him. Muhammadﷺ did not respond to his insults, for by nature he was not a man to use evil language and the Arabs revered their elders.

Muhammadﷺ had an uncle called Hamza who was at the same time his foster brother. Hamza was a brave and fearless man fond of hunting. Every day when he returned from the hunt, he would go around the Ka'ba. That day when he returned, he was informed of what Abu Jahl had done to Muhammadﷺ. So he did not go around the Ka'ba, but went straight to where Abu Jahl sat and struck him with his bow. Abu Jahl fell wounded and people from his clan, Banu Makhzum, tried to stand between him and Hamza, but, fearing a blood feud between the tribes, he begged them not to interfere and admitted what he had done. Then Hamza went to Muhammadﷺ and swore allegiance to Allah and to Muhammadﷺ as His Messenger.

6.3 Calling Quraysh to Allah

After being commanded to call his close kin to Allah, the Messenger was commanded to call the whole of Quraysh to Allah. They all knew him well, they all knew how truthful and sincere he was. So Muhammadﷺ used this knowledge they had of his character (he had lived among them for forty years) to convince them of the truth of his mission. He stood upon a prominence called Al-Safa (where Hajar had stood so many years earlier to search for water) and called them by the names of their clans. The clans heard and said, 'Muhammadﷺ upon Al-Safa,' and they came to him from all directions.

When they had gathered, he began with these words, 'Tell me, if I were to inform you that there was a band of horsemen behind this mountain, would you believe me?'

'Certainly,' they said. 'To us you are above suspicion. We have never heard you utter an untruth.'

'I am a messenger of warning,' he said, 'Coming to you before impending painful punishment! Banu 'Abdu'l-Muttalib, Banu 'Abdu Manaf, Banu Zuhrah, Banu Taym....' he kept enumerating the clans of Quraysh, calling each by name, then he continued, 'Allah has commanded me to call my tribe to Him. I can do you no good in this world or give you a share in the eternal until you say that Allah is One.'

Abu Lahab, who was a fat man quick to anger, rose up in a temper and cried, 'May your hand perish forever! Have you called us for this!' When the Arabs refer to a man's hand they are employing a figure of speech which denotes the whole by the part and by this he meant his life.

Muhammadﷺ did not answer as Abu Lahab was his uncle and the Arabs were brought up in the ancient tradition of respecting their elders, but then to all those who hurt him he was kind, patient, and forbearing. He knew they were hurting themselves more than they were hurting him. Soon afterwards some verses of the Qur'an were revealed to answer Abu Lahab, his insults as well as his misconceptions, for when Muhammadﷺ had pointed out that those who do wrong were destined for eternal torture, Abu Lahab had said that he would ransom himself and his children from such torture - he was a very wealthy man. The holy verses say:

May the hand of Abu Lahab perish, and perish he!
What can his money and what he has made spare him?
He shall enter fire of burning flames
and his wife, the carrier of the thornbush kindling
upon her neck a rope of palm-fibre. (111:1-5)

Abu Lahab is one of the few people from Quraysh mentioned by name in the Holy Qur'an and is the prototype of the man who collects much wealth but does not do anyone any good with it. He was singularly narrow-minded and prejudiced. The last two verses mention Umm Jamil, his wife, who used to cast thornbushes in the Messenger's way whenever she saw him.

When she heard the holy verses describe her as the carrier of thornbush, Umm Jamil was furious and decided to throw stones at Muhammadﷺ the next time she saw him. She collected some stones and took them to the Ka'ba where he often taught and prayed. Muhammadﷺ was sitting by Abu Bakr near the Ka'ba. Umm Jamil walked to where they were sitting and spoke to Abu Bakr, saying that his friend (meaning the Messenger) had insulted her, and if she ever saw him, she was going to throw these stones at him, then she walked furiously away. Abu Bakr was much amazed and said, 'But, Messenger of Allah, didn't she see you?'

'No,' said Muhammadﷺ, 'Allah has blinded her perception of my presence.'

6.4 Hostility of the Makkan Nobles

Abu Lahab and his wife were not the only people hostile to the new religion. Many of the eminent people of Quraysh began to feel it was a threat to their privileges and their way of life. They were not willing to sacrifice their privileges for the sake of the wronged; they were not ready to give up the customs of generations, customs that had secured their honorary titles and high status, for the sake of the truth. And they saw no reason why they should jeopardize their economic interests for the good, even if it was the good of all humanity.

They had no objection to following Muhammad☀ as he came from a long line of men who were chiefs of the Quraysh and rulers of Makka. He was the most noble of birth among them and he had dignity, intelligence, wealth, and was well-connected. They were quite willing to follow him, if he would only stop these ruinous ideas. If only he would become more understanding and make a compromise with them. The Qur'an repeats their words, saying:

> **When Our clear words are read to them,**
> **those who do not fear the meeting with Us say,**
> **'Bring us a writ other than this or alter it.'**
> **Say, 'It is not for me to alter it by myself.**
> **I only follow what is communicated to me.**
> **I fear should I disobey my Lord, the suffering of a great day.'** (10:15)

Many of them could not grasp the great and terrible portent of these words. They did not realize that the Truth was not to be tampered with; they could not conceive that one does not compromise the ideal. They thought Muhammad☀ was just being perverse, that he did not want to come to an understanding with them. But his ideas would cost them, indeed were already costing them much. They would have to stop him by arguments or by force, and if he did not stop, they would have to kill him.

The hostility of Abu Lahab and those like him did not prevent those who sought the truth from believing. This is what some had yearned for as parched earth yearns for water - to be free from evil superstition, from the degrading worship of stone, to worship with a pure heart Allah, the Creator of all the universe, and to be connected with all His beings in a bond of love and brotherhood. No more slaves, no more masters, all were brethren in Islam.

How different was this message of the Truth from Quraysh's love of wealth, lineage, and ostentation. They considered Muhammad☀'s call to love all mankind a base idea unworthy of their greatness. They buried their daughters alive and sacrificed their children to Hubal, their chief god, yet saw nothing base in this. Islam came and revealed that to bury daughters alive was a great wrong - daughters were jewels to be nurtured and brought up with care, children were a gift from Allah, they had no right to kill them. Allah, the Provider, provided for both parents and children. It was a religion of enlightenment, justice, and mercy. Those whose hearts echoed these qualities were happy to follow it and to endure and sacrifice for its sake.

6.5 Arguments and Objections

The enemies of Islam began to take active and orderly steps in opposition. The Arabs were poets by nature, never so moved as by a good poem, so they gave their poets money and set them upon Muhammad⁂ to insinuate that he was a liar, crazy, or bewitched. Muhammad⁂ did not answer them as he was too busy explaining what had been revealed to him to take any notice of them, but Muslims who were poets, men who had hearts as well as the gift of poetry, answered with such convincing arguments that they silenced them.

They reverted to another trick. They said that if Muhammad⁂ was truly a prophet, let him change Al-Safa to gold for them, or let the earth gush out into springs of water, or let him bring forth the angels for them to see, or let a book from heaven be sent down for them, or (joking further at his expense) let him tell them which merchandise would rise in price and which would be scarce.

The Qur'an bid him to tell them,

Exalted be my Lord, am I anything but a man, a messenger. (17:93)

In other words, I am only a man, I cannot do miracles, those belong to Allah alone. They were demanding a miracle, but Allah in His wisdom denied them this single proof. A miracle meant breaking the laws of nature. This was easy for Him who had created all the laws of nature, yet He forebore for three reasons mentioned in the Qur'an.

The first was that when prophets had been sent to earlier peoples, and after they had performed, by the will of Allah, miracles, they were deified after their death and worshipped alongside with Allah, the One. Much superstition and erroneous beliefs had been the result.

The second was that in earlier times when people had demanded a miracle, and Allah gave them what they asked, many would still not believe. They had promised to believe, if only they would get a certain sign and when they were given the sign they had asked for and still did not believe, the judgment passed upon them was destruction. In the Arabian peninsula itself there were the ruins of

several civilizations who had suffered such a fate. When Allah wants
to spare a people, He does not give them a miracle.

The third reason was that if people would only observe the world
around them, they would see hundreds of the tokens of Allah's power
and wisdom. The whole of creation is co-ordinated in a most perfect
and orderly design; to those who believe this is a greater sign than
any instance of breaking the laws of nature. The Qur'an says:

In the creation of the heavens and the earth,
the alternation of night and day,
the boats that sail the seas bringing benefit to man,
the water Allah sends down from the sky
to give life to the earth after its death,
and the dissemination of every species upon it,
the distribution of the winds,
the clouds ordained between the sky and earth,
there are tokens to those who reason. (2:164)

6.6 The Challenge

Quraysh, the masters of poetry and oratory in an age which is
considered the golden age of those arts, continued to argue and
quibble with, or without, reason. Muhammadﷺ, continually
receiving the Revelation, continued to teach and help people and to
bring them 'out of darkness into light.' He taught them morals,
manners, and principles far above anything their fathers had known.

He related to them stories of ancient peoples, the stories of those
before them who had believed and those who had not believed. The
Qur'an gave accurate information about preceding generations,
about ancient peoples within the pale of history and those outside its
range, peoples only Allah could recall. Such knowledge could only
come from the source of all knowledge. The Qur'an has related these
stories not to amuse people or to teach them mere history, but to
point out to them the moral behind these stories. First a story, or
several instances of the same kind are related, then the moral behind
them is pointed out, and last of all the law or theory behind it is
given. These stories are used as examples to help people grasp the
significance of the theory.

People were very much interested and flocked around
Muhammadﷺ. The eminent Qurayshis were worried and, in order to
divert people from the Qur'an and its great wisdom, they concocted
a lie. Seeing that the Messenger who was always considerate,

particularly to the neglected, stopped occasionally and said a kind word to a poor Christian boy called Jabr, they propagated the rumour that Muhammad⁕ sat by this poor boy day after day, and it was he who dictated the Qur'an to him. In answer to this the Qur'an gives them a clear and infallible argument. It says:

We are aware they say, 'But he is taught by a man.'
The tongue of him they allude to is foreign,
and this is a clear Arabic tongue. (16:103)

The Arabs were very sensitive to the shades and variations in their language. Not only could no foreigner master these very fine literary arts, but the Qur'an surpassed anything that they, the masters of the language, could produce. Then how could it be taught by a foreigner? The Qur'an was beyond anything that man could produce and it challenged them in the verses below to produce anything like it.

If you are in doubt about what We have sent down on Our slave,
then produce one surah like it,
and call your witnesses, apart from Allah, if you are truthful.
If you cannot, and you shall not,
then beware of the fire, prepared for deniers,
whose fuel is people and stones. (2:23,24)

Try as they might,Quraysh could not produce anything like it. No one, in the last fourteen hundred years has been able to do so. If one examines the Qur'an from any angle, upon any level, it is always so beyond anything that man can produce as literature, as thought, as historic and scientific knowledge, that neither the years nor new scientific discoveries can tarnish it.. The Qur'an points this out to them in the following words:

Had it come from other than Allah,
you would have found in it many incongruencies. (4:135)

CHAPTER SEVEN

7.1 Muhammad ﷺ Attacks Idols

The Messenger began to attack the idols of the Ka'ba, saying that they could see nothing, hear nothing, and had no power to do any good or harm. Apart from these idols, the Quraysh worshipped the angels and jinn. Muhammad ﷺ taught that whatever man worshipped other than Allah, whatever he took as patron or aid, could do him no good or harm unless it was the will of his Maker. The fate of man rests in the hands of Allah alone. It is He who provides or withholds provision, it is He who gives life and death, all good is in His hands, and when He desires anything He says to it, 'Be!' and it becomes.

> **Should Allah touch you by harm,**
> **none can relieve you from it except Him.**
> **Should He desire good for you,**
> **none can deter His bounty,**
> **He bestows it on whom He will of His slaves.**
> **He is the Merciful, the Forgiving. (10:107)**

The leaders of Quraysh could bear it no longer. Muhammad ﷺ was corrupting their dependants. Was he not doing enough harm already with his ideas of forgiveness and charity? If he were to divert people from their 'most sacred gods', and teach them that only Allah could do them good, then why should people obey them, the nobles of Quraysh? What would become of their honorary titles and privileges? What would happen to their trade when the Arabs stopped coming to visit their idols from far and wide?

Had it been just any man, a slave or dependant, who was saying these words, they would have meted out a slow death by torture. But Muhammad ﷺ was not a nobody, he came from the most noble of the great houses of Quraysh. He had been held in high esteem among them before he began calling people to Allah. If harm touched him, his tribe would immediately retaliate. Makka would be torn apart by a feud of vengeance, a civil war in which neither side would rest until the other was annihilated. In such a feud both victor and vanquished were losers. They were trying desperately to avoid such dire measures, but the Messenger was breaking up their world.

They went in a body to his uncle, Abu Talib, the aged and revered head of Banu Hashim and said that they were willing to relieve him of his embarrassing nephew. Abu Talib had not entered into Islam, but he was very fond of his nephew, who as a little boy had been entrusted to his care by his father, 'Abdu'l-Muttalib, and who had grown to be a man of such courage, wisdom, dignity, and intelligence. Even this strange inspiration of Muhammad ﷺ's that he could not understand was noble and elevated. Abu Talib spoke pleasantly but firmly to them, giving them to understand that all Muhammad ﷺ's clan, those who had entered into Islam and those who had not, stood firmly behind him, and so the Messenger continued to call to the Truth, to Allah's eternal principles and merciful rule, and to the rejection of idol worship.

7.2 The Blind Man

In spite of his kindness, one day Muhammad ﷺ happened to frown upon one of the poor people he was continually striving to help. That particular day he was standing with one of the chief men of Quraysh, trying to convince him to enter Islam. When a man of such consequence entered Islam, his family, his dependants, and sometimes his whole clan followed him. Muhammad ﷺ wanted as many people as possible to follow the right path; he wanted to save as many as possible from the degrading worship of stone and from eternal suffering. More than once the Qur'an gently reproved him for his anxiety for people, his extreme concern for them.

Perhaps you will kill yourself from grief, following their trail
because they do not believe these words. (18:6)

While Muhammad ﷺ was speaking to this prominent Qurayshi, a poor blind man came up to him. He was the son of Umm Maktum, a poor woman. Unable to see that Muhammad ﷺ was busy with another, he kept saying, 'Teach me something of what Allah has taught you,' over and over again. Muhammad ﷺ saw his opportunity of convincing this dignitary of Quraysh slipping away, but the blind man kept on insisting, 'Teach me something of what Allah has taught you.' Muhammad ﷺ turned and walked away from him. On the way home he felt ashamed for not having stopped and talked with the son of Umm Maktum, then immediately after this, these holy verses were revealed to him:

He frowned and turned away,
when the blind man came to him.
How can you tell? Perchance he might become a better man,

or recall and the reminder would help him.
As for him who is indifferent,
you stop and address him,
when you are not charged with his salvation;
as for him who comes hurrying to you,
while apprehensive,
you are diverted from him.
Nay, this is a reminder,
so remind him who wishes it. (80:1-12)

To Allah it is not only the important personages who are of consequence, but all those who want to walk in the straight way, who desire to know Him and to be taught His words. Muhammad was commanded not to address people according to their position in this world, but according to their earnestness in seeking guidance. A man may be humble and poor but great in the sight of Allah; and a man may be very great in the sight of his fellow men and of no consequence to Allah. He assesses people according to what is in their hearts and not according to their appearance, wealth, position, or influence among other men.

The Messenger taught his followers these verses just as he taught them every word that was sent down of the Qur'an. He did his very best to deliver everything accurately, neither diminishing nor adding anything. These verses contained a reprimand for him, nevertheless he repeated them and explained their implications as he explained everything else from the Qur'an.

Whenever the blind man passed by him after that, Muhammad used to be very cordial and attentive to him. Smiling he used to say, 'You, on account of whom my Lord has taken me to task.'

The personality of Muhammad, so frank and open, so intelligent, tactful, and modest, helped attract people to Islam. 'Ali ibn Abi Talib said of him: 'No one saw him without being awed by his presence; and no one came to know him without loving him.'

7.3 The Struggle Continues

Muhammad became more and more active in calling to Allah as more verses of the Qur'an were sent down and the number of his followers continued to increase. So once again Quraysh went to his uncle. This time they took the handsomest youth of all Quraysh, called 'Umara, with them and asked him to take that youth as a son and deliver Muhammad to them. Abu Talib refused and

Muhammadﷺ continued to call to the new religion with vigour and wisdom.

Muhammadﷺ was protected outside his home by his tribe. Inside his house he was comforted and consoled by a most understanding and affectionate wife who had total trust in him. Patient and wise, Khadija dissipated the slights, the injuries, the insults he received outside his house. Although the deniers would not kill him, fearing his tribe's retaliation, they did all the mean and spiteful things they could. They used to throw the innards of animals they had killed as offerings to their gods over him while he prayed. They threw filth at his house. He had particularly vicious neighbours in Abu Jahl and Abu Lahab. At first he used to keep someone on guard in front of his house, but one day the holy verses said that Allah had made him immune from men so he stopped keeping a guard. His life was protected, but he was not safe from their injuries. Like all prophets he had to drink from the bitter cup of rejection.

The leaders of Quraysh did not fight Muhammadﷺ for the sake of their gods alone, but to maintain the reign of the strong over the weak in Makka that Muhammadﷺ's teaching was bound to break up. There was a certain monopoly of rich merchants who ruined smaller merchants, particularly strangers from other tribes. They controlled the economy of Makka by force and fraud.
The Qur'an teaches:

You shall not eat your money unrighteously between you,
or hand it to the rulers
to eat up the money of a group of you in sin,
when you know. (2:188)

There was much in the teaching of the Qur'an that was against the practices of the powerful Qurayshis. It was against injustice, against usury, against the strong tyrannising the weak. It struck at the very root of the evils of their social and economic system. Even without attacking the idols and proclaiming the worship of Allah alone, Muhammadﷺ had made powerful and implacable enemies.

7.4 Muhammadﷺ Claims Redress from Abu Jahl

A man stood in the heart of Makka and cried, 'People of Makka, I am a stranger among you. I came to you with camels that I sold to Abu Jahl. I have waited and pleaded until my patience has run out but Abu Jahl will not give me the price of my camels. Which of you will intercede with him on my behalf?'

Some of the group of people he was addressing were friends and intimates of Abu Jahl, but they did not see why they should exert themselves and perhaps displease Abu Jahl for the sake of this stranger. Then someone, thinking it would be a capital joke, pointed out Muhammad⌘ to him. Muhammad⌘ was at some distance from them, praying by the Ka'ba. They said to him, 'Do you see that man over there? He will intercede for you with Abu Jahl.'

They did not tell him that Abu Jahl was Muhammad⌘'s bitterest enemy, who had plotted time and time again against him. They thought they were going to have an amusing time at the expense of Muhammad⌘ and the stranger.

The stranger went to Muhammad⌘, not knowing who he was nor his relationship to Abu Jahl. Muhammad⌘ listened to the man's story. He could have excused himself, saying that his intercession could not be expected to be successful in enabling the man to find favour with Abu Jahl, but he would let nothing stand in the way of justice - there was wrong to be redressed. He rose with the man, saying that they would go to ask for the money together.

Quraysh followed at a distance to see what would happen. Perhaps Muhammad⌘ and Abu Jahl would fight, which might in turn lead to civil war among the tribes, so they sent, from among them, a spy to discover exactly what the two men would say to each other.

When Muhammad⌘ and the stranger reached Abu Jahl's house, he knocked at the door.

'Who is it?' said Abu Jahl.

'Muhammad⌘.'

Abu Jahl came out trembling and pale-faced.

'Could you give this man his money?' asked Muhammad⌘.

'Certainly,' said Abu Jahl, 'if you wait a moment.'

He went in, brought the money and gave it to the stranger, and the stranger went on his way.

As was often the case with these Qurayshis, they plotted behind his back, but when face to face with Muhammad⌘, they cowered and obeyed although Muhammad⌘ was gentle, patient, and forbearing.

7.5 Quraysh go to Abu Talib a Third Time

Quraysh went to Abu Talib for a third time and said, 'Abu Talib, you are our elder, the most honoured among us, the highest of rank.

We have asked you to stop your nephew but you have not succeeded. We shall bear this no longer for he has insulted our forefathers, belittled our aspirations, and spoken against our gods. Either you stop him or we shall fight you and him until one of the two parties perishes.'

Abu Talib called Muhammad☼, repeated to him the words of Quraysh, then said, 'Stop, for my sake and yours. Do not force me to bear what I have not the power to endure.'

Muhammad☼, mute with compassion, looked at his uncle for he understood his position well. But there was more at stake than the feelings of men, more than their lives. There was the salvation of their souls, the hope of eternal happiness for them. So he answered in these memorable words, 'Uncle, if they placed the sun in my right and the moon in my left to abandon this affair, I would not until Allah made the truth prevail or I died in the attempt.'

He rose and turned to go for his heart was heavy with compassion and sorrow. Abu Talib saw how much Muhammad☼ cared and how great the thing must be for which he was jeopardizing his life and the life of all those he loved. He called him back and said, 'Nephew, say what you will, for I shall never deliver you up to anything you would not like.'

Then Abu Talib called the tribes of Banu Hashim and Banu 'Abdu'-Muttalib, whose head he was and who were Muhammad☼'s nearest kin, and asked them to swear to protect Muhammad☼. This was one of the customs of the Arabs. If a man protected by his tribe was harmed by a man from another tribe, his tribe were bound in honour to retaliate. They all agreed, except Abu Lahab who declared his enmity to all and went over to the opposite side.

Some of Muhammad☼'s people believed and some did not, but Muhammad☼ was their own flesh and blood and they felt he had a right to say what he wanted just as any of the orators around the Ka'ba and in the market-places did. They were not going to stand by and allow men from other tribes to deprive him of this right.

7.6 Quraysh Persecute Muslims

As more and more people began to listen to the words of Allah, Quraysh became increasingly alarmed. They began to take vicious and spiteful action against the Muslims in their tribes. Each tribe fell upon those of its members who had entered Islam. They tortured them, they beat them, they starved them, they abandoned them to die in the wastes of burning rock surrounding Makka. There were those who were tortured so severely that, no longer in control of themselves, they said whatever Quraysh wanted them to say, and there were those who held on, steadfast, no matter how extreme the torture.

A humble family, Banu Yasir, which consisted of father, mother, and son, entered into Islam, so the leaders of their clan, the Banu Makhzum, used to torture them in the rocky wastes around Makka. The Muslims numbering less than forty men could do little to protect their own. Seeing Banu Yasir being tortured, the Messenger said, 'Banu Yasir, our appointment is Paradise.' The mother died of torture without giving in. The father and son also refused to submit, but somehow they survived the terrible ordeal. Years later when the Muslims were ordered to fight their oppressors for the sake of the freedom of religion, the son became a very brave soldier of Islam.

The viciousness of Quraysh knew no bounds. One man, Al-Walid ibn Al- Mughira, put Bilal, his black slave, out in the desert sun with a great stone over his chest and left him there to die a slow death because he would not return to idol worship. Bilal persisted in repeating, 'The One, the One, the One,' as he lay dying in the sun.

Abu Bakr passed by, and seeing him in this condition, bought him and set him free. Bilal turned out to have a strong, clear voice. Years later when the Muslims emigrated to Madina, he became the first man to call the believers to prayer. The majestically beautiful words of the call to prayer were called out in his clear, melodious voice. He was the first mu'adhdhin. After the Prophet passed away, he excused himself to the first Khalif, Abu Bakr, and would call to prayer no more. He loved Muhammadﷺ with such great and passionate devotion that fulfilling the special task the Messenger had given him was too painful a reminder of his loss.

Abu Bakr made it his job to buy such unfortunate slaves and set them free. Another such case was Ibn Fahayra whom he set free and even employed as a shepherd for his flocks.

A slave whose craft was forging iron entered into Islam, so the woman who owned him took the very tools he used in his trade and tortured him with them. She would not kill him - slaves cost money - but she would torture him day after day. One day Muhammadﷺ passed by and saw the sight. He felt great pity for the man but could do nothing since slaves were the property of their masters. All he said was, 'My Lord, save him, save him!'

55

The word 'ansur' in Arabic means to save, to revenge, or to give victory. It implies all these three together.

The woman was bitten by a mad dog, and the only recourse physicians had at that time in such cases was cauterization with the same hot irons she had used on the smith.

7.7 The Overt and Covert of the Human Heart

A certain man who had been very badly tortured, broke down and told Quraysh whatever they wanted him to say. But in his heart he was of deep faith and was certain that the message Muhammadﷺ had brought was from the Lord of all creation. He felt devastated about what he had been forced to say and went to the Messenger in a pitiable plight, trembling lest what he had said under torture would jeopardize his relationship with his Lord. It was on this occasion that the following verses of the Qur'an were revealed:

Those who deny Allah after belief,
not he who is compelled while his heart is secure in faith,
but those who are glad in their hearts to deny,
upon them is the wrath of Allah
and for them there is great torture. (16:106)

This verse affirms that it is the human heart that is of consequence. What a man is compelled to say under duress is not binding before Allah, what he harbours in his heart is what matters. A man is not only responsible for what he says, without being coerced, but for what he feels and thinks, for what his heart conceals. On the day of judgment nothing will be of any avail, neither money or children, nothing in fact except a pure heart.

The day neither money nor children are of any benefit,
except going to Allah with a sound heart. (26:88,89)

The word 'sound' in Arabic means free from all blemish or impurity, hence sincere, pure, honest, righteous. It implies much.

To Allah belongs all in the heavens and all on earth.
Whether you reveal what is in your hearts or conceal it,
Allah will take you to account for it.
He forgives whom He will and punishes whom He will.
Allah is able to do anything. (2:284)

While to Allah a statement or promise made under duress is not. binding, the opposite tendency, that is to pretend belief is a very grave sin. It is hypocrisy to deny Allah inwardly and then to pretend to believe before people in order to to appear better than what one, in reality, is. No wonder that hypocrites are assigned to the deepest fire of Jahannam. In this assessment of the behaviour of men there is deep perception and justice.

7.8 Persecution of Muslims Continues

Although Quraysh, for fear of tribal retaliation, would not kill Muhammad☆, they did all the mean and spiteful things they could to hurt him. What was beneath their dignity they incited their rabble and riff-raff to do. They harassed, insulted, and annoyed him in every possible way. They accused him of being a liar and a magician and they did all they could to distract him as he taught the believers. For a man of such noble birth, brought up to be looked up to and respected, it was not easy to bear, but Muhammad☆ bore it all with very great patience and endurance. He was a man entrusted with the greatest responsibility that any human being has ever been entrusted with and he let nothing distract his attention from his noble mission of bringing people out of darkness into light.

While Muhammad☆ bore injuries and insults to himself with equanimity, he found it more difficult to bear the suffering that those who followed him had to undergo. By nature very kind-hearted, he felt for them more than he felt for himself. The Qur'an says:

There has come to you a messenger from among yourselves.
Painful to him are the hardships you suffer, careful of you,
merciful and compassionate to those who believe. (9:128)

The more Quraysh tried to coerce the Muslims into abandoning the worship of Allah, the more they adhered to their religion as being the only salvation for them and their people. They became people who cared for nothing, sought nothing except the great light that had dawned upon them, the truth that proclaimed itself to the heart and mind at the same time. They became patient and persevering in the effort to save as many of their people as possible from superstition and the false gods they worshipped. Many of these men had lived a life of luxury before Islam. They no longer cared for this idle way of life or for money or for the advantages and titles they used to enjoy. To be acceptable to Allah was far more important to them than this world and everything in it. Islam liberated them from the petty fetters of custom, tradition, prejudice, and material desires. They were born anew, remodelled to owe allegiance to none except Allah, the One, the Creator of all. They served Him in humble devotion and considered no sacrifice too great for His cause.

One day the Muslims said to each other, 'Quraysh have never really heard the Qur'an.' They were opposing it chauvinistically for the sake of their traditions and their idols, but very few of them had had a chance to hear it. Who would volunteer to recite it to them?

Ibn Mas'ud, a young man not yet twenty, immediately volunteered. The Muslims objected saying that they needed a man who had a strong clan to protect him, otherwise he might be injured or tortured. But Ibn Mas'ud insisted that it should be him. In the end they allowed him to try. He sat by the Ka'ba and started to recite the Qur'an in the soft melodious tones that Muhammadﷺ had taught them to use. They listened for a moment enthralled, then someone said, 'But this is part of what Muhammadﷺ has brought.' So they got up and started hitting Ibn Mas'ud about the head, while he continued to recite the Qur'an. When he could continue no longer, he returned beaten and bruised to the Muslims. 'But we told you so,'they said. He answered that he was willing to do it again if they would let him. They refused, however. It was characteristic of the Muslims that each tried to do the difficult and unpleasant job in order to spare his brothers. They saw Muhammadﷺ's example and were quick to follow.

7.9 'Utba ibn Rabi'a is sent to Muhammadﷺ

Quraysh did not know what to do about Muhammadﷺ and his followers. They were increasing in strength and number every day and they were willing to bear persecution and injury for the sake of their religion. They did not object to Muhammadﷺ as an individual, on the contrary, they trusted him beyond all others and when travelling they would leave their valuables and precious things with none but him. What they objected to were the new principles and concepts that he had introduced. In the narrowness of their perception, they thought he would stop if they gave him whatever it was that he wanted. They did not realize that spreading the words of the Most High to save the whole of mankind from the evil and base life it led was to him a far more precious thing than the world and all it contained.

They sent one of the greatest and oldest among them, 'Utba ibn Rabi'a, to negotiate with him. He said, 'Nephew, you are one of us, you have the highest rank and lineage among us, but you have brought your people something very grave that has split their ranks, so listen to me: I shall make three offers to you, perhaps one of them will be acceptable to you. If the aim behind your call is money, we can collect for you all the money you ask so that you become the richest among us. If it is honour, we are ready to make you ruler over us, nothing shall be done without your command. If it is kingship that you want, we are ready to make you king over us. If that which comes to you is a phantom that you have no power to ward off, we are ready to call doctors to your aid until you are cured.'

When he finished Muhammadﷺ said nothing, but read him the chapter from the Qur'an called Surat Al-Sajda. The man sat awed by the beauty of the words, the truth and majesty of the content. Before him was a man who was not mad and who desired neither money nor influence nor honour. This was a call to justice, charity, kindness, and the eternal truth that Allah is One. He sat and listened in reverence, feeling the intensity of what was before him. He said nothing more to Muhammadﷺ but went back to Quraysh and counselled them to leave Muhammadﷺ alone. In the diplomatic language of the Arabs, he said, 'Leave Muhammadﷺ to the rest of the Arabs. If they overcome him, you will be relieved of him. If he overcomes them by his strange words, then all the honour will go to you for you are his people.

Quraysh did not like 'Utba's counsel, nor the state of mind he returned in, but all they could do was to keep persecuting the unprotected Muslims. They tortured, they molested, they killed, making life a misery for them. Whenever they heard that someone had entered into Islam, they went to him and said, 'We shall destroy your hopes and blacken your honour.' If he was a merchant, they said to him, 'We shall stagnate your trade and destroy your capital.'

7.10 Emigration to Abyssinia

Many Muslims had to hide and pray secretly whereas what they needed was to pray in peace and freedom and to be able to learn more about their religion without fear or worry. So Muhammadﷺ counselled these vulnerable Muslims to flee for the sake of their religion, to leave Makka and go to Abyssinia. He said that in Abyssinia there was a king in whose realm no one was wronged. They slipped quietly out of Makka, fourteen men and one woman. Through the king's hospitality, they lived for some time in peace and plenty until they heard that Quraysh were no longer torturing the Muslims. They returned to find matters worse than ever so they went back to Abyssinia. This time there were eighty men with their women and children.

They had left Arabia to escape the Quraysh but Quraysh would not leave them in peace with their religion. They sent emissaries to the Negus of Abyssinia bearing precious gifts. They said to him, 'Great King, some of the rabble of our land have come to your country. They have deserted

the religion of their forefathers and have not entered into your religion (the king was a Christian). We have sent their masters, their uncles and their fathers, the heads of their people who know them best, and we beg that they be handed over to them.'

The Qurayshis had given precious gifts to the patriarchs of the Negus and begged them to deliver the Muslims to them without their having to meet the Negus. But the Negus, against the patriarchs' counsel, insisted on hearing what the Muslims had to say for themselves. He called them and said, 'What is this that has made you forsake the religion of your forefathers yet not enter into any of the known creeds.'

The man who spoke for the Muslims was Ja'far ibn Abi Talib, Muhammadﷺ's cousin. He said, 'Great king, we were an ignorant people. We worshipped idols, ate dead things, committed abominations, rejected our kindred, were bad neighbours, and the strong among us tyrannised the weak. We remained thus until Allah sent us a messenger, one of us, whose lineage and integrity we all know. He called us to worship Allah alone, and reject the idols and sacred stones our fathers had worshipped. He commands us to be true to our word, to return a trust to its owner, to be good to our kindred, to our neighbour, and to stop sin and bloodshed. He forbids us abominations and perjury; he forbids us to eat the money of the fatherless or to slander innocent women. He commands us to prayer, charity, and fasting. So we believe in him and follow what he has brought us from Allah. Now we worship Allah alone, forbid ourselves what He forbids us, and allow ourselves what He allows us.

'However our people have aggressively assaulted us, persecuted us, tortured us in order to compel us to return to the worship of idols and the evils we used to do.

'When they overpowered us, wronged us, coerced us, and tried to stand between us and our religion, we came to your land and chose you from all other kings to seek your protection, hoping that in your land we should not be wronged.'

'And have you anything of what he has brought from Allah to read to me?' said the Negus.

'Yes,' said Ja'far, and he read him the verses in Surat Maryam which describe Maryam and Jesus.

So she pointed to him.
They said, 'How can we speak to a baby in the cradle?'
He said, 'I am the slave of Allah
He gave me the Book and made me a prophet.
And He blessed wherever I be,
and charged me with prayers and charity so long as I live.
Benevolent to my mother, He has not made me a miserable tyrant.
Peace unto me the day I was born,
the day I die and the day I am resurrected.' (19:29-33)

When the patriarchs heard these words, they were appalled and said, 'These words come from the same source as the words of our Lord Jesus Christ.'

The Negus said, 'This and what Moses brought come from the same niche. No, I shall never deliver you to them.'

So the Muslims lived in peace and hospitality in Abyssinia until the Prophet settled in Madina, then they joined their fellow Muslims there.

Many years later, after the whole of the Arabian peninsula came under Muhammadﷺ's domination, a delegation was sent to him by the Negus of Abyssinia. Muhammadﷺ insisted on serving them himself. When asked why he, rather than any of his followers or servants, should serve them, he said, 'They were good to my people.'

7.11 'Umar ibn al-Khattab Enters into Islam

'Umar ibn Al-Khattab was in the prime of manhood, powerfully built, of large frame, and with a quick, violent temper. He loved drink, wrestling, and sports. He enjoyed company and reading poetry in late night revels. He was good to his family and relations, but he was one of the men the Muslims feared and many suffered at his hands. He molested them, spoke ill of them, and took every opportunity to harass them.

But behind 'Umar's rough exterior and harsh manner was a soft and sensitive heart. When he found the Muslims had fled to Abyssinia, he felt a pang of remorse and he began to miss them. Then he thought of Muhammadﷺ, this man who had divided Quraysh, and decided that the only thing to do was to kill him. After

Muhammad's death, he believed, these people would return to their homes and land, to the religion of their forefathers, and all would be happy and united again.

He heard that Muhammad and the Muslims met at the house of Al-Arqam, so he took his sword and headed towards it. On the way he met Nu'aym ibn 'Abdu'l- 'Uzza. When the latter learned his intention, he said, 'Really, 'Umar, you are deceiving yourself. Do you think you can kill Muhammad and that then Banu 'Abdu Manaf and Banu Hashim would leave you unharmed on the face of the earth? Besides, shouldn't you put your own house in order first?'

'Umar learning from Nu'aym that his own sister and her husband had entered into Islam, marched off to their house in fury. He heard someone reading the Qur'an. As soon as he approached, it stopped. He entered in a rage and said, 'What is this noise I hear?'

When his sister and her husband denied there had been any noise, he began to beat Said, his brother-in-law. His sister rose to stand between him and her husband, but he pushed her aside. She fell and wounded her forehead so that blood streamed over her face. 'Umar looked at what he had done and felt remorseful. He had not meant to hurt her.

His sister and her husband were furious with him. They admitted that they had entered into Islam and, defying him, bid him do what he would. He asked to see the text, but Fatima, his sister, would not let him see it until he promised to return it safely.

It was the opening verses of Surat Taha. 'Umar was thrilled and taken aback by the power and majesty of what he read, by the truth that would reveal itself, whether deniers liked it or not. He sat shaken for a moment, then rose and headed towards where Muhammad taught in the house of Al-Arqam.

As he approached, people whispered, 'It is 'Umar.' But Muhammad who feared no man told them to let him in. He entered, professed himself a Muslim, and swore allegiance to Allah and His Messenger. Muhammad was overjoyed, for he had often prayed that Allah would strengthen the new religion by either 'Umar ibn Al-Khattab or Al-Walid ibn Al-Mughira, two men of great power and influence among Quraysh.

'Umar was not a man to do anything by halves. Just as he was terrible to the Muslims before, now he stood terrible and magnificent in defence of Islam. He dared any man to prevent him or any Muslim from prayer. He prayed openly at the Ka'ba for all to hear and see and led the Muslims in prayer there, bringing them out of their hiding place in the house of Al-Argam.

He was a man of iron will and a clear, just perception. Now that he was convinced of the truth of Islam he resented that Muslims should be deprived of freedom of worship when they were in the right. He made no compromises about his beliefs. The Muslims found in him, as they found in Hamza, a shield against the ever-growing spite of Quraysh.

CHAPTER EIGHT

8.1 Calling All Arabs to Islam, Quraysh's Reaction

After being commanded to proclaim the worship of Allah to his kin, then to all Quraysh, Muhammad☻ was commanded to call all the Arabs to Allah, as he was later commanded to call all men. Like everything introduced by the Qur'an, the process was gradual, in phases. There is nothing arbitrary, nothing abrupt or exorbitant in the legislation or the concepts that the Qur'an introduces. It is free of the characteristics of haste and tyranny that often mark the work of the human legislator. It is a gradual and- steady transition, a wise guidance from wrong towards right, from falsehood towards truth by Him who has the time and the destiny of all men in His hands.

In answer to the command to call all the Arabs to Allah, Muhammad☻ thought of addressing the Arabs who came every year on pilgrimage to the Ka'ba, from different parts of the Arabian peninsula. Quraysh heard of this and decided to prevent him. But how were they to go about it? There were now in each tribe, in each family of Quraysh, men who believed in Allah and His Messenger. Men for whom, if any of them was touched by harm, a whole tribe would retaliate even if it had not entered into Islam. If they could not prevent Muhammad☻ by force, then let it be by cunning. The first weapon they chose was propaganda. Years earlier they had set their poets upon him and had not succeeded. Now they wanted a way to vitiate his call and belittle him in the eyes of the Arab pilgrims who were coming in the Sacred Months.

In one of their meetings, they plotted together in order not to say contradictory words and belie each other thus proving the falsehood of all their statements. Someone suggested that they tell the pilgrims that Muhammad☻ was a soothsayer, but Al-Walid ibn Al-Mughira, who was heading the meeting, rejected the idea, saying that Muhammad☻'s clear, majestic words were very different from the mumblings of the soothsayer. Another suggested that they say that Muhammad☻ was mad, but this idea was also rejected as Muhammad☻'s words, so orderly and reasonable, were obviously not madness and his whole bearing and manner further proved his sanity. Then it was suggested that they say he was a magician, but

Muhammadﷺ never practised magic. At last Al-Walid ibn Al-Mughira came up with the idea that they should say that Muhammadﷺ was a magician of words for he bewitched people by his words and made them desert the religion of their forefathers. He separated father and son, mother and daughter, brother from brother, and this, at least, they could prove. There were so many examples among them. The visitor had only to look at Quraysh who were once the epitome of unity and solidarity - that should be sufficient warning to the tribes who came. If they listened to Muhammadﷺ it would be at their peril; he would bewitch them, divide them, and break their unity. As an extra precaution they hired a man to relate to the pilgrims the ancient legends of Persia, just in case they listened to him out of boredom.

8.2 Al-Tufayl al-Dawsi

Al-Tufayl ibn 'Amr Al-Dawsi was approaching Makka. He was a chieftain of noble birth, a poet, and a man of sound judgment. So Quraysh went out to meet him and warned him to keep away from Muhammadﷺ so that he and his tribe should not suffer what they were suffering.

Muhammadﷺ used to sit by Al-Marwa, and Al-Tufayl, after entering Makka, heard some of his words to the people. He liked what he heard but he hesitated to come forward because of the warnings of Quraysh to him. Then he said to himself, 'May my mother grieve for me! I am a poet, a man of mature thought, I can distinguish between good and bad, so why should I not listen to what he has to say? If it is good, I will try to learn more; if it is bad, I can always reject it.' He listened and was interested in what he heard so he followed Muhammadﷺ to his house, revealed his identity and asked to know more. Muhammadﷺ recited the Qur'an to him and the man became Muslim, then went back to his country.

Many years later, after the liberation of Makka, Al-Dawsi came to see Muhammadﷺ in Madina at the head of a great delegation of his tribe who were all Muslims, for he had spent those years calling his people to Islam. Some had responded readily and some had not, but he had persevered and succeeded in converting many to Islam.

Al-Dawsi was an example of what happened to many, and it was not only idol worshippers who entered Islam, but also Jews and Christians. They felt that the Qur'an explained the things they were in doubt about.

A delegation of twenty Christian men from Najran was sent by their people to discuss religion with Muhammadﷺ. They sat, talked with him, and got up Muslims. Quraysh were furious. They said to them, 'May Allah humiliate you, you shameful delegation. Your people have sent you to 'bring them news of the man, but no sooner did you sit with him than you left your religion and believed in him!'

8.3 The Three Questions

In their war of propaganda against Muhammadﷺ Quraysh sought the aid of the Jews of Khaybar. They were people of the Book and had knowledge from ancient books and writings that were available to no-one else. The Jews of Khaybar responded readily for Quraysh had great influence in the Arabian peninsula. They advised them to ask Muhammadﷺ three questions for, according to their ancient books, no one but a prophet would be able to answer these three questions correctly.

Quraysh were delighted. They thought they were giving Muhammadﷺ a test beyond his powers. They asked him these three questions. Who was the man to whom Allah gave power and enabled him to journey around the world in ancient times? Who were the young men who had deserted their people because their people worshipped other than Allah, and what happened to them? What was the spirit?

The Jews' ancient books gave them information about the first two, but said that no prophet would pretend to know what the spirit was, since knowledge about it belonged to Allah alone.

Muhammadﷺ waited, confident that Gabriel would soon come and give him all the information he needed concerning these three matters. But Gabriel did not appear. He waited and waited, and Quraysh jeered at him in derision; he had nothing to tell them. At last when his patience was wearing thin and he had begun to despair, Gabriel appeared. Mystified, Muhammadﷺ asked him what had kept him away for so long. He answered that angels did not descend unless it was the will of Allah - He alone regulated all their movements and knew all their actions. Then he added a gentle reproof and reminder to Muhammadﷺ, saying, 'And your Lord is never forgetful.'

The verses Gabriel brought are in Surat Al-Kahf and they give clear and accurate information about the first two matters, but about the spirit the holy verses point out that such knowledge was not granted to man:

They ask you about the spirit.
Say, 'Knowledge of the spirit belongs to my Lord,
and of knowledge you have not been given except a little. (17:85)

Allah has given man knowledge that suffices his physical, mental, and spiritual needs but what is beyond his capacity, or perhaps not for his good, has been withheld. The realm of the supernatural is one of the realms where he was not granted knowledge.

Years later, when Muhammadﷺ emigrated to Madina with the Muslims, the Jews of Madina used to sit and study what he taught to the Muslims. The above verses puzzled them. They asked, 'Messenger of Allah, do these verses refer to us or to your people?'

'These verses refer to you both,' replied Muhammadﷺ:

The Jews argued that they had been given the Torah which contained much knowledge, and Muhammadﷺ answered that it contained sufficient knowledge for their needs if they adhered to it but that, in comparison with the knowledge of Allah, this was very little.

CHAPTER NINE

9.1 The Nobles of Quraysh Listen to Islam, Quraysh's Reaction

Although the leaders of Quraysh fought Muhammadﷺ with every means at their disposal, by propaganda and lies, by persecuting his followers, by tempting them with money, slave girls, and allurements, by threats and rages against those of their class who entered into Islam, and by paying poets and entertainers to relate to people the tales of ancient civilizations in the hope that they would be diverted, many in their heart of hearts were not sure they were in the right, many felt uneasy, and many experienced internal conflicts and doubts.

One night four of the leaders of Quraysh, Abu Sufyan ibn Harb, Abu Jahl ibn Hisham, Al-Akhnas ibn Shariq, and 'Amr ibn Wahb decided, each separately and unknown to the other, to go and listen to the wondrous words that Muhammadﷺ read to himself during the night, for the Messenger used to spend the night in prayers and reading the Qur'an, stopping only after the dawn prayers.

Each of the four men sat listening in the dark, thinking he was the only listener, but when it was dawn and each rose to go to his house, they all met at the crossroads. They reproached each other and assured each other that this was the first time they had succumbed to such a temptation and that it would be the last. But the next night something stronger than them seemed to draw them to Muhammadﷺ's house again and each went thinking he would be the only listener. In the morning they again reproached each other and agreed never to be seen listening to Muhammadﷺ in case the common people heard of it, as it would encourage some to enter Islam. On the third night they met each other again sneaking away from Muhammadﷺ's house. They were truly alarmed and feared they were capitulating, so they swore a solemn oath, binding on the four of them, never to approach his house again.

The next morning Al-Akhnas was disturbed. He could not get out of his mind the grandeur and majesty of what he had heard, its deep wisdom and infallible truth. He put on his cloak and went to Abu Sufyan's house. He asked Abu Sufyan what he thought of what they had heard. Abu Sufyan answered that he did not know, he could understand some of it but some he could not.

Al-Akhnas left him and went to Abu Jahl and asked the same question. Abu Jahl said, 'So what! We and Banu 'Abdu Manaf (Muhammad🕊's tribe) competed with each other for honour. They fed the poor and so did we. They carried water to the Ka'ba (an honorary office) and so did we, until we became like two race horses, neck to neck. Then they say, "Among us is a prophet who receives the message from heaven." When are we going to be able to do something like that? By Allah we shall not believe him or believe in him ever.'

9.2 The Jealousy of His Peers

These words of Abu Jahl are most significant. One of the main reasons why Muhammad🕊's peers would not believe was because they were jealous of him. He was one of them, a man, not an angel, who had grown up among them, lived the same life, and belonged to the same tribe. Why then was he followed, honoured, and obeyed? Why did people listen to his teaching? They thought only with a narrow tribal mentality full of competition and struggle for supremacy in honour and power. They seemed to know very little about Muhammad🕊's real aims.

9.3 Reasoning of Quraysh's Leaders

At first the leading men of Quraysh had no objection to Muhammad🕊 personally but only to the revelation he brought and the concepts it contained. When they saw how Muhammad🕊 was revered, how people listened attentively when he taught and when he read the Qur'an, they became jealous of him. They could no longer deny the beauty and majesty of the Qur'an, they could no longer ignore the truth and justice of its precepts, so they began to tell each other that they would have believed in the Qur'an if only it had descended upon someone other than Muhammad🕊. Why was he chosen from among all the men of Quraysh? And they named two men in particular, two men of great wealth and power, one in Makka, the other in Ta'if, a rich city which the nobles of Quraysh had made their summer resort. The Qur'an quotes their own words to them, then answers them with the following arguments:

And they said, 'If only this Qur'an were sent down
upon one of the chiefs of the two cities.'
Are they distributing your Lord's mercy?

**It is We who distribute their livelihoods upon them
in the life of this world
and raise some above others in degrees
so that they subjugate them,
and your Lord's mercy is better than all they collect. (43:31,32)**

9.4 The Choice of a Prophet

The choice of a prophet is a very carefully planned matter. There is nothing arbitrary about it. He is chosen from birth from millions of beings and nurtured for his great office. Then he is tried and tested until he is ready for the great task, the greatest that man has ever been given. Muhammadﷺ, the last and greatest of the prophets, was no exception. He

used to say, 'It is my Lord who has brought me up, and He has brought me up well.' In an age when men were gross and brutish, he was refined, cultured, tactful, and considerate, and he instilled these qualities in his followers. Like all prophets, Muhammadﷺ was very severely tested and tried and he endured his trials with manliness, patience, and perseverance.

When the Quraysh demanded one of the two great men in Makka or Ta'if to be Prophet, they were demanding what they had neither the right to demand or the ability to choose. As the Qur'an points out, **'Allah knows best where to place His message.'**

CHAPTER TEN

10.1 The Boycott

Quraysh were constantly seeking an effective means of paralyzing Muhammadﷺ's call. After much deliberation they decided to make a covenant against Muhammadﷺ, his clan and tribe, Banu Hashim and Banu 'Abdu'l- Muttalib, and all the Muslims. There was to be a complete boycott, social and economic. They would not buy or sell to them, they would not marry with them nor give them their daughters in marriage. They wrote down this covenant and hung it, like all important proclamations, on the wall of the Ka'ba. This covenant meant the financial ruin of both Muhammadﷺ's people and the Muslims, but they never thought of abandoning Muhammadﷺ and his message. They had to take refuge in a gulley in the mountains where they lived a life of hardship and severe deprivation, but they were strengthened by their faith and with the belief that they were doing the right thing.

Then Quraysh went to the three men who were married to Muhammadﷺ's three eldest daughters and asked them to divorce their wives. They said, 'You have taken a burden off Muhammadﷺ, return them to him. Let him be occupied with them.'

Two of the Prophet's daughters were married to the two sons of Abu Lahab, Muhammadﷺ's uncle and bitter enemy, a man who collected much wealth but did nobody any good by it. The third daughter, Zaynab, was married to Abu'l-'As, a cousin of Khadija. The two sons of Abu Lahab divorced their wives, according to the wishes of Quraysh and their father. But Abu'l-'As, although he had not entered into Islam, refused to take orders from Quraysh or divorce his wife according to their bidding. Abu'l-'As was a courageous and honourable man, as will be revealed later.

This boycott began in the seventh year of Muhammadﷺ's calling and it lasted for three years. During those three years, Muhammadﷺ's people lived in a state of near starvation, besieged in the mountain heights. They were eating up their capital, their children were growing hungry and thin, their elderly were becoming weaker day by day, but they would not bow to the tyranny of Quraysh.

Quraysh had meant this boycott to be a lesson for would-be Muslims, a deterrent against Islam, but the Muslims suffered it with patience and courage. What Muhammad☀ himself suffered with perseverance and fortitude (he used to place stones inside his waistband to quell the pangs of hunger), earned him the sympathy and respect of many. He used to descend once a year during the Sacred Months to address the pilgrims, and the pilgrims responded with sympathy and admiration for the man who had endured so much for what he believed.

Some of the Qurayshis themselves were appalled at their own cruelty to their kin. One of them, Hisham ibn 'Amr, used to sneak out at night with camels carrying food until he reached the place where they lived. Then he would whip the camels to run forward into the Muslim camp.

10.2 Breaking the Covenant

When Hisham ibn 'Amr could no longer bear to see the Muslims in this condition, he decided to campaign against the hard-hearted and unfair behaviour of Quraysh. So he went to another of the Qurayshis called Zuhayr and said to him, 'Zuhayr, are you content to eat food and marry women when your uncles are starving in the mountains? If they were my uncles, I would not endure this wrong.'

The two men agreed to work diligently together to break this unfair boycott. They spoke secretly to three others and the five men set to work to sway public opinion.

Then one day, when they felt the time was ripe, Zuhayr went seven times around the Ka'ba, then called out to the people, 'People of Makka, shall we eat food and wear fine clothes when Banu Hashim are perishing in the mountains? By Allah, I will not rest until this unfair and wrongful covenant is broken.'

As soon as Abu Jahl heard these words, he cried, 'Never, it shall not be broken!'

The other four rose up to support Zuhayr. Abu Jahl then saw by the hostile faces around him that he had no support and that, by the persistence of the five men, the matter had already been settled. He feared speaking up when he found himself alone, so he said no more.

They went inside the Ka'ba to tear up the hateful covenant but found the work had already been done. Termites had eaten up all of the covenant except the first line which read: In Thy name, O Allah,

Now Muhammad☀'s people could come down from the

mountains, buy, sell, and resume a normal life. But those three years in the mountains had taken a heavy toll from them physically and financially. Khadija, genteel and delicate, was not used to the hard life of privation and her health had suffered. Abu Talib, who was in his eighties, had also felt the strain and soon after they returned he lay on his death-bed.

10.3 Quraysh meet the Messenger at Abu Talib's

The Quraysh feared that the situation between Muhammad☙ and them would deteriorate further after the death of Abu Talib. They went to the dying man and asked him to intercede between them and his nephew so that after he was gone Quraysh would not be rent by strife.

Muhammad☙ met the leaders of Quraysh at his uncle's house and said to them, 'In truth, all I ask is one word, one word that you shall give me, with it you shall dominate the Arabs and have ascendance over all foreigners.'

'Ten words, not one,' said Abu Jahl, 'ask all you wish.'

'Say, "Allah is One," and reject the idols you worship.'

They were scandalized, and one of them said, 'But, Muhammad☙, do you want us to make the gods only one?'

Then they agreed with each other that it was no use, they were never going to get anything out of such a man who was not ready to budge an inch. They left Abu Talib's house without coming to an agreement with Muhammad☙.

10.4 Abu Talib on His Deathbed

As Abu Talib approached death, Muhammad☙ went to see him. This old man was very dear to him. He had brought him up from childhood, guided him through youth, and even after he had become a man, Abu Talib had stood resolutely between him and the evil spite of Quraysh. Remembering this period of his life in later years, Muhammad☙ used to say, 'Quraysh were never really able to do me harm except after the death of Abu Talib.'

Now that Abu Talib was about to leave this world, Muhammad☙ wanted to help him gain a place in Paradise. He was going to him with the hope that perhaps now that he was so close to death his uncle would be able to accept the truth. Unfortunately he found Abu Jahl and some other of the Qurayshi chiefs with him. Muhammad☙ pleaded with Abu Talib, coaxed him, begged him just to say one statement, 'Allah is One.' 'If only you would say it, I could plead for you with it before the Throne.'

Abu Talib loved his nephew, loved him as dearly as a son, but he could not understand what Muhammadﷺ had been struggling and was still struggling for. He protected him because he loved him and because Muhammadﷺ was his own flesh and blood. He trusted and respected him, but this strange, spiritual contact with the unknown was beyond Abu Talib. His old mind, fixed in its habits, could not at this late hour strike out on a new route but, because he loved his nephew, he said, 'If I did not fear that the women of Quraysh would say that I said it out of fear of death, I would say it to please you.'

Here Abu Jahl and the other men intervened saying, 'Nay, nay, the religion of 'Abdu'l-Muttalib.'

'Abdu'l-Muttalib, Abu Talib's father and Muhammadﷺ's grandfather, had been a polytheist who worshipped the stone idols of the Ka'ba. To these visionless men the greatest virtue was to adhere to the religion of their forefathers. They did not ask themselves whether it was true or not, sound or not, or whether there was something better. They followed blindly in the groove that preceding generations had left and considered this to be steadfastness and faithfulness.

Again Muhammadﷺ pleaded with his uncle. To save the soul of the man he loved like a father was so important to him, but again, whenever Abu Talib began to lean towards him a little, the Qurayshi chiefs would remind him, 'The religion of 'Abdu'l-Muttalib.'

Muhammadﷺ found himself powerless to move the rigid, fixed mind of the old man, reinforced as it was by the constant interruptions of the others. The weight of tradition and the habits of years stood against him. He returned home sad and discouraged, and Abu Talib died a polytheist.

On this occasion these holy verses were sent down to console Muhammadﷺ for his failure to save the old man, so close to his heart,

You do not guide those you love.
Allah guides whom He will,
and He knows best those who would be guided. (28:56)

10.5 Khadija Passes Away

A few months after the death of Abu Talib, Khadija, whose health had suffered from the years of privation in the mountains, passed away. Khadija, the affectionate and understanding wife, the companion in struggle, the sincere friend, the first person on earth to believe in him. Khadija, who had dedicated her whole life to the service of her persecuted husband and her Lord, who had cheered his heart and tended his wounds, who was part of Allah's mercy to him, was no more. Muhammad🌺 felt no loss so greatly as this one. External support had been weakened by the death of Abu Talib, and now love, comfort and understanding at home were lost with the death of Khadija. Muhammad🌺 was a lonely man. He left a cheerless house to preach and struggle for Allah's sake and returned to a cheerless house. At this very time, when he had suffered such grievous bereavement, Quraysh augmented their campaign against him. He walked, a solitary light, gleaming in the dark evil of Qurayshi superstition.

After Abu Talib's death the insults and injuries of Quraysh had grown more bold and vicious. The least of it was that one of their rabble poured dust over Muhammad🌺's head, which was considered a great insult, but he bore everything with courage and perseverance for the sake of his mission. Patiently he would go to Fatima, his daughter, for her to clean him. Fatima could not bear to see her father suffer such humiliation. She used to sob and sob as she removed the dust, while Muhammad🌺 kept comforting her, saying, 'Do not cry, my child, Allah protects your father from men."

He meant that Allah protected his life. But suffering, insults, and injuries were the price of standing against evil.

10.6 Muhammad🌺 Goes to Ta'if

Quraysh were stubborn and heedless. Those of them who had the ability to understand had already entered into Islam, those who did not persisted in their idol worship and superstitions. Muhammad🌺, whose duty it was to spread his call as far and as widely as possible, looked to new horizons hoping his words would find more responsive hearts elsewhere.

He went to the tribe of Thaqif who lived in Ta'if. This tribe enjoyed a temperate climate and fertile lands. They were opulent and engrossed in matters of this world. Moreover, they had an idol that they cherished and boasted of before the other tribes.

Ta'if's equable weather made it a summer resort for the rich of Quraysh, while the Thaqif themselves visited Makka in the Sacred Months. The good will of Quraysh was therefore very important to them. Muhammad☀ was aware of the situation, but he was trying to break the narrow circle Quraysh had woven around him, and to him the message from Allah was far more important than this world and all the riches in it. He hoped they would be able to grasp the magnitude of the gift sent down to man.

He went alone to speak to Thaqif. They received him with expressions of resentment and derision. He explained, gave examples, preached but they were deaf, blind, and dumb. At last Muhammad☀ realized that they would not believe, so he asked them not to mention his visit to Quraysh for he knew they would gloat over his misfortune, but immediately they spread the news far and wide.

As he was leaving they incited their rabble to pelt him with stones, so he fled from them and took shelter behind a wall which belonged to the two sons of Rabi'a. Then he looked heavenwards and said:

'My Lord, to Thee I complain of my weakness and lack of ability, my being scorned by men. Most Merciful of the merciful, thou art the Lord of the downtrodden and my Lord. To whom hast Thou entrusted me? To a stranger who frowns upon me, or to an enemy in whose hands Thou hast given me? If Thou art not angry with me, I do not mind, but Thy pardon is the greatest to me. I seek the aid of the light of Thy face that dissipates darkness and rectifies the condition of this world and the eternal world lest Thou let Thy wrath befall me or Thy displeasure overtake me. Thine is reproach until Thou art content. There is no power and no right without Thee.'

The two sons of Rabi'a sat and listened in wonder. Here was a man who was once the most honoured of the honoured. Whatever made him expose himself to the insults, jeers, and sneers of the rabble? He could have been the highest among his people if only he had renounced these strange ideas. Out of pity they sent their boy 'Addas to him with a bunch of grapes.

Before taking the grapes, the Prophet said, 'In the name of Allah.' Then he began to eat.

The boy started and said, 'The people of these parts do not speak like this.'

The Messenger asked him what country he came from, and the boy said that he was a Nestorian Christian, that his name was 'Addas. 'From the country of the righteous man, Yunus son of Matta?' asked Muhammad☀.

'Do you know of him,' asked 'Addas.

'Yes,' said Muhammadﷺ, 'we are brethren. He was a prophet and I am a prophet.'

'Addas bent down and kissed Muhammadﷺ's forehead, hands, and feet, while the two sons of Rabi'a watched on in wonder. They had seen what happened to those who did not follow the ways of their fathers, so they called 'Addas and said to him, "Addas, be careful! Don't let that man lure you away from the religion of your forefathers for it is better than this.'

When they heard from Thaqif what had happened, Quraysh were in ecstasy. They increased the venom of their attacks, but whatever he had to suffer, whatever he had to endure for Allah's sake, Muhammadﷺ bore with a patient courage and indomitable will. Even after his hostile reception at the hands of Thaqif he did not give up but continued to address the tribes who came on pilgrimage to Makka. Abu Jahl, however, would not let him alone and went wherever Muhammadﷺ went, to try and belittle him and his message in the eyes of the tribesmen.

The Messenger was not content to wait for the tribes to come to Makka, but went to them in their own homes where he talked to them, read the Qur'an, explained that he was a messenger sent to them, but in vain. They were unmoved. Some of them answered ungraciously, while Banu 'Amr said they would follow him provided that if he were victorious they would rule after him. When Muhammadﷺ replied that such matters were in the hands of Allah, they lost interest.

10.7 The Celestial Journey

The more a prophet is rejected by men, the more he is loved by Allah; the more he is despised by men, the more he is honoured by Allah. Muhammadﷺ had suffered and struggled much, and proved steadfast and unswerving; then came solace and encouragement.

One night when asleep in the house of his cousin Umm Hani, the daughter of Abu Talib, he was summoned away by the angel Gabriel who took him first on a visit to the Aqsa Mosque in Jerusalem, then accompanied him on a journey through the seven heavens. It was a stupendous journey whose memory sustained him through the years of struggle, patience, and privation that lay ahead of him.

He had prayed the evening prayers with Umm Hani and her family, then they all went to sleep. At dawn he said to them, 'I prayed the evening prayers with you in this valley, then I went to Jerusalem where I prayed, and here I am praying the dawn prayers with you.'

'Messenger of Allah,' said Umm Hani, 'do not tell people this lest they reject and injure you.'

'Indeed I shall tell,' said the Prophet.

Then he went to the Ka'ba where he began to recount his experience to the people. Fearless and of indomitable spirit, he cared not what they thought of him nor what they said about him, so long as he delivered every message he was commanded to deliver. On another occasion he received the following admonition:

Honourable Messenger,
deliver what was revealed to you from your Lord.
If you do not, then you have not delivered His message.
Allah gives you immunity from men;
Allah does not guide deniers. (5:67)

He resolved to relate this most extraordinary experience even if half of Makka laughed at him and the other half did not believe. He had to do what he had been ordered by Allah to do.

More than once the Qur'an reminds Muhammad ﷺ of the patience and perseverance of the prophets in past times; more than once he is addressed compassionately and told that he has to continue, no matter how hard or depressing it may be.

Makka listened in wonder. Those who did not believe were exultant. At last Muhammad ﷺ had said something so wild and extraordinary that it proved him to be a liar. What! Go to Jerusalem and return on the same night, when it took their camels one whole month to go and one whole month to return. Impossible! It was as impossible to them as travel to another universe is to us today. As for the ascent to the seven heavens, it was so far from their imagination they could not even conceive of it.

Even some of those who believed wavered and went to Abu Bakr with the story. Amazed, at first Abu Bakr told them that they were inventing tales about the Messenger. When they assured him that it was Muhammad ﷺ himself who was saying these things, Abu Bakr said, 'If he has said it, then he has said the truth. He informs me that the command comes to him from Allah during any hour of the night or day. That is much less accessible than Jerusalem.'

Of deep faith and broad vision, Abu Bakr was immediately able to transcend above the material knowledge of his day. They knew of no conveyance to Jerusalem quicker than a camel, but he realised that to receive revelation from Allah was more extraordinary than a night journey to Jerusalem.

He went to the Ka'ba and found the Makkans asking the Prophet to describe the Aqsa Mosque to them. Muhammadﷺ had never been there before this visit while Abu Bakr, who was a merchant and had travelled much, knew the place well. Muhammadﷺ was describing it, part by part, when Abu Bakr cried out in delight, 'You have spoken the truth, Messenger of Allah!'

From that day Muhammadﷺ gave Abu Bakr the name As-Siddiq, 'the True', because his faith was so deep that it knew no reservation and had no limits. All through Abu Bakr's life, both during the Prophet's lifetime and after it when he was the Khalif, it was this limitless faith that carried him through the worst crises.

Materialistic, with an envious nature and narrow vision, Quraysh continued to question Muhammadﷺ and demand concrete evidence, as if the vast realm of the supernatural could be explained with the terms of the limited, circumscribed material universe, but obligingly the Messenger complied. He told them that on the the way he had seen a lost camel and further on its owner looking for it. He had called out to the man and directed him to where the camel was. At another place he had descended to drink, then replaced the cup in a particular way. On the return journey he had seen a caravan on its way to Makka which would arrive towards evening. The caravan did indeed arrive towards evening, and a desert Arab came in, dazed, to relate that a most amazing thing had happened to him. He had lost his camel, then a voice from the clouds had spoken to him and told him where to find it. Quraysh then went to the place, far away from Makka, where he had descended to drink, and found the cup placed as Muhammadﷺ had said it would be. Quraysh continued to ask questions, then check and re-check Muhammadﷺ's answers, in the hope of finding something they could use against him, but in vain, for every time they found that the material evidence supported his words. This did not make them more responsive to his call but, on the contrary, those who hated Muhammadﷺ envied him even more than before. The Qur'an, inimitable and vast, was beyond anything they could produce, but this journey to the seven heavens was so beyond their limited conceptions that the fact that Muhammadﷺ could produce material evidence simply made them furious.

Quraysh's insults, mockery, and invective against the Messenger increased, but tranquil and patient, he continued with his mission.

This extraordinary journey had acted as a revitalizer and inspiration to him. It made him see beyond the immediate struggle, beyond the slow and painful passage of those days.

When he used to recall this decisive journey, he said that if he were ever allowed to return to that realm of splendour he would never willingly come back to this world, and he used to say also that no prophet had ever been tested as he was, for to return to this world of cares after the glimpse of everlasting joy above was a most painful experience.

10.8 The Gift Descended to Man

From the highest spheres, from that journey that had reached far beyond where human feet had ever been, far beyond where human eye had ever seen or human mind imagined, the Messenger brought back a gift for those who believed. It is significant that the gift he brought was not for himself, but for his people, for Muhammad☙ cared much more for those who followed him than for himself; it is significant that it was nothing worldly, no diamond or bar of gold, but something of far greater value to those who understood. It was the gift of prayer and contact with the Most High. Muslims were to call upon their Lord - that is stand before their Lord and perform the rituals of prayer - five times a day. These five prayers, Allah, out of His bounty, would count as fifty. To pray five times a day is expiation and purification for the human soul, it can also be a very great spiritual pleasure.

The Messenger found in nothing more solace and pleasure than in prayers, and when it was prayer time he used to tell Bilal, 'Bilal, relieve us by prayers.' The pressures, pains, and disappointments of this world are very many, so he found in prayer, in the moments he spent with his Lord, the greatest joy of his life. Whenever he had to face the impossible, a dilemma too great for the human mind, or a catastrophe too powerful for human hands, he sought refuge and solace in prayers.

Prayers are a very important spiritual aspect of religion to all Muslims. They are one of the five pillars of the faith.

One of the Companions once asked the Messenger about the prayers and Muhammad☙ told him to compare a stream of running water and a pond. The stream of running water changed its water five times a day while the water in the pond was stagnant. Which would have purer water? The Companion answered that the running stream would. Muhammad explained that the action of prayer upon the human soul was as the action of running water on the stream.

The second great gift the Messenger brought back concerned human actions. Man is liable to err, so Allah in His mercy encourages him by the following bonus. He who starts to do a good deed and then stops, this shall be counted for him just the same as a good deed, but if he accomplishes it, it shall be counted as ten good deeds. He who starts to do a bad deed but refrains, this shall not be counted against him, but if he actually commits a bad deed, it shall be counted as just one bad deed. And we learn from the Qur'an that a good deed is sometimes rewarded up to seven hundred times. Such is the grace of Allah.

CHAPTER ELEVEN

The Prophet's followers in Makka were fewer in number than before. Some had fled to Abyssinia with their religion; some had wavered and turned back; but those who remained were of deep and sincere faith. Isolated and surrounded by the great numbers of Quraysh, they were a united and strong group, working together in harmony. So few were they, they lived in fear of being wiped out, but Muhammad ⁕ never gave up. He was certain that Allah would make His religion prevail, even if the deniers hated it.

11.1 The Dawn from Yathrib (Madina)

At this dark hour the dawn of hope began to break from a direction no one had expected. It came from the direction of Yathrib. Next to Makka, Yathrib was the city Muhammad ⁕ had most connection with. His uncles of Banu Najjar were from Yathrib. His father was buried there and his mother in a nearby village. He had gone to Yathrib when a little boy to visit the grave of his father and once a year the aged and stately chief of Quraysh, Muhammad ⁕'s grandfather, used to go there to visit the grave of his beloved son.

Yathrib was a more pleasant city than Makka, with a temperate climate and cool green shade. Its inhabitants were the two tribes of Al-Aws and Al-Khazraj. There were also some Jewish tribes in the city. The Jews, who were a minority, had created misunderstanding and hatred between the two tribes in order to be safe from them and to be the dominant power. The two tribes lived in a state of constant warfare, strife, and raids..

The Jews mocked the Arabs for their idolatry and foretold the appearance of a great prophet, described in their ancient books, who would lead those who followed him to dominate over all. Believing themselves the chosen people, they assumed that this prophet would appear from amongst them, and they told the Arabs of Yathrib that, when he appeared, they would exterminate them as 'Ad and Thamud and other Arab tribes had been exterminated in ancient times, or keep them as slaves. They thought that day was soon approaching.

A war of hatred and vengeance broke out between the Al-Aws and the Al-Khazraj, and each tribe resolved to exterminate the other if it was victorious. So some of the Aws went to Makka to seek the aid of Quraysh. There they met the Messenger and listened in hope and wonder to his words. One of them said, 'My people, this is much better than what you have come for,' and he entered into Islam. The rest, though very much attracted to the new religion, did not commit themselves for they were preoccupied by the impending battle and feared to do anything that would offend Quraysh as the fate of their own people hung in the balance.

This battle proved to be a life and death struggle. At first Al-Khazraj were victorious, then Al-Aws by a mighty effort turned the tide of defeat into victory. As they were about to burn down the houses of their enemy and to cut down their palm trees, one of their leaders intervened, saying that as both Al-Aws and Al-Khazraj had become so weak neither could stand alone without the other, and that it was better to have Al-Khazraj as neighbours than be in the neighbourhood of the foxes. He meant the Jews, for he knew that the Jewish tribes of Yathrib would soon dominate whichever tribe survived and use them as slaves.

An uneasy truce resulted between Al-Aws and Al-Khazraj. They could not trust each other, nor could they trust the Jews. Al-Khazraj were honour bound, according to the rules of war of the tribes, to revenge this defeat. Another battle would have been the end of both tribes.

11.2 The First Oath of Al-'Aqaba

As the year progressed, many people from Yathrib came as pilgrims to Makka. Twelve men came secretly to swear allegiance to the Messenger. They said to him, 'If Allah should unite us through you, then no man on earth would be dearer to us than you.' They had been often threatened by the Jews with a prophet who would come in the last or latter days. He would lead those who followed him to dominance. The Jews prayed and waited patiently for such a day and the tribes of Yathrib were apprehensive, for the Jews in their old books knew of. things that the Arabs found obscure and mystifying.

In the oath of allegiance they swore to worship no other gods than Allah, not to steal, not to tell lies, not to commit adultery, not to kill their children, and not to disobey the Prophet. If they fulfilled these commandments their reward would be paradise; if they neglected or forgot any of them, Allah might forgive them or punish them for it.

The Prophet sent one of his Companions, Mus'ab ibn 'Umayr,

with them to teach them the Qur'an and the practices of Islam. Mus'ab came from one of the noble clans of Quraysh. Before Islam he had lived a life of luxury and pleasure, a pampered and idle youth. People used to point him out for his fine appearance and rich dress. After becoming Muslim he left everything, left his family who would not enter into Islam, and dedicated his whole life to the service of Allah. With his clear perception and sincere belief he was an excellent guide to the precepts of Islam. He went to live with the people of Yathrib and every day some of them would enter into Islam at his hand. The choice of Mus'ab for this office was an auspicious one for he was singularly suitable for the job.

As the following year progressed, the sacred months approached once again. These were the months when the Arabs from all parts of the Peninsula came to make the pilgrimage. Mus'ab came a little earlier to Makka with good news. He told the Messenger how well the people of Yathrib, both Al-Aws and Al-Khazraj, were receiving Islam, how numerous were those converted to it, and how eager they were to hear the words of Allah and to know more of the Qur'an.

11.3 The Second Oath of Al-'Aqaba

That year many pilgrims came from Yathrib, among them those who came on business, for it was the season when much trade was done, and those who came to offer sacrifices to the gods of Quraysh, but there were also seventy-five Muslims - seventy-three men and two women. They had a secret appointment with the Messenger on the third day of Al-Tashriq, that is the third day after the great feast. In the dead of night they rose, left their tents, climbed the mountain to the place of rendezvous and waited there for the Prophet.

He came accompanied by his uncle, Al 'Abbas, who had become the head of Banu Hashim and Banu 'Abdu Manaf after the death of Abu Talib. Banu Hashim and Banu 'Abdu Manaf had sworn to protect Muhammad؛, and Al- 'Abbas came to demand a solemn oath from the people of Yathrib to protect Muhammad؛ should he decide to live among them, so that Banu 'Abdu Manaf and Banu Hashim would not be embroiled in a war they were unequal to in the event of the people of Yathrib deserting him.

'People of Al-Khazraj!' he said, 'Muhammad؛, as you know, is one of us and we have protected him from our people who do not share our opinion concerning his religion. He is here immune among his people and powerful in his land, but he insists on joining you and becoming one of you. If you are sure you will fulfill what you have called him for and that you will protect him from all who differ from him then you are free to carry this responsibility, but if you are going to desert him and betray him after he has gone to you, then it is better to leave him now.'

The people of Yathrib said, 'We have heard your words. Speak, Messenger of Allah, demand what you will for yourself and your Lord.'

The Messenger recited from the Qur'an to them and spoke of Islam. Then he said, 'Swear to protect me from what you would protect your women and children.'

Al-Bara' ibn 'Amr, who was the head of his people and their greatest man, had sworn allegiance the year before at Al-'Agaba and observed all the rites required of a Muslim. Now he spoke, 'We swear, Messenger of Allah. We are a people with knowledge of war that we have inherited from father to son.'

'Prophet of Allah,' one of them said, 'there are treaties between us and the Jews that we shall break. If Allah gives you victory, will you return to your people, leaving us?'

The Prophet smiled and said, 'My blood is your blood, my ruin is your ruin. I am of you and you are of me. I fight those you fight and befriend those you befriend.'

After many years and many victories, after Makka lay open under his feet, after all the peninsula was under his dominion, Muhammadﷺ still held those words dear and binding. In his farewell speech before he left this world, he charged those who would come in power after him to be good to the people of Yathrib.

They rose to swear allegiance, but Al-'Abbas ibn 'Ubada stopped them, saying, 'People of Al-Khazraj, do you know what you are swearing allegiance to this man about? You are swearing to fight the red and black of people (that is all peoples, all races). If you think that the loss of your money and the death of your leaders would make you deliver him to the enemy, better leave him now. But if you do so, by Allah, it is ignominy in this world and the next. If you are certain you will fulfill your vow to him, even in loss and death, then take him for he is the good of this world and the next.'

'We take him,' they answered, 'accepting loss of our money and the death of our leaders. What will be our reward, Messenger of Allah, if we fulfill our obligations?'

'Paradise will be yours,' answered the Messenger.

They gave their hands to him and swore allegiance. Then he said to them, 'Choose twelve deputies from you who will stand surety for your people!'

They chose nine men from Khazraj and three from Al-Aws. Then the Messenger said to them, 'You are deputies for your people as the disciples were to Jesus, son of Maryam, and I am deputy for my people.'

The deputies then swore to follow and obey in wealth and in poverty, in sickness and in health, to tell the truth always and fear the attacks of no one for the salve of Allah.

On a mountainside under the stars they swore this oath and felt that Allah was their witness. They swore with hearts that yearned for the right and souls that hungered for the truth. It was an oath that oriented the fate of mankind and changed the history of the earth. Millions came after them, generation after generation, in all the lands to swear with pure hearts that Allah is One and that Muhammadﷺ is His Messenger.

Suddenly they heard a loud cry that disturbed the solemn stillness of the night. They were brought down from the world of lofty ideals to the world of mean, petty strife. The cry came from a man who had gone out on an errand and overheard some of their words. 'People of Quraysh,' he cried at the top of his voice, 'Muhammadﷺ and the defectors are conspiring to fight you.'

This was a test from Allah for those Muslims so new in faith. They were a minority in the land of Quraysh but they proved true to their Lord and His Prophet. They neither faltered nor turned back but stood firm awaiting his orders. Al-'Abbas ibn 'Ubada said, 'By Allah who has sent you with the truth, if you wish we could fall upon the people of Mina tomorrow with our swords.'

'We were not ordered to do so,' said the Prophet. 'Let each return to his tent.'

They returned and slept peacefully until morning.

Before dawn broke on the dark valleys of Makka Quraysh had heard the news. They went to the tents of the people of Yathrib to question, torture, or kill, but on reaching the first of those Yathribis who were polytheists and had slept soundly throughout the night, they were met with innocent stares, followed by oaths of protest and indignation. They could see that the people before them were telling the truth. The Muslims who had sworn an oath to tell the truth remained silent.

The Quraysh returned, not knowing whether to believe or disbelieve what they had heard. By the time they found out the truth and went after the people of Yathrib, the latter had a headstart and were out of reach. They were able to catch one man, however, who had tarried behind on business. They tortured him until two of their nobles whose trade he used to protect on the summer journey to Al-Sham offered him their protection and saved him from their clutches.

CHAPTER TWELVE

12.1 The New Horizon

The oath of Al-'Aqaba marked an opening for the new religion enabling it to grow unmolested in a city where people could worship Allah in hope and freedom and without fear. To worship openly before all men, whether believer or not, without being tortured, persecuted, or molested had been the dream of the Muslims of Makka and after thirteen years of patient struggle Allah made their dream a reality.

Muhammadﷺ gave his followers permission to emigrate to Yathrib. They were to emigrate discreetly in twos and threes so as not to attract the attention of Quraysh, but Quraysh, always suspicious and alert, tried to prevent anyone they could from emigrating. They tortured them, imprisoned them, seized their money and possessions, or they flattered them, plied them with goods and money and beautiful slave girls. They used every method and means to stop those who wanted to emigrate from leaving. They tempted them in every possible way. They told one man, 'You came to us a pauper and now you are a rich man. You will never leave this city.'

'If I give you all my money will you let me emigrate?' he said

'Yes,' they answered.

So he left all his money to them and emigrated with only his religion to sustain him. Muhammadﷺ met him with a hearty welcome and the words, 'Well done, well done.'

All the deterrents of Quraysh did not stop a steady stream of Muslims from emigrating to Yathrib. Their religion was dearer to them than their wealth, their homes, their families, and their motherland. They were content, happy to escape with their religion, to flee to Allah, leaving their city and its strife behind them.

No one knew for sure whether Muhammadﷺ intended to emigrate to Yathrib or to remain in Makka. He remained, calm and dauntless, in Makka as the number of Muslims there began to dwindle. One day Abu Bakr asked permission to emigrate to Yathrib. All Muhammadﷺ said was, 'Be patient! Perchance Allah will give you a companion.'

12.2 The Qurayshi Plot

The number of Muslims in Yathrib had grown considerably through the sincere efforts of the Muslims the Messenger had sent to teach the people there the Qur'an. They had substantial power and were now supported by the Muslims who had begun to arrive from Makka. If Muhammad۩ were also to emigrate, they would have the wisest and most indomitable leadership and would become a power to be reckoned with. Quraysh feared this above all else. The Muslims might return to attack Makka and threaten its trade route to Al-Sham. Muhammad۩ had, therefore, to be prevented from joining his followers at all costs. Once again they sat in the House of Debate to discuss what was to be done about Muhammad۩. If they kept him in Makka by force, the people of Yathrib might come to fight them for the sake of their religion and their Prophet. If they let him go, he would become dangerous, free, and powerful in Yathrib. If they killed him, his clans, Banu Hashim and Banu 'Abdu Manaf, would demand blood for blood. This would mean a civil war in Makka.

After much debate they contrived a devilish plan to murder him in such a way that his blood could not be demanded of any single clan and no single person would be held responsible for the deed. They selected a large group of young, able-bodied men, one from each clan of Quraysh. They gave each a sword and ordered them to surround Muhammad۩'s house. The moment he came out they were to strike all together as one man. In this way his blood would be upon all the clans of Quraysh, and his people would have to accept blood money for him, for they would not be able to fight the united might of all the clans of Quraysh.

The Messenger was aware of what they had prepared for him, but he was waiting for permission from Allah to emigrate. He waited calmly, full of faith that Allah would enable him to arrive safely in Yathrib. The holy verses told him:

When those who deny plotted cunningly
to restrain you, kill you or drive you out.
They plot and Allah plots
and Allah is the best of plot-makers. (8:30)

His support was his Lord who rules over all the universe, therefore he feared no man. When the permission came, he went to Abu Bakr and asked him to be his companion on this perilous journey. Abu Bakr was overjoyed since to travel with the Prophet was a sign of heavenly favour; to die with him, should that happen, was to die a martyr, the highest honour. Since the day that the Messenger had suggested that he might have a travelling companion, he had kept two camels ready.

It was impossible for them to slip out of Makka unobserved during the day, and when night fell the group of youths came and surrounded the Messenger's house. Muhammad✥ asked 'Ali ibn Abi Talib (the little boy who had sworn to support him was now a man ready and able to carry responsibility) to sleep in his bed that night and wear his green mantle. When morning came, 'Ali was to restore the trusts people had left with Muhammad✥ to their owners.

Quraysh would not believe Muhammad✥, but, curiously, they would trust no one else with their valuable possessions. 'Ali took the Prophet's place, knowing full well the danger involved.

12.3 Muhammad✥ Escapes

During the second part of the night the Messenger, by the power of Allah, was able to walk unseen through the ranks of the encircling youths. He went to the house of Abu Bakr who was expecting him. The two men climbed out through a window at the back of the house. All they had with them was five thousand dinars belonging to Abu Bakr. Muhammad✥ had spent all his own and Khadija's money in the mission. Abu Bakr had made much money in trade and once had forty thousand dinars put aside, but after embracing Islam and after three years of boycott, he had only five thousand dinars left. He had spent most of his money in freeing persecuted slaves and relieving the poor and distressed Muslims.

They headed southwards towards Yemen, the opposite direction to that of Yathrib, and hid in the cave of Thawr. They knew that as soon as morning came, Quraysh would search for them everywhere.

Asma', the daughter of Abu Bakr, used to bring them food while his son 'Abdullah used to spend the day with Quraysh, then bring them news at night of what Quraysh were doing. Ibn Fuhayra, a slave that Abu Bakr had set free and given a job as a shepherd, went each evening to them to milk his goats and give them milk to drink, then he would let his flock walk over 'Abdullah's trail after he left so that no one would notice where it led.

When morning came and 'Ali woke up, the youths of Quraysh discovered the sleeper was not Muhammad✥ but 'Ali ibn Abi Talib. All night they had kept watch, looking at the sleeper in the green cloak, and were convinced that their quarry was within their grasp.

Now they were furious, realizing that they had been outwitted. They divided themselves into search parties, with each party taking a different route. Every day the search parties would go out and return, having accomplished nothing. Quraysh announced a prize of one hundred camels to whosoever would bring them Muhammad☙, dead or alive, or inform them of his whereabouts.

At last one of the search parties took the road to Yemen, the unfrequented route past the cave of Thawr. They approached the cave and found a shepherd standing near it. They asked him if he had seen men answering Muhammad☙ and Abu Bakr's description. Casually he answered that they might be in the cave but that he had seen no one. One of the party went towards the mouth of the cave.

Inside Abu Bakr was listening to the conversation outside, while the Messenger was praying. Abu Bakr, fearing for Muhammad☙, went and stood very close to him. Muhammad☙ whispered in his ear, 'Do not grieve, for Allah is with us.'

The Qur'an describes the scene:

When those who deny drove him out,
one of two was he in the cave,
when he told his companion,
'Do not grieve, for Allah is with us.'
So Allah sent down His peace upon him
and supported him by soldiers you could not see,
and let the word of the deniers go under,
and the word of Allah is the highest.
Allah is of the highest wisdom, of invincible will. (9:40)

When the young man of Quraysh went to the mouth of the cave, he found it covered by a tree with a spider's web built over it and he found a wild dove that had built its nest in the tree. No one could have entered the cave without twisting the branches of the tree, breaking the spider's web and driving the dove away. So he said to his companions, 'There is no one in the cave. Why it has been covered by cobwebs since before Muhammad☙ was born!'

A tree, a spider's web, and a dove's nest were all that appeared of the invisible action that saved Muhammad☙ and his friend. Things so natural that they seemed accidental. Quraysh saw no angels and no soldiers. They returned thinking there was no one in the cave.

12.4 The Long Journey to Yathrib

After three days when they learnt that the search had petered out, the Messenger and his party started out for Yathrib. Asma', the daughter of Abu Bakr, came to them bringing food for the journey. When they were about to start she could find nothing to tie it to their saddles with and so she undid her waistband, tore it in two, wore half and tied the food with the other half. Muhammadﷺ smiled and said, 'She of the two waistbands.' And ever after the Muslims knew her by that name.

A guide from the Banu'l-Duwil came with three camels. They still had to be very careful for many would be tempted by the prize Quraysh had offered.

The guide led them southwards first, towards Tihama by the edge of the Red Sea. When they reached a less-frequented route, the guide then led them northwards, going parallel to the sea but at some distance from it. They rode all the night and most of the day, travelling on in the burning desert heat amid gleaming sand and hard, hot rock. They would rest at noon, the worst part of the part of the day for travel, then with the cool of late afternoon they would start out again. It was a hard, slow journey but with faith and patience they persevered.

12.5 Suraqa ibn Ju'sham

While the Prophet and his party were proceeding at this slow pace, a desert Arab went back to his tribe and said that he had seen three men on camel- back by the Red Sea whom he believed to be Muhammadﷺ and his friends, for whom Quraysh offered a reward. A warrior, called Suraqa ibn Ju'sham, wanting the prize for himself said that he knew who these were, they were so-and-so from such-and-such a tribe and not Muhammadﷺ and his party.

Suraqa was a powerful warrior skilled in the use of weapons and he knew the Messenger and those with him were unarmed. Appearing nonchalant, he went back to his house, saddled his horse without the aid of his groom, armed himself to the teeth, and rode secretly out of the encampment.

He rode furiously in order to catch up with them. On the way his horse jolted him badly. It was a pure Arab steed that normally would not have behaved in this way to its master, but Suraqa had his eye on the prize and drove it on. Again it gave him a bad jolt, but Suraqa galloped on until he could see them at a distance.

At that moment Muhammadﷺ and his party had rested from the

noon-day heat and with the cool of the late afternoon they were about to get on their camels and continue their journey. With a triumphant cry, Suraqa drove his horse closer to them, but as he approached within hailing distance his horse fell into quicksand. The earth began to suck up both man and horse. A strange awe fell upon Suraqa. He felt that all nature, including his beloved horse, were the allies of the Prophet. The great mountains, the hard rocks, and the sands seemed to stand sentinels for Muhammad's safety. Woe unto any who approached him! Suraqa cried for forgiveness, swearing that no harm would ever come to them through him. The Prophet, kind and forgiving, forgave him immediately. The earth began to be more solid under him and the horse started to extricate its legs from the sand. Suraqa asked for a word from Muhammad, a token of security and peace. With the Messenger's permission, the guide wrote something for him on a piece of parchment and the Messenger asked Suraqa to stay where he was and not allowanybody to reach them.

12.6 Umm Ma'bad

They journeyed on, until they reached the camp of Umm Ma'bad, a good woman who used to feed people and give them water to drink, a very important thing for travellers in the desert. But on that day Umm Ma'bad had nothing to offer. They asked for some dates but she had none. They asked for a little milk but her husband had taken all the strong goats out to pasture and those left were too weak to go out or give milk. Muhammad asked for permission to milk one of them and she said, 'As you please.' So he put his hand on the goat's back and said, 'In the name of Allah.' Then he began to milk it. Milk flowed. He gave the first bowl to Umm Ma'bad in spite of her protests, the second to Abu Bakr, and third to the guide. He was the last to drink. Then he milked the second goat in this manner and left Umm Ma'bad with bowls full of milk.

When her husband came home he was amazed to see the bowls of milk, for he had left behind only the goats too feeble to go to pasture or give milk. So he asked her where it had come from. She said, 'I saw a blessed man who came here with two of his friends. His face was luminous like a full moon, his expression serene. When he is quiet, there is a strange dignity about him, when he speaks his words are like sprinkled pearls. His friends obey his every wish and listen to his every word.'

'Ah,' said the husband, 'this is the man Quraysh are looking for. Had I been here when he came, I would have entered into Islam.'

'And why not now? Let us follow him to Yathrib and enter into Islam.'

So they followed the Prophet to Yathrib. Both became good Muslims. Umm Ma'bad's brother also entered into Islam, fought for it, and died a martyr.

12.7 The Miracle of the Qur'an

The life of Muhammad☺ is full of such incidents, but most historians do not dwell upon them. They mention them because they did occur and were witnessed by those who testimony is undoubted. Had they not occurred at all, Muhammad☺ would still be the Messenger of Allah and His prophet. Muhammad☺'s message needs no miracle to corroborate it; it is itself the Miracle. The Qur'an is not prose, yet it has the stately majestic flow of the best prose; it is not poetry, yet it has a very subtle rhythm, peculiarly its own, that makes it easy to quote, easy to remember. If we add to this its very great power of expression, its lucid and infallible logic, its imagery of very great sensibility, and that there is in it a nameless spiritual quality that affects the heart as well as the head, it is not surprising that the Arabs, who were experienced critics in an age that is considered the golden age of poetry, should decide that its composition was beyond the power of mortals to achieve.

In the world today, when men have lost the ability to appreciate the literary excellence of the Qur'an, it is the scientific data in it that scholars find amazing. Whatever branch of science one specializes in, one can find accurate knowledge in the Qur'an about it.

CHAPTER THIRTEEN

13.1 Islam in Yathrib

When news reached Yathrib that the Messenger had been able to escape from Quraysh and was making his way towards them, the Muslims of Yathrib waited with both hope and fear in their hearts. They knew the journey was long and that their enemies were numerous and powerful. Every day they would go to the outskirts of the city in the hope of welcoming their honoured guest.

Muhammad's Companions, whom he had sent on before him, were dedicated men of understanding and vision. Many of the people of Yathrib became Muslim through their teaching, and the following incidents show how certain of the nobles of Yathrib entered into Islam.

Two of the Messenger's Companions, Mus'ab ibn 'Umayr and As'ad ibn Zurara, were sitting by a wall teaching the Qur'an to a group of the men of the city. Two Yathribi nobles seeing their clansmen gathered around the two strangers, were disturbed at the sight. 'Go and drive these two men away before they make fools of our common people. I can't go because one of them is my cousin,' one said to the other.

Off went the man with the intention of driving them away, but when he approached, Mus'ab invited him to sit down and listen.

'If you like what you hear, well and good,' he said, 'but if you do not, then you can take the people away.'

The Yathribi noble found this an equable proposition, so he stuck his spear in the ground and sat down to listen. He got up convinced of the truth of Islam and returned to his friend in a very different manner from how he had left. His companion was furious and went to drive away the foreigners himself. He too was invited to sit and listen as his friend had been and, like his friend, he got up a Muslim.

The second of these two men, Sa'd ibn Mu'adh, was to play a distinguished role in the support of the Prophet and fight in many a battle for Islam. After becoming Muslim, he went immediately off to his clan. 'Banu 'Abdu'l- Ashhal,' he said, 'what do you think of me?'

'You are our greatest man,' they answered, 'noblest in birth, wisest in judgment, and keenest in perception.'

'Forbidden to me is speech to any of you, man or woman, until you believe in Allah and His Prophet.'

So all Banu 'Abdu'l-Ashhal entered into Islam, all its men, women, and children.

13.2 'Amr ibn al-Jumah

'Amr ibn Al-Jumah, one of the nobles of Banu Salama, had wooden idol that he kept in his house, as was the custom of Arab nobles at that time. Some of the young men of Banu Salama who had become Muslim used to take it at night and throw it in one of the pits used as a latrine. When morning came and 'Amr missed his idol, he used to go and look for it in the pits, clean it up and purify it, and put it back in its place of honour in his house, threatening and raging all the while.

This happened night after night until he became so exasperated that he hung a sword around the idol's neck and said to it, 'Defend yourself, if you can.'

The next morning he found it in a well tied to a dead dog and the sword gone.

When some of his people then approached him on the subject of Islam, he was only too happy to become a Muslim, having thoroughly experienced the degradation and futility of idol worship.

CHAPTER FOURTEEN

14.1 Reception of the Prophet in Yathrib

At last the Prophet reached the settlement of Quba', just beyond the boundaries of Yathrib and remained there four days to rest, during which time the mosque of Quba' was built. He set out for Yathrib on the fourth day, a Friday. The people of Yathrib were on the look-out as usual. Suddenly a Jew shouted to the waiting crowd, 'People of Yathrib, here he comes!' They all went out either singly or in groups to meet him, hurrying forward in hope and awe, in joy and fear. They had heard so much of Muhammadﷺ, but few of these men and women who mentioned him five times a day in prayer had ever seen him. The women came in a group with musical instruments, singing a poem of joy:

The full-moon has risen above us from the direction of Sanyat Al-Wada Thanks is due from us whenever we call upon Allah,
O you who have been sent to us, you have come to be obeyed

On and on they chanted, verse after verse as Muhammadﷺ entered the city. All wanted to have a glimpse of this great man, both those who believed and those who did not believe. This man, who was so wise, who had endured so much, and had been able to escape the ring of assassins - this man who, although from the noblest of the clans of Quraysh, had accepted to be as one of them and to come and live amongst them.

They followed his camel wherever it went. The nobles of Yathrib vied with each for the honour of having him as their guest, but the Prophet tactfully excused himself. He gave his camel free rein and let it go where its Maker would guide it. It went on and on, while the Muslims followed, until it reached a plot of land where it stopped and kneeled. Muhammadﷺ asked to whom the land belonged and was informed that it belonged to two orphan boys from Banu Najjar, Muhammadﷺ's maternal uncles. Their guardian said they would offer it to him as a present, but he insisted on buying it. He then ordered that a mosque be built on the site, and beside the mosque was built a simple house for the Messenger.

Yathrib, where his grandfather had been brought up, and where his father had been buried, was now the home of the Messenger of

Allah, and henceforth it ceased to be known by its old name, but took on a new and noble designation - the 'Illuminated' City, Al-Madina al-Munawarra, or as we known it in English, Madina.

14.2 Muhammadﷺ's Indifference to Luxury

The Prophet joined in building the mosque and his home, which were so simple that they required neither much money or much effort. The mosque consisted of an wide space, fenced in and partly roofed over with palm fronds, and it was only lit for night prayers. The house was much smaller and equally simple, being single-storied with a roof of palm fronds.

The Messenger had little concern for material comforts. All his energy, all his thoughts were directed to helping people to believe in Allah, to bringing them out of darkness into light. Although his peers at that time lived a life of idle luxury based upon the service of many slaves, he was content with his simple and frugal life, and whenever slaves came under his control, he set them free or, with Salman the Persian, showed them how to set themselves free, legally, without rebellion.

What he considered a very great pleasure and a luxury that few could afford was the time to be alone, time to spend in contemplation or calling upon his Lord. A solitary moment away from society, in the mountains, was to him far more precious than silks, gold, or brocade. It is not that Islam forbids the good things in life. The Qur'an states that they are among Allah's gifts to his slaves. This frugal life on Muhammadﷺ's part was a matter of preference rather than divine decree. The Qur'an does advise moderation however, and those who believe are to be neither niggardly nor prodigal but to steer a course in between.

Years later when the Messenger acquired much wealth, he spent it all upon the poor, in freeing slaves, or in the furtherance of religion generally, and he used to say that the inheritance of prophets was not of this world nor in it, but of the eternal one to come. The men close to him were influenced by his example: Abu Bakr, the first Khalif, 'Umar, the Amir of the Believers, in whose reign the Arabs were to become extremely rich, 'Uthman, and 'Ali ibn Abi Talib, the third and fourth Khalifs, all lived frugally and simply, preferring to give than to take, to distribute rather than to hoard. Khalifs did not start living in luxury except after these early Muslims were gone and the clan of the Umayyads took the leadership of the Muslims. The founder of this dynasty was Abu Sufyan, of whom we shall soon hear more.

14.3 Life in Madina

Madina, teeming with life, had four groups of people living in it. There were those people from the tribes of the Aws and the Khazraj who had entered into Islam. These were called the 'Ansar' or Supporters, because they were people who supported the Messenger when other tribes had rejected him. Then there were the Muslims who had emigrated from Makka who were known as the 'Muhajirun' or Emigrants, because they had left their homes and city and emigrated to Madina to support Allah and His Messenger. There were also people from Al-Aws and the Al-Khazraj who had not entered into Islam. These were becoming fewer in number and of less consequence as they held no sway over the Muslims who had been strengthened by the arrival of the Makkan Muslims. However a group of them, who professed to believe in Allah and His Messenger, plotted secretly against the Muslims and were dangerous in an insidious and·underhanded way. These were headed by a man called 'Abdullah ibn Ubayy, who had hoped to be made king before the coming of the Messenger to Madina. He resented the Messenger's influence over most of the inhabitants of Madina and he resented the presence of so many Emigrants from Makka, but he stayed his tongue and bided his time. This group of people we shall call 'the Hypocrites', as they were called later by the believers. Apart from these groups there were also three powerful Jewish tribes. How could harmony be created among the four groups? The answer could only be found in the teachings of Islam.

The Messenger made a treaty giving the Jews freedom to practise their religion and binding all the parties together in a pact of mutual protection.

14.4 The Covenant of Brotherhood

In order to give the Muslims the strength to uphold these teachings which were new and alien to the spirit of the world at the time and in order to make these principles a living force and a way of life, the Messenger brought all the Muslims together by assigning to each Muslim a brother in Islam. This bond had all the sanctity of the blood brotherhood that the Arabs revered. He brought together one of the Emigrants with one of the Supporters in these contracts, so that the Emigrants would not feel like strangers in the land, and so that the Supporters would forget their old feuds and vendettas. Muhammad✿ chose as his brother 'Ali ibn Abi Talib, the young cousin he had brought up and loved as his own son.

This act proved beneficial to all. The natives of Madina explained to their Emigrant brethren the customs of the city, and many even shared their homes and purses with them. The natural hospitality of the Arabs, combined with the new faith, made these men completely selfless. Both Emigrants and Supporters thought only of the good of their small community and not of themselves. The Emigrants who had been learning and teaching the Qur'an for thirteen years helped their brothers from Madina with their studies in religion.

At first the Emigrants were the guests of their brethren but very soon they were able to find work and become independent. Some worked in the fields of the Supporters and shared the harvest with them, while others worked as traders. The Makkans were expert traders and many of them became wealthy in a short time and began to help their less fortunate brethren. Abu Bakr continued to work in commerce, to make much money, and to spend most of it in helping the distressed or in the furtherance of Islam.

They were people who worked hard and were content with little of this world. They had not left a life of ease in Makka for the sake of material gain, and so long as they were allowed to learn and understand the words of Allah in peace and freedom they were happy.

14.5 Solidarity through Intermarriages

The Arabs were very careful about their marriage connections because they were not a union of two individuals only, but of two clans. They had obligations to, as well as rights over, their relations by marriage. In this interval of peace in Madina, Muhammad✿ gave his daughter Fatima in marriage to his cousin 'Ali ibn Abi Talib, who had become a mighty warrior and a learned scholar. He married his daughter, Umm Kulthum, to 'Uthman ibn 'Affan, a rich merchant who had wielded great influence among the Makkans, but who had become a devout Muslim, renowed for his generous spending for the sake of religion. Then Muhammad✿ himself married 'A'isha, the daughter of Abu Bakr who had been bethrothed to him since they were in Makka. Sometime after, when the daughter of 'Umar ibn Al-Khattab became a widow, Muhammad✿ asked for her hand. By these four marriages, the four most important men in Islam were gathered into one strong unified whole. It also placed Muhammadﷺ's two closest companions, Abu Bakr and 'Umar; upon an equal footing.

14.6 The Men around the Messenger

A study of the biography of any of the men mentioned above who, after the Messenger passed away, carried the burden of spreading the word of Allah far and wide, shows how truly great each of them was in his own right. The historian who tries to understand this age is struck by the number of exceptional men surrounding the Messenger: Abu Bakr with such gentle, refined ways, yet firm as steel if ever the principles or the decrees of Islam were involved, 'Umar ibn Al-Khattab, a man who reshaped himself anew in order to be able to serve the religion of Allah with the quintessence of justice and mercy, 'Uthman who had the talent to make large amounts of money and used his wealth to buy wells and equipment for the Muslims. Apart from these very close Companions, there were hundreds of other men who would be considered great in any age and against any background, men like Abu 'Ubayda, whom Muhammadﷺ called 'the trustee of this nation', or Khalid ibn Al-Walid whom he called 'the Sword of Islam'. Allah gathered around His Messenger a group of men worthy and able to fulfill their tremendous task.

CHAPTER FIFTEEN

15.1 Relationship with the Jews

At first the Messenger was well received by the Jews of Madina. They saw how powerful his followers were and thought they could eventually use them to fight in their wars against the Christian tribes of Najran. Muhammad☀, benevolent and trusting, met their show of friendliness most cordially, and made treaties with them, mentioned earlier, that gave them freedom and security. He used to sit with their elders discussing religion, teaching and explaining, just as he did with his own followers.

As the Jews were not sincere in their attempts at understanding, instead of being delighted, they began to fear Muhammad☀. This new religion was so clear and logical that they feared the reaction of their own people. They had, however, given them permission to attend the Messenger's sessions and they could not abruptly withdraw it.

One day there occurred a momentous and significant event that brought the Jews' resentment out into the open and showed what their true feelings were. Their most learned scholar and devout rabbi went to discuss religion with the Messenger. This rabbi had found in the ancient books of the Jews that the last and greatest of the prophets was yet to appear and that he was clearly described. The rabbi applied the description to Muhammad☀ and finding that it fitted him so well, he had become more and more convinced that Muhammad☀ was indeed this last and greatest prophet.

This Rabbi, who was re-named 'Abdullah ibn Salam by the Prophet, professed his belief and made one request. He asked the Messenger to hear the opinion of his people about him before he announced to them his entry into Islam.

Accordingly, the Messenger called them and asked what they thought of their rabbi. Not understanding the reason for the question, they replied, 'He is our most learned scholar, our master and the son of our master, and our greatest man.' Whereupon 'Abdullah ibn Salam appeared and announced his entry into Islam, inviting them to do the same, but they rejected him and the truth he had embraced. They rapidly changed their tune and began to revile him among their people in an attempt to prevent any of them following him. When the Jews realized that they were not going to be able to make Muhammadﷺ and his followers fight their wars for them and that they were not going to be able to regain dominance in Madina, they began to wage a devious war upon the Prophet, which makes the slanders against him seem crude. It was a war of cunning insinuations and subtle arguments, and because of their knowledge of previous revelations they were experts at this. Their aim was to make people doubt and to waste the Messenger's time and energy upon questions whose answers they already knew and which could be found in their own books. They sat with the Muslims, pretending to believe, and then asked questions that served only to deprive others of the Messenger's teaching. Such questions were, 'If Allah created everything, then who created Allah?' Thereupon the holy verses were sent down to say:

Say, 'Allah is One, Allah the Everlasting.
He has not given birth, He was not born.
He has absolutely no peer. (112)

The Jews were well aware that Allah is One. Most of the precepts of Islam were not new to them, for, in principle, the precepts of Allah are unchangeable, eternal and the same for all peoples. The Qur'an differs from the Torah and the Bible only in the parts of the previous revelations that have been altered by man. Their aim was to quibble and cast doubts in the heart of those who believed.

15.2 Jewish Plots

They began to ask questions about things that had happened centuries earlier which had for them a symbolic value and that only a prophet would know about. Some of the holy verses sent down in the Qur'an were in answer to these questions. Muhammadﷺ was able to answer these questions correctly as he was truly a prophet, supported by the invincible power of Allah. As the only way to destroy him was to make him err in the sight of Allah, they devised a wicked plan to this end. Some of their elders and rabbis went to him and said, 'You know our position among our people. If we follow you, they would all follow you.' Then they explained that they differed with their people on a certain issue. If Muhammadﷺ would accept to be arbiter between them and their people, then take their side, they would follow him and all their people would follow him. He would thus be saving many human souls. This they knew to be the Messenger's dearest wish.

In spite of his wish to save them, the Messenger refrained from their suggestion, for Islam decrees that a Muslim shall judge fairly, even if it is against himself or his own parents. He used to say, 'It is my fate to see people try to rush into the fire and my duty to try and pick them out.' On one such occasion the holy verses tell him to be on his guard against them, saying:

**And decide between them according to what Allah has shown you,
and do not follow their wishes.
If they turn away, then know that
Allah desires to strike them for some of their sins.
Of men many are trespassers. (5:49)**

At the same time, the Jews tried stirring up the old feuds between Al-Aws and Al-Khazraj as this had always been a successful way of dominating them both in the past. Now, however, Al-Aws and Al-Khazraj had become brothers in Islam and were often to be seen discussing religion and earnestly studying the Qur'an together.

One day a Jew, Sha's ibn Qays, passed by some of Al-Aws and Al-Khazraj conversing amiably together. He was annoyed by the sight, so he called a Jewish youth who had been standing with them and told him to find an opportunity to mention a certain battle from the past. He did so and they began to differ, boasting of their respected warriors until it became a full-blown dispute. When news reached the Messenger of what was happening, he went to them and reminded them of the lofty aims of Islam and of their bond of brotherhood. Brought to their senses, both stunned at their own stupidity and overjoyed with re-affirmation of their faith, they wept and embraced each other.

On another occasion some of the Jews who pretended to listen to the Messenger's teaching were caught whispering and conspiring in a corner of the mosque and Muhammadﷺ had to order that they be sent out.

The Jews did not know what to do about Muhammadﷺ. Realizing that they would never be able to dominate the inhabitants of Madina so long as he was there, they went to him and said that all the great prophets had been to Jerusalem. Since he was a prophet, it was only proper that he should go there as well, and consider his stay in Madina only as an interval between Makka and Jerusalem. It did not take the Messenger long to realize what their real aim was. Then a momentous revelation came to him from Allah which left him in no doubt about the matter.

15.3 The New Orientation

Until that date, seventeen months after the Hijra to Madina, the Muslims had made their orientation in the prayer the same as that of the Jews. Muhammad☆ had felt increasingly uneasy about this and had longed for a direction to face that was characteristic of the pure, unspoilt faith that was his in common with his forefathers, Ibrahim and Isma'il. Where could a faith so very old, yet reborn and revived, turn? Muhammad☆ had turned towards Allah for guidance, and the command had come:

We see your face scanning the sky.
We shall give you an orientation you approve.
Turn your face towards the Sacred Mosque.
Wherever you are, turn your faces towards it.
Those given the Book know it is the truth from their Lord.
Allah is not unaware of what they do. (2:144)

The Muslims were overjoyed because the implications of the new orientation were very great; the hopes it revived even greater. Makka was the Messenger's homeland and in Makka had been built the first sanctuary for the worship of Allah. The Emigrants were homesick for this place that had spiritual connections stronger than anywhere else in the world, but they would not admit it even to themselves. Allah, who knows the secret of every heart, would give them back what they had sacrificed for the sake of their religion. He would give them back the Sacred House, cherished and sought out by pilgrims throughout the centuries.

If their orientation was to be the House of Allah, then surely one day Allah would let His Messenger return to it. If they were given permission to pray towards it, then surely one day they would be allowed to go there as pilgrims and circle the Ka'ba as their ancestors Ibrahim and Isma'il had done. It was a day of hope and rejoicing for the Muslims; a day of connecting the very new with its ancient roots.

15.4 Jewish Reaction

While it was a day of hope and joy for the Muslims, it was a day of mourning and mortification for the Jews. Mortification because the different orientation implied that the Muslims had become completely independent of them, and mourning because their old books said that the last of the great prophets would change the orientation of the religion of Allah from Jerusalem to the Ancient House of Ibrahim. Their knowledge of this prophecy is what the holy verses in the previous section refer to.

So long as Muhammadﷺ had not done so, they could deny his prophethood and feel justified in not being committed to follow him, but once the prophecy had been verified at his hands, they could no longer deny that he was the very prophet they had waited centuries for and had been ordered to obey. Their arrogance as the chosen people stood in the way of their following an Arab. Their desire for power prevented them from admitting that this prophecy had come about in case it led the common people to follow him. They had to find a means of stopping it happening, thus proving that he was not the prophet they had waited for.

Their elders went in a body to the Messenger and said that if he would change his orientation back to Jerusalem, then they would follow him. Once again the revelation guided the Messenger:

> **If you bring the People of the Book every token,**
> **they will not follow your orientation,**
> **nor will you follow theirs.**
> **You will not follow each other's orientation.**
> **Should you follow their wishes**
> **after the knowledge that has come to you,**
> **you would be of the wicked. (2:145)**

The Muslims began to have a distinctive character, while the Jews began to grow closer to the hypocrites and the polytheists.

15.5 The Meeting of the Three Religions

At the time when religious discussion and arguments had reached a peak between the Messenger and the Jews, a delegation of sixty horsemen came from Najran. They were Christian priests and nobles, who had come to join in the discussions, and among them were priests honoured and revered by the Roman Emperor.

The three revealed religions at last met in one place. The Jews denied the prophets who came after them and denied that Jesus was the son of God as the Christians maintained, claiming that 'Uzayr (Ezra) was the son of God.

The Messenger pointed out that the decrees of Allah were eternal and unalterable. What was communicated to him was the same as had been communicated to all the prophets before him, Noah, Abraham, Job, Moses and Jesus, son of Maryam. It is that Allah is

One, He has no son and no mate and He is the Creator of the whole universe. The difference found between the Christians and the Jews was due to human invention. The Messenger challenged them to bring the Torah and to recite it, for in it is written that Allah is One.

When he saw that they would not admit the truth of his words, even though they realized that he spoke the truth, he asked them to do what the holy verses had bid him ask them:

To those who argue with you about him (Jesus)
after the knowledge that has come to you, say
'Come, let us call our children and your children,
our women and your women, ourselves and yourselves,
then call upon Allah to let His curse fall upon the liars.' (3:61)

The Christians of Najran were aware that he spoke the truth, and so they refused to pray with him for the curse of Allah to fall upon those who had not told the truth. They saw how upright and fair he was in dealing with them, and they asked him to send back with them one of his Companions to be the arbiter between them and their people in certain matters on which they differed. The Messenger chose Abu 'Ubayda ibn al-Jarrah to go with them, a man of profound faith and upright judgment, whom the Messenger used to call 'the Trustee of this nation.'

Although they were convinced of the truth of the Messenger's words, the Christians of Najran would not announce their belief in him. When they were asked why they did not, Abu Harith, one of the most learned among them, summed up the situation in the following words, 'What prevents me is what these people (the Romans) have done to us. They have honoured us, made us rich, and given us influence. If I were to disagree with them, all this would be taken away.'

CHAPTER SIXTEEN

16.1 Permission to Fight Back

For thirteen years, the messenger had struggled in Makka to eradicate idolatry and corruption, and for thirteen years the Muslims had been severely persecuted by the Makkans. On more than one occasion they had asked permission to fight back, but the Messenger had replied that they had not been ordered to do so. Aggression breeds aggression, and had the Muslims fought back while they were in Makka, life in the holy city would have turned into a nightmare of violence, and the Muslims to whom the Messenger was trying to teach forgiveness, tolerance and mercy would have had to resort to force to resist Quraysh who far outnumbered them. In such a war both sides would have been the losers. Allah in His mercy had planned something much better for them. All those who were destined to believe by peaceful means were given the opportunity to believe and all those who had the power to emigrate to Madina were given the opportunity to emigrate. Two years after the emigration of the Messenger to Madina the only Muslims who remained among the polytheists of Makka were those who were too weak or too dependent to carve out a new life for themselves. The Messenger and the Muslims thought of these poor Muslims under the yoke of Quraysh, and also of their aged parents who could not emigrate, the young children for whom the new life was too rough, and for the homes, possessions, and businesses they had left behind. Quraysh continued to torture or kill any of the Muslims they could lay hands on.

Islam is a religion that seeks goodness and justice, not passively, but actively. It is not enough to be good - to be truly good one has to stand against wrong. In many verses the Qur'an describes the believers as those who 'command the right and forbid the wrong.'

In order to forbid corruption or command justice one has to be in a position to do so. One has to have the material strength and the power to fight for what one believes in, and until this juncture the Muslims had not been given permission to fight those who attacked them. At last, after fifteen years of patient endurance they were given permission to fight back in the following words:

**Permission is given to those who were attacked, for they were wronged,
and Allah is able to give them victory,
those who were driven out of their homes unfairly,
only because they said, 'Our Lord is Allah.' (22:39,40)**
The above verses give permission only to those who were
wronged. Islam is based upon justice and mercy and it abhors
aggression. The holy verses say:
**Fight for Allah's sake those who fight you,
but do not be the aggressors.
Allah does not like aggressors. (2:190)**
While Islam abhors aggression, it equally abhors weakness and
submissiveness. Muslims should fight for the rights Allah has given
them, should struggle to uphold justice and an equable peace, and
should gather all the power they can to do so.

Throughout his life Muhammadﷺ was patient and forbearing. He
avoided battles and engaged in them only after other means had
failed. When the use of arms was necessary, however, he was the first
to face the enemy with a dauntless courage and an untiring
perseverance. He did his very best, then trusted completely in Allah.
When in battle we notice that he fought with restraint, in accordance
with the decrees of the Qur'an. He never went beyond the necessary
and showed great mercy to his enemies when they fell into his hands.

On the new soil of Madina, the Muslims were in a much better
position to oppose Quraysh, as they had been greatly strengthened by
the Supporters and in Madina they had a stronghold from which they
could go out to make treaties or fight. Had they been given
permission to fight in Makka, they would have had to despoil their
own city, the city of Allah; they would have had to injure women and
children, which is against the decrees of Islam. Allah in His infinite
wisdom spared them all these miseries. Now if they fought Quraysh,
they would fight only men and only those who came to fight them.

The Muslims had only half the numbers of Quraysh and they did
not possess the military equipment or the wealth that war demanded,
for most of their possessions were in the hands of Quraysh. But the
holy verses say:
**Allah will support those who support Him.
Allah is the Almighty, the Invincible. (22:40)**
They were willing to stand and fight for Allah's sake, even though
they were fully aware of the might of Quraysh and of their own
weakness. Once the Holy verses had given permission to them to

fight, it was their duty to do so. Muslims should always be ready to struggle for what they believe in, for faith is not a matter of words but of deeds.

The holy verses above give a promise of victory. This promise proved true throughout the history of Islam. Every time the Muslims have fought for Allah's sake, for the sake of justice and righteousness, they have been granted victory even when material circumstances have been against them. The moment they begin to fight for worldly considerations, victory is withheld, even when material circumstances are in their favour. The reader will notice this in every battle the Muslims fight.

16.2 'Abdullah ibn Jahsh's Raid and the Decision of Allah

Having been given permission to fight, the Muslims went out in groups of twenty men or more to threaten the trade routes of Quraysh, the jugular vein of their livelihood, hoping to make Quraysh come to terms with them. Muhammadﷺ made treaties with many of the tribes around Madina and some of the coastal tribes, so that in case of a war with Quraysh, these tribes would not support the Makkans, as they had formerly done. These armed parties used to go out on sorties, then return to Madina.

One day in the month of Rajab, the Prophet sent 'Abdullah ibn Jahsh at the head of one of these groups and asked him not to open the document containing his instructions and destination until he was already two day's march away from Madina, so as to outwit the spies of Quraysh. After a two days' march, when 'Abdullah opened his letter, he found the following words, 'Go to Nakhla, watch for Quraysh there, and bring us news of their movements.' Nakhla is between Makka and Al-Ta'if.

All the men with him had volunteered to go on this mission, for joining in a mission was optional and Muslims were always consulted on any mission or battle they were to attend. Two of them went to search for a camel they had lost, and were taken captives by Quraysh.

Arriving at Nakhla, 'Abdullah and those with him observed a caravan carrying goods belonging to Quraysh, led by 'Amr ibn Al-Hadrami - Quraysh who had persecuted them, taken their property, and driven them out of their homes. This seemed to be an opportunity to exact revenge, but they hesitated as it was the last day of Rajab, one of the four holy months during which the Arabs did not fight. At least they were unsure whether it was the last day of Rajab or the first day of the month after it, as such matters cannot be decided in advance and depend upon the sighting of the new moon. If they waited until the next day, however, the caravan would enter the precincts of Makka and be out of their reach. They thought of all they had suffered at the hands of Quraysh, and then charged forward, capturing the caravan. During the fight one man fired an arrow at 'Amr ibn Al-Hadrami, killing him.

'Abdullah and those with him returned to Madina with the caravan and two captives. Muhammadﷺ was aghast. He said, 'I never commanded you to fight in the Sacred Months.' He refused to take a share of the caravan. All the Muslims reproached their brethren for having fought in the Sacred Months and without the Prophet's permission.

'Abdullah and his comrades felt they had done wrong, and all the Muslims were upset. Quraysh was exultant. This was an opportunity they would not allow to pass by. They spread the news far and wide that Muhammadﷺ and his followers had fought, taken captives, and killed a man in the Sacred Months. The Muslims answered in defence of their brethren that it was the first of Sha'ban and not the last day of Rajab, but they felt humiliated by this trespass. Deep in their hearts they knew they were the wronged party, they had been wronged over and over again, persecuted, tortured, and robbed, but their limited perception could not transcend above the customs and traditions they had been brought up to respect. Then these holy verses were revealed.

They ask you about the Sacred Month, does one fight in it?
Say, 'There was great fighting in it,
and driving people from the way of Allah, and denying Him.
The Sacred Mosque and driving its people out of it
is to Allah a worse sin.
Persecution is worse than killing'
They will continue to fight you,
until they make you deflect from your religion, if they can. (2:217)

This was justice, finer, clearer, more certain than anything that the Muslims could think of. It was Quraysh who were the trespassers, it was Quraysh who had infringed the sanctity of the Sacred House by not allowing its visitors to enter it. It was Quraysh who had trespassed against the Muslims' sacred right to believe and worship in freedom. It was they who had broken the sanctity of the Holy City.

To Allah, driving worshippers out of His House was a worse sin than fighting in the Sacred Months. To Allah, tempting a man away from His worship, whether by torture and persecution or by allurements, was a sin worse than killing, for it jeopardized his immortal soul. Quraysh had no right to complain since it was they who had started trespassing against things which were sacred.

The Muslims were much relieved to know they had not done anything that Allah did not approve of. Deep in their hearts they had felt it all the time but, blinkered by tradition, they could not express themselves or point out the finer principles involved. On more than one occasion we find observations and judgments in the Qur'an different from what Muhammadﷺ had felt or thought as an individual and from what his contemporaries thought.

The Muslims rejoiced but Quraysh were adamant. They continued to complain and spread evil propaganda against the Muslims until the Messenger realized that he would never come to an understanding with them. They would not listen to reason nor would they be guided by justice. Quraysh disregarded their own interests and the interests of the Muslims for the sake of their pride and they underestimated and belittled Muslim power. The hope that a threat to their trade route would let them come to an understanding was stillborn. If the Muslims were ever to attain freedom of worship for themselves and their families in Makka and be able to return there and if they were ever to go as pilgrims to the Sacred House, it would have to be by force of arms. They were not numerous enough or strong enough to attack Makka but they could harass its main trade route which passed near Madina on the way to Al-Sham.

16.3 Qurayshi Caravan

There was a rumour that a caravan belonging to Quraysh would pass near Madina on its return journey. Muhammadﷺ sent out two men to find out all they could about it, but, while they were gone, he learnt that it was a great caravan that nearly everyone in Quraysh had a share in, worth at least fifty thousand dinars (an enormous sum of money at that time). He did not wait for the two scouts' return but called the Muslims together and told them that perhaps Allah would let it fall into their hands and that they should get ready to intercept it. Some of those who did not believe wanted to join in for the sake of the booty, but the Messenger rejected their help even though he was short of men and weapons. As the battle was between the

Muslims and those who had wronged them, Allah would decide the issue, and Muhammadﷺ wanted no aid from polytheists.

Just as Muhammadﷺ received warning of the caravan's approach, so had Abu Sufyan, who led the caravan, heard that the Muslims intended to intercept it. Only thirty men from the Quraysh guarded this great caravan and, after having gained so much in trade, Abu Sufyan feared for its safety, so he hired a man called Damdam to go and warn Quraysh and call them to his assistance.

Arriving in Makka, Damdam cut his camel's ears and tore open his shirt front, then stood on a prominence and cried, 'Help, help, Quraysh! Muhammadﷺ and his followers are going to attack your caravan, but you may be able to prevent them yet.'

He did not have to cry for long, Abu Jahl heard him. Abu Jahl was a man of sharp features, sharp eyesight, and sharp tongue. He began to call the people of Quraysh to come out and fight for their caravan. Quraysh needed no urging - each of them had a stake in this caravan. But some of them, who felt how cruel they had been to their Muslim kin, hesitated, hoping that the caravan might come in safely without their having to fight those they had already wronged. They pointed out that there was a feud between them and the tribe of Kinda. What guarantee had they that, should they all go out to war as Abu Jahl desired, Kinda would not take this opportunity to attack Makka in their absence?

Sometimes the fate of men hangs on seemingly unimportant coincidences. For at that moment, Malik ibn Ju'shum, one of the leaders of Kinda, was visiting Quraysh and hearing the dispute, he gave his word that he would stand surety against Kinda attacking them. Because of the words of Malik, Abu Jahl and his party prevailed.

16.4 Quraysh Go out to War

Quraysh marched out of Makka displaying all their military might, with their clients and their slaves, their feared javelin throwers, and their famous warriors. They did not do this to frighten the Muslims whom they knew to be weak, few in number, and badly armed, but to display their power before all the tribes of Arabia, both to those who would see their progress and those who would hear of it later. So sure were they of their superiority that they took provisions to feast upon after victory and musicians to play for them in the celebrations. They marched out in ostentatious pride, as if marching on parade.

The Messenger left Madina, putting Abu Lubana in charge of the city. The Muslims had only three hundred and five men and they were short of arms and camels, each three men sharing one camel, two men walking beside it and one riding. Muhammad☙ insisted on sharing a camel like everybody else. He never allowed himself anything that the other Muslims did not have.

16.5 The Messenger Consults His Men

The Muslims feared the caravan would slip by, so they hurried as fast as their limited means allowed until they reached the valley of Dhafiran where they rested. There they learnt that Quraysh had come out to defend their caravan. Muhammad☙ called the Muslims together and informed them of the news. He first consulted his two close advisors, Abu Bakr and 'Umar ibn Al-Khattab, and then he consulted all the Muslims after giving them time to consider this new development. He invariably consulted his men, for according to the Qur'an the affairs of Muslims are best decided after mutual consultation.

Al-Miqdad ibn 'Amr rose and spoke. He said, 'Messenger of Allah, go ahead with what Allah has commanded you, for, by Allah, we shall not say to you as the Jews said to Moses, "Go, you and your God, and fight and we will remain here." But we shall say to you, "Go, you and your God, and fight and we shall fight with you."'

The people listened to his words in silence. Muhammad☙ asked again, for he always wanted them to speak out and to act freely. If they were to fight, they were to fight willingly. He repeated, 'Tell me your opinions?'

Then Sa'd ibn Mu'adh, the chief of the Supporters, spoke, 'Do you want our opinion, Messenger of Allah?'

'Yes,' said Muhammad☙.

'We believe in you and know that you speak the truth. We have given you a solemn oath and covenant to listen and obey. So go ahead with what you desire, for by Him who sent you with the truth, if you were to ask us to cross the sea, we would cross it with you, and not a single man of us would tarry behind. Lead us forward with the blessing of Allah.'

The Prophet smiled and said, 'March forward and be of good cheer, for Allah has promised me that one of the two groups will be ours.' He meant that they would either capture the caravan or Allah would give them victory over Quraysh.

When they reached the well of Badr, Muhammadﷺ went on ahead to discover fresh information. He found an old man whom he asked about Muhammadﷺ and his followers, to see what news had leaked out to these parts, and then he asked him about Quraysh. Muhammadﷺ, learning from him that Quraysh were nearby, sent out 'Ali ibn Abi Talib with three others to find out more. They brought back with them two boys, servants of Quraysh, who had gone out to get water. When the two boys came, the Messenger was praying. The Muslims asked the boys for information, and when they would not answer, some started beating them. The boys said whatever came into their heads to avoid being beaten and the men stopped.

When Muhammadﷺ finished his prayer, he said, 'Wondrous! When they tell you the truth, you beat them. When they tell you lies, you stop beating them!' Then he asked the boys how many Qurayshis there were, and they answered that they did not know. So he asked them how many cattle they slaughtered a day, and they answered that they killed either nine or ten a day. Muhammadﷺ was able to infer from this that they were around one thousand strong: He also learnt from the boys that all the nobles of Quraysh had come out to fight him.

Two of his men went to the well at Badr and overheard two slavegirls talking. One of them was asking the other for money she owed her and the other was telling her to wait one or two days until the caravan came in. They returned with this bit of information to Muhammadﷺ.

Abu Sufyan who was leading the caravan was very wary and cautious. He went a little ahead, fearing that Muhammadﷺ and his men were on his route. Reaching the well, he met a man whom he asked if he had seen anyone. The man said that he had seen no one except two men who had come to water their camels. Abu Sufyan went to where the two men had stood and, looking at the camel droppings, said, 'Ah! This is the kind of food the people of Madina give their camels!' So he returned quickly to his caravan and took another route towards safety. Next day the Muslims learnt that the caravan had slipped away and that only the warriors of Quraysh remained nearby.

Some of the men hesitated, for they realized that they were no match for Quraysh. They were three hundred and five men, ill-equipped, poorly supported, while Quraysh were one thousand strong, well- equipped, with clients and slaves to attend to their needs. Many of them were experienced warriors, while for many of the Muslims this was the first time they had attended a battle.

Muhammad🌸, once he made a decision, never hesitated or turned back. He trusted in Allah to fulfill the destiny written for him. If it was the will of Allah that they fight Quraysh, then they would fight Quraysh. The Muslims had hoped to regain some of what Quraysh had taken from them by intercepting the caravan, but He who decides the destiny of men had other reasons for this fateful meeting.

In the meantime Abu Sufyan had sent a messenger to Quraysh to inform them that their caravan had escaped and that they would do well to return. But Abu Jahl would not hear of it; he would not be cheated of his quarry. He hated Muhammad🌸, his very uprightness and manly courage were a reflection on Abu Jahl's cowardly and cunning behaviour. Muhammad🌸 and the Muslims must be exterminated and here was the opportunity to do it. He must detain Quraysh by any means, so he swore that they would not return before they had remained three days by the well of Badr to celebrate, so that none would make the mistake of thinking they had returned out of fear, and so that all the Arabs would hear of their illustrious march.

All Quraysh liked Abu Jahl's idea, except the Banu Zuhra, who returned to Makka. Quraysh occupied a good strategic position behind a hill which they used as a shield. Seeing this, the Muslims decided that if Quraysh wanted to engage them they would stand and fight. A downpour of rain facilitated the march towards Badr for the Muslims and when they reached the first of its wells, they stopped and dismounted.

When Al-Hubab ibn al-Mundhir saw where the Prophet had stopped, he said, 'Messenger of Allah, is this by Allah's command, in which case we should not move an inch from it, or have you chosen this place for strategic reasons?' Muhammad🌸 answered that it had been chosen for strategic reasons whereupon Al-Hubab suggested that they descended lower down and filled in the wells lower than them, so that they could drink and the enemy could not. They moved down towards the well, and Al-Hubab built a basin for them to drink clear water from.

The Messenger took this opportunity to point out to them that he was a mortal man liable to error. In Islam men are helped to avoid the pitfalls that have distorted preceding religions. The Qur'an points out that Muhammad🌸 was only a mortal and lived the life of an ordinary man, the same as those around him, so that he would not be deified after his death. He was not too far removed from other men to be followed. The Qur'an says:

In the Messenger of Allah you have a good example
for him who seeks Allah and the Eternal Day. (33: 21)

Sa'd ibn Mu'adh suggested that they build a small shelter for the Prophet where he could remain during the battle, adding that if Allah granted them victory, well and good, but if they were defeated, then the Prophet could join his followers in Madina who supported him and who loved him as much as those who were fighting with him that day. The Prophet thanked him and accepted the suggestion.

Muhammadﷺ was no coward, on the contrary, he was absolutely fearless. 'Ali ibn Abi Talib said of him that in the heat of the battle he was always first and closest to the enemy. He always adopted a modest and inconspicuous role, far from the conquering hero's, except in situations too difficult for anyone else, when his true mettle appeared (as later at the Battle of Hunain). He tried to foster courage and self-confidence in those around him by assuming a minor role, to the extent that some historians point out that Muhammadﷺ's greatness lay in his ability to create great men. He saw the best in each man and started to build him up from there.

Now the Muslims were facing a vicious enemy far superior to them in numbers and weapons, so their first concern was for the safety of the Messenger, whom they all loved dearly, and indeed many would and did sacrifice their lives for his sake. It is at such moments that the hearts of men are revealed, their love for their Lord and His Messenger blazing like a lighted torch.

16.6 Abu Jahl Stirs the Tribes

Having taken positions for combat, Quraysh sent out spies to bring them information about the Muslims. They were informed that although they were men who had nothing but their swords, not one of them would fall without taking a man with him. Now Quraysh hesitated, and those of judgment among them, seeing so many of their nobles in the front row, feared they might have to pay a heavy price for victory. The men of noble birth would be plucked out and Quraysh would suffer a loss of prestige among the Arabs. 'Utba ibn Rabi'a, one of their nobles, rose and said, 'O men of Quraysh, we achieve nothing by confronting Muhammadﷺ and his Companions today. Even if you defeat them, each of you will look upon his neighbour and see a man who has killed his brother, his uncle, his cousin, or a man from his clan. It is far better to return and leave Muhammadﷺ to the rest of the Arabs. If they defeat him, then that is what you wanted. If they do not, then you have not exposed yourselves to what you would hate.'

When Abu Jahl heard these words, he rose in fury and went to 'Amr whose brother had been killed by the Muslims in the Rajab raid and said, 'Look at your ally, wanting to return with the people when your revenge is within your grasp. Rise quickly and bewail your brother.' So 'Amr rose to bewail his brother, stirring the emotions and reminding all his blood relations that they were honour bound to avenge him.

Before the battle Muhammadﷺ had ordered his Companions not to kill those who had been good to them during the days of persecution in Makka. Granted that that they came as enemies, ready to kill and be killed, but it was characteristic of Muhammadﷺ that he never forgot those who had done him or his followers a good turn. He had the ability to transcend beyond the emotions and excitement of the moment and see the broader issues and nobler course.

16.7 The Battle of Badr

The battle started when a man from Quraysh tried to break the basin the Muslims had built. Hamza, the Prophet's uncle, raised his mighty sword and quickly despatched him. Now the leaders of Quraysh challenged the Muslims to single combat. Some of the youths of Madina went out to meet them, but they said to them, 'We have no quarrel with you, we want our people!'

They cried, 'Muhammadﷺ, let our peers from our people come out to us!'

Out came 'Ali ibn Abi Talib, Hamza, and 'Ubayda ibn al-Harith. Hamza, a lion in combat as in hunting, quickly despatched his opponent as did 'Ali. Then Hamza, in accordance with the rules of battle, aided 'Ubayda, who was in difficulties. The two armies rushed towards each other: those who fought for Allah's sake and those who fought arrogantly to prove their might and superiority. The deep faith of the Muslims made them stand firm in spite of their paucity in arms and men; the pompous pride of Quraysh made them so sure that the day would be theirs.

At last the Muslims faced their tormentors man to man, or more accurately, each Muslim opposite three men of Quraysh, for Quraysh were three times their number, moreover Quraysh had cavalry, which played a vital role in the battles of old, while the Muslims had only one horse to represent the cavalry. Each of the Qurayshi warriors was served by his slaves and attendants, while each Muslim stood alone with nothing but a sword in his hand to face the superior equipment of the Qurayshi nobles. In spite of all these factors, the Muslims were willing to fight them. It was their duty to themselves, to their relations held in bondage in Makka, and to their Lord. They were willing to fight the idol worshippers and let Allah decide the outcome. Quraysh, who insisted on fighting them even after they knew that their caravan was safe, piled aggression onto years of aggression, wrong onto years of wrong.

When Muhammadﷺ was in the front ranks, placing his men in positions for combat, he saw how few they were in comparison with the number of Quraysh and how ill-equipped. His heart went out to them and after having done his work, he returned to the shelter they had built for him, to seek the aid of Him who is invincible. With his hands raised upwards he started to pray and pray, to plead and urge, calling, reaching out towards his Maker with his whole being, 'My Lord, this is Quraysh who have come out in all their vainglory to attack Thy Prophet. My Lord, give us Thy victory, the victory that Thou hast 'promised me. My Lord, if Thou lettest this group of men perish today, Thou wilt not be worshipped.' He prayed and pleaded until his garment fell off his shoulders and, unaware of it, continued to pray and plead.

Abu Bakr, who was with him in the shelter, took it and placed it over his shoulders again, saying, 'Messenger of Allah, do not take it so hard. Allah will fulfill His promise to you.' But Muhammadﷺ continued to pray until a serene calm came over him, a peaceful drowsiness in which he saw for a second a vision of the Muslims' victory.

He rose with all his fears and doubts dispelled, for ever since he became a prophet, he had not seen a vision that had not come true. He left the shelter and went out to tell his Companions to be of good cheer, encouraging and giving hope of victory. 'By Him who holds sway over Muhammadﷺ's soul, the man who fights them today, steadfast and persevering, Allah will let into Paradise.'

The Muslims became dauntless, like charging lions. Each man seemed equivalent to ten of the enemy. Each sword reaped the heads before it, oblivious of time, place, connections. It was one of the days of Allah, the days of truth when His hand holds the reins. The chief among the deniers fell, but not indiscriminately. Those who were particularly cruel, those hardened in opposition to Allah were plucked out from the fighting hosts while Muslim swords seemed the scythe that reaps the wicked to Jahannam. Muhammadﷺ took a handful of gravel and cast it at the enemy ranks. It was a simple gesture, but it played havoc in the enemy ranks, both men and horses. They fell, they could not see, they stumbled, and the horses shied away.

16.8 The Holy Verses Concerning this Battle

The Muslims were amazed to see such confusion created by a handful of gravel. They were equally amazed to see the great and mighty fall so easily by their swords. After the battle, when they had routed the enemy completely and returned to Madina, they kept relating what they had seen to those they had left behind, as if unable to believe their own eyes. Then these verses were sent down:

You did not kill them, but Allah killed them.
You did not throw when you threw.
It was Allah who threw. (8:17)

The first sentence, addressing the Muslims, tells them that it was not they who killed the polytheists with their swords but Allah who killed them. The second sentence, addressing the Messenger, tells him that it was not he who made the handful of gravel scatter and disrupt the enemy ranks but Allah who did. Man acts and it is the will of Allah that makes his actions powerful and significant or impotent and insignificant.

Nameless terror spread among Quraysh, the great and mighty fled before the angelic onslaught and the Muslims followed them in hot pursuit, killing and taking captives. The proud 'kings of men', as the Arabs called them, fled in fear, shame, and humiliation. The great host was scattered far and wide, fleeing in terror from the battlefield. They had waited at Badr to torture and terrify the Muslims, now it was they who were being pursued, captured, or killed. They had ridden out in arrogance and pomp to show off before all the Arabs, now they had only their shame and defeat.

Many of the things that took place in this battle that changed the face of history had been referred to years earlier by Qur'anic verses when the Muslims were weak and few in Makka. Then the Qur'an had said,

The host shall be defeated and turn round in flight. (54:45)
'Umar ibn Al-Khattab had said, wondering, 'What host is that?'For at that time the Muslims lived in fear that they would be winnowed out. Such a battle and such a victory no one could have then imagined.

The holy verses spoke also, in those early days in Makka, of Abu Jahl. He persecuted Muslims and incited others to do so. It was he who would not let Quraysh return to Makka; but insisted on them remaining for three days at Badr, in the hope of wiping out the Muslims. The holy verses said about him years earlier in Makka:

We shall mark him on the trunk. (68:16)
Who could injure or chastise the great Abu Jahl ibn Hisham on the nose? For the word trunk is used in Arabic as a pejorative epithet for the nose of the arrogant, narrow-minded. After the battle of Badr, Abu Jahl was found dead, killed by a blow on the nose.

After the battle, the Muslims spent the night at Badr. They dug a large pit for the dead of Quraysh and buried them in it. In the dead of night, people heard Muhammadﷺ calling out to those in the mass grave, 'People of the grave, 'Utba ibn Rabi'a, Umayya ibn Rabi'a, 'Utba ibn Khalaf (he kept calling them one by one by their names) have you discovered what your Lord.promised to be the truth? For I have found what my Lord promised me the truth.'

The Muslims said to him, 'But Messenger of Allah, these are corpses. Do you speak to the dead?'

'They hear me as you do, but they cannot answer,' he said.

People began to dispute as to how the booty should be distributed. Those who had collected it said it was theirs. Those who had pursued Quraysh said they had more right to it, and those who had stood guard over the Prophet in case Quraysh counter-attacked said they had more right to it. Muhammadﷺ asked them all to give up the booty they had gathered. Then he put it in a heap and divided it fairly among them, after putting aside one fifth for the needy, the poor, and the orphans. Those who had been left in charge of affairs in Madina were also given a share, as well as the families of those who had been killed in battle. Those who had been given permission to stay behind for a reason the Prophet had accepted were also given a share. No one who had a right to have a share was left out, for Islam is a religion of brotherhood and sharing whatever comes of good or evil.

The Muslims had never had captives before and did not know what to do with them. Two men who used to torture the Muslims cruelly and had been an incessant source of evil to them when they were in Makka were put to death before the army returned to Madina. The rest of the captives were taken back to Madina with them. Muhammad ﷺ commanded his men to be kind to the prisoners until they could decide what to do with them.

CHAPTER SEVENTEEN

17.1 News Reaches Madina

Muhammadﷺ had sent two men on ahead to Madina with the news of victory. They entered the city through different gates and began to call out the good news. The Muslims in Madina were overjoyed and much relieved, for they were aware of the might of Quraysh and the meagre condition of their own army, but the Jews, the Polytheists, and the Hypocrites (those who had pretended to enter into Islam but had not) were shocked and grieved. At first they did not believe the emissaries and they could not bear the idea that the Muslims should have been victorious. They saw Zayd ibn Al-Haritha, Muhammadﷺ's retainer, on the Messenger's white mule and assumed that Muhammadﷺ and his men had all been killed and that Zayd was overwrought because of the horrors he had seen at the hands of Quraysh. They pointed out that Zayd would not be riding Muhammadﷺ's mule if the latter were alive. When they discovered that Zayd spoke the truth and the names of the Qurayshi nobles who had been killed in battle were read out to them, they were alarmed and depressed. The Muslims already had considerable influence in Madina and if they really had defeated Quraysh, then they would soon be masters of the city. They could not hide their envy and frustration. One of the Jews said, 'It would be better to be under the earth today than on top of it, now that the noblest and greatest of men after the kings of the Arabs, the inhabitants of the Sacred Sanctuary, have been killed.'

It seems curious that the Jews' sympathy should be with the polytheists who worshipped idols, rather than the Muslims who worshipped Allah like them, but they believed that they were the chosen people and that no other people had a right to receive a Messenger from Allah. They resented the Muslims because they worshipped Allah like them, and could never forgive Muhammadﷺ for being a prophet. Add to this their struggle to be the dominant power in Madina and their reaction becomes understandable.

17.2 On Entering Madina

The body of Muslims entered Madina a day ahead of the captives.

When the captives were brought in, the Prophet distributed them among his Companions and charged them to treat them well, until it was decided what was to be done with them. During this period of respite, the Muslims dispersed to their own homes. The captives, who feared the severity of 'Umar, sent for Abu Bakr to plead with him to speak for them, saying that they were his kin and of his clan. Surely he would not let them be killed. They persuaded him to speak to the Messenger on their behalf.

17.3 Abu Bakr and 'Umar

The Messenger called his two counsellors, Abu Bakr ibn Abi Quhafa and 'Umar ibn al-Khattab. They were both men of exemplary character and deep faith, but in temperament they were the exact antithesis of each other. While Abu Bakr was small, with a light frame and mild, gentle ways, 'Umar was tall, with a heavy, powerful build and a rough, fierce temper. Abu Bakr was affectionate, merciful, and kind, with a pleasant, polished manner to both friend and foe, while 'Umar was stern and sober, capable of severe, unflattering words. While Abu Bakr let his intuition and his kind but penetrating heart judge affairs, 'Umar had an unerring sense of justice, and he exhausted his intellect to arrive at the facts. But he had a heart of gold that he hid beneath this severe exterior in case it made him deviate by a hair's breadth from absolute justice. Abu Bakr understood events with his heart as well as his head and he was considered one of the two men of great wisdom in Quraysh. 'Umar, however, would examine every issue again and again until he was absolutely satisfied that he had reached the truth about it. What the Messenger says about each is significant. To Abu Bakr, he gave the epithet 'the True' because his faith was so true and deep it could see beyond all obstacles and barriers, while about 'Umar, he said that the truth had descended on his heart because it shunned anything other than the absolute truth. As we shall see in due course, sometimes the holy verses came down to corroborate 'Umar's judgment, even when it differed from the Messenger's.

Muhammadﷺ loved and trusted both men, though Abu Bakr was closer and dearer to him, for each of them was of noble character, and each of them was unswerving in his service of Islam. Each saw matters from a different angle and the opinion of two such men, so good yet so different, helped to make the Messenger see things from two widely different perspectives.

17.4 The Captives

When the Messenger asked their opinion about the captives, Abu Bakr, always benevolent, spoke of mercy and forgiveness. Perhaps if these misguided men were given a second chance they would take advantage of Allah's mercy to them, instead of dying unbelievers and going to the eternal fire. He spoke of the bonds of kinship between them and the Muslims.

Muhammad࿐ listened attentively, but said nothing,then he asked 'Umar's opinion. 'Umar said, 'Messenger of Allah, these are the leaders of the rejectors. If you execute them, Allah will make Islam triumph by it.' 'Umar was thinking of the years of torture that the Muslims had suffered at the hands of these men and also, as his words denote, of what would happen if these men were set free and allowed to return with larger forces and a greater desire for vengeance. It was only fair that those who had persecuted and killed should be killed, it was only prudent not to give those bitter and vicious enemies a second chance to destroy the Muslims.

Then Abu Bakr responded, gentle, benevolent, and conciliatory. Justice was a good thing, but mercy was even better. Does one kill one's own kin when they were poor misguided souls? Again he spoke of pardon and forgiveness, for to pardon when in a position to punish is the true spirit of Islam as so many verses in the Qur'an commend.

The Messenger made no comment on what he had heard but said he would go into seclusion for a while to think the matter over, and he asked all to reflect about it likewise and to discuss it among themselves. It is possible that Muhammad࿐ knew what he wanted to do all along, but he insisted on making his Companions think and judge for themselves. Just as in the battle he assumed a minor role and encouraged them to be the judges, he would not let his superior judgment dominate theirs, but on the contrary he used his insight to make them mentally active and independent.

The Muslims discussed the matter amongst themselves. These men were their relatives, their uncles, their cousins, their brothers, but these men had also tortured them for thirteen long years. Some, like Abu Bakr, believed that mercy and kindness would aid these misguided creatures towards faith; others, like 'Umar, believed that death was their just desert for all those they had persecuted, tortured, and killed. The Muslims were in need of money as they had left most of their possessions in Makka, so some of them believed that to accept ransom would not be a bad idea, for what would they gain by killing these captives? They debated, they discussed, they pondered over the matter, then the Prophet came out to them.

He said that among the angels Abu Bakr was like Michael who descends with Allah's mercy and forgiveness, and among the prophets he was like Ibrahim who asked forgiveness for his people and would say nothing against them, even after they cast him into the fire. While among the angels 'Umar was Like Gabriel who descends with the wrath of Allah and with retribution from heaven, and among the prophets he was like Noah who prayed that Allah leave no house for the deniers on the earth, or like Moses who prayed that Pharaoh's wealth would perish. Then he mentioned that they were in need and that, should they decide to accept ransom, they should let no rich man go free without paying it.

They discussed it amongst themselves again and decided to accept ransom. One of the captives was a poet and he went to the Prophet and said, 'Muhammadﷺ, I have five daughters. Will you give me as a present to them and I promise never to fight you or speak against you again?'The Prophet allowed him to go free without ransom, but he broke his word, fought the Muslims again at Uhud and was killed.

On this occasion the verses from Allah came to show that the Muslims had not chosen wisely. Allah in His mercy forgave them and allowed them to keep the ransom they had chosen to take, but it would have been more just, as 'Umar had declared, to kill these captives. The Muslims had sought the wealth of this world, but it was not the best thing for them. Allah desired for them something much better than this: immortality and eternal happiness.

It is not for a prophet to take captives
until he makes the earth warm with blood.
You desire the delights of this world;
and Allah desires the eternal.
Allah is the Invincible, of highest judgment. (8:67)

Very often one meets in the Qur'an ideas and thoughts completely different from Muhammadﷺ's as an individual. This next verse discusses the captives.

Our Prophet, tell the captives in your hands,
'If Allah knows that there is good in your hearts.
He will give you better than what was taken from you,
and forgive you Allah is the Merciful, the Forgiving. (8:70)

126

If one compares these two verses, one can infer that Allah in His mercy had no intention of having the captives killed. Had He had any such intention then the command would have been communicated to His Prophet, but verse 67 serves a very important purpose. It warns the Muslims that they should not care about money and material goods and then it makes the captives realize that death is their just desert, but that Allah is granting them life in spite of all they have done, a gift from Him, the Merciful, the Forgiving. Those with any good in them would respond to such generosity. Then verse 70 gives them hope and solace, telling them that Allah will replace what was taken from them by better if He finds there is good in them. No one is forgotten. The door of hope and forgiveness is never closed in the face of man, even when he denies the existence of Allah and fights those who worship Him.

17.5 The News Reaches Makka
News of the disastrous defeat reached Makka. At first the Makkans did not believe it. Surely the Muslims were far too weak to compete with Quraysh; they had fewer weapons and fewer men and they were less experienced in war. When they finally learnt the facts, they were thunderstruck. Abu Lahab, the only one of the Qurayshi nobles who had not gone out in person to fight, but had sent a man who owed him money instead, was so shocked that he was struck down with a high fever, took to bed and never recovered. He died within a week.

The women of Quraysh decided not to mourn their dead in case the Muslim women heard of it and gloated over them. They would not shed tears until they had attained their revenge. The men decided not to begin negotiations with the Muslims concerning ransom for their captives until the right occasion presented itself, in case they asked too high a sum. Then they allotted all the money gained by Abu Sufyan from trade in the caravan that had escaped the Muslims to make preparations for war and buy equipment for the battle that would restore their honour and their prestige - a battle that would give them the revenge they craved.

17.6 Quraysh Pay the Ransom
After waiting patiently and biding their time, Quraysh began to seek freedom for their captives and to pay ransom for them. One of the captives was a foul-mouthed man who used to say evil things

about the Messenger and the Muslims. 'Umar ibn al-Khattab hated to see him set free and said to the Prophet, 'Let me pull out his two front teeth so that his tongue sticks out, then he will never dare to speak in public against you.'

'If I mutilate him, Allah will mutilate me, even though I am a Prophet,' Muhammad 攤 answered.

Among the things brought in to ransom the captives, Muhammad 攤 recognized a medallion that belonged to his daughter Zaynab. He was deeply moved, for he remembered that it had belonged to his beloved Khadija and that she had given it to her daughter on her wedding day. Zaynab had sent it to ransom her husband, Abu'l-'As, who was among the captives. Muhammad 攤 said, 'If you could set her prisoner free for her and return her medallion to her, then do so.' After that he came to an understanding with Abu'l-'As, who had not entered into Islam, to give Zaynab her freedom. (A Muslim woman is forbidden to a man who does not believe.) He sent Zayd ibn al-Haritha with two other men to conduct her safely to Madina.

17.7 Abu'l-'As

Some months later Abu'l-'As was carrying trade money belonging to Quraysh to Al-Sham, when he was taken captive by a group of Muslim soldiers. They appropriated his money which belonged to Quraysh, so under cover of night, he went to Zaynab's quarters and asked her to intercede for him. She agreed and through her mediation the Muslims returned the money to him and he was able to return it to Quraysh. He gave each of the Quraysh their share, then he stood and cried, 'Men of Quraysh, has anyone not received his money back?'

They all answered that they had received their money. Then he said, 'Now I testify that Allah is One and that Muhammad 攤 is His Prophet. The only reason why I did not profess my faith while in Madina was lest you thought I had done it to take your money.' Then he went to Madina and swore the oath of allegiance to Allah and His Messenger, and Muhammad 攤 returned his wife Zaynab to him.

17.8 'People Who Do Not Know'

Although the polytheists tortured and killed Muslims whenever they fell into their hands, disregarding completely their rights as individuals and their relationship to them as kin, the Qur'an commanded the Muslims to protect and treat well the polytheists they captured for they were people who did not yet understand. Very often they opposed the words of Allah without knowing what they were opposing. So they should be allowed to hear the words of Allah, then put where thay felt secure. If, after returning to their people when there was no pressure upon them, they declared themselves to be Muslims, they should be accepted as such.

On this the holy verses say:

Should any of the polytheists ask your protection,
give it to him, so that he may hear the words of Allah,
then deliver him to where he feels safe.
This is because they are people who do not know. (99:6)

There were many who came to jeer and sneer, and remained to worship; there were many who came suspiciously to test and try, and then bowed in reverence. There were those who came as captives, then returned Muslims to spread the word of Allah among their people.

CHAPTER EIGHTEEN

18.1 Alcohol

Just as the Messenger was commanded to proclaim the worship of Allah in stages, so were many of the evil habits of the Arabs eliminated by degrees. The Muslims were very gradually and systematically weaned away from all that was wrongful, unjust, unseemly, or unrefined. The Arabs were very fond of drinking, so the first verses that mention alcohol say that from palm trees man acquires goodly provision and also alcohol. The provision is described as goodly, while alcohol is left without comment. The Muslims paid no attention to this silence concerning the epithet of drink, and continued to drink alcohol until they emigrated to Madina. Allah in His wisdom was teaching them the right thing at the right moment and not overtaxing them with side issues when they were being persecuted and tortured by the Makkans for the sake of their religion.

When they had settled in Madina and could pray in freedom and without fear, they had the time and peace to study the precepts of their religion, the next verses concerning drink revealed that there was both good and bad in drink and gambling, but that the harm and sin in them was greater than the benefit. People began to think that, if there was more sin in them than benefit, it would be better to keep away from them as much as possible. Their minds were being prepared to accept that such an activity was incompatible with spiritual awareness.

Sometime later these holy verses were revealed:

**You who believe, do not approach prayers in your drink,
so that you are not aware of what you are saying.**

The Messenger delegated someone to walk through the streets of Madina proclaiming that those intoxicated should not attend prayers. The Muslims had become devoted to prayer and study of the Holy Qur'an, and as the obligatory prayers were five times a day, the person who prayed had no time to drink during the day. Many forsook drink altogether in order to be able to gain the greater pleasure of prayer during the day and night for, like the Messenger, most of the early Muslims spent long hours in prayer at night. By the

time the verses below were sent down, it was quite natural and relatively easy for the Muslims to give up drink. The holy verses say:
O you who believe!
Alcohol, gambling, idols set-up, and arrows for divination
are filth of the devil's doing,
so avoid them perchance you succeed.
For the devil seeks to cast enmity and loathing
between you in gambling and alcohol
and to divert you from remembering Allah and from prayers.
So will you be finished with them? (5:90,91)

18.2 Women in Islam

Amongst the Arabs at this dark and cruel period of human history, so many human beings of both sexes and all ages were considered possessions, that women, by nature less strong, were considered per se as belonging to someone. A woman might be rich, even respected, but only as the daughter of so-and-so, the wife of so-and-so, or the sister of such-and-such a chief or ruler. No one thought of her as an individual in her own right.

With the advent of Islam and the gradual revelation of the Qur'an women were given one right after another. First she had a right to think for herself, to believe what she would and to proclaim her belief. Next, she was an individual before Allah who had both rights and responsibilities towards Him and towards the society she lived in. As a person responsible before Allah, she was not to blindly follow her husband's or father's belief, but to think for herself. If she did believe then she was to go to Muhammad ﷺ and swear allegiance to Allah and His Messenger as men did.

She had a right to be educated and to demand education and it was the father's or guardian's duty to educate his ward. If a husband found his wife uneducated, it was his duty to have her educated. Amongst the Arabs before Islam women were inherited from father to son as a possession. After Islam such marriages became forbidden and a man was no longer able to marry his father's widow who now acquired the status of a mother. Women were given the right to choose their own husbands so that if a father or guardian married a woman to someone against her will or without consulting her, the marriage was considered invalid and she had the right to annul it.

A woman was given the right to inherit from her relatives - father, mother, husband, or brother (if the latter has no son). She had a right to have property of her own apart from her husband, and to manage it alone as she wished. In every aspect of life she was given clear and just rights.

Amongst the Arabs before Islam a man could marry any number of wives. Islam limited the number of wives a man could keep to four wives. As a woman could not live alone in that tribal society, marriage was a matter of social convenience and accommodation rather than an individual choice. It was the union of two tribes. While man is allowed freedom of choice, he is made fully responsible for the women he marries, whether one, two or more. He is to support his wife or wives and children and to treat all his wives with equal fairness (a condition that most Muslims find impossible to meet and so very rarely do they marry more than one). Legally, morally, and financially he is responsible for his family or families. It is a system that discourages more than one marriage, without making it impossible for a man to meet certain circumstances he may encounter in life. Adultery is a very grave sin in Islam, and the punishment for it is being stoned to death. It is a better system for women than one where one woman is betrayed and another is deprived of all rights and reduced socially to a depraved and humiliating position.

The laws of Islam liberated women from their bondage and they became active companions to men in the struggle for Allah's sake. Before the Battle of Tabuk, when the Muslims did not have enough cash, the women of Madina collected all their jewelry, bracelets, earrings, anklets, made a great pile and sent it to the Messenger. Men began to look upon them as companions in the struggle. In other battles they used to walk among the rows of fighters to give them water to drink. In the battle of Al-Yarmuk when the Muslims were outnumbered four to one by the Romans, the women joined in the fighting with the men.

Muslim women used to carry the wounded from the battlefield to nurse them. A certain woman called Rufayda used to erect a great tent behind the battle lines and collect other women as volunteers to nurse the wounded.

The Qur'an revealed verses giving women rights unheard of in the world at the time, and Muhammad taught the Muslims to follow the decrees of Islam in word and spirit by setting the best of examples. Upon every occasion he treated women with chivalry and gentleness. 'The most gracious among you is he most gracious to his womenfolk,' he used to teach his followers. In his farewell speech, one of the last commandments he urged men to observe was to be good and fair to women.

The Qur'an decrees that one should be humble and kind to one's aged parents, but mothers in particular are given a most elevated status. 'Paradise is under the feet of the mothers,' Muhammad💍 taught his followers.

At the conquest of Makka, a polytheist asked Umm Hani', Muhammad💍's cousin, to place him under her protection although, before Islam, only men could offer such protection. 'Ali ibn Abi Talib, Umm Hani's brother, thought the man deserved to be killed. Muhammad💍 ruled that Umm Hani' had the right to protect him, saying, 'We safeguard he whom you safeguard, Umm Hani'.' And who would dare touch a man to whom the Messenger of Allah had promised protection?

18.3 Slaves in Islam

Makkan society was based upon slave labour; as were most societies at the time. To liberate slaves 'en masse' would have disrupted the economic system and ruined both masters and slaves, as too much labour in the labour market can be as injurious as its being too scarce. Islam approached the subject with compassionate wisdom. First Muslims were taught that their slaves were their brethren in religion. Then they were informed that to liberate a slave was an act most pleasing to Allah. The next step instructed them when and how to liberate slaves to prevent them being cast helpless upon society. A Muslim may liberate his slave or he may allow him to buy his freedom by paying a certain sum of money after he is established in business and gaining his own living. Not all slaves are fit to be liberated, however, but only those who can take care of themselves while those who are unable to do so are not to be cast as a burden upon society, their master has to take care of them.

Very many slaves were liberated by the Muslims in an attempt to please Allah. Such liberated slaves were called 'Mawali' and since they were liberated in peace and without coercion, they felt very great regard for the man who had set them free and considered it an honour to belong to him and his tribe. It was quite normal among the Muslims to see a former master and mawla praying side by side, or fighting shoulder to shoulder to uphold the word of Allah. They were no longer master and slave, but brothers in Islam.

18.4 Orphans in Islam

Concerning orphans, Islam decrees that a guardian should treat an orphan as he would like his own children to be treated should he die. An orphan is to be guided and given sincere and wise counsel. If he has money, it is to be employed for him in the best possible way and not spent extravagantly before he comes of age. If the guardian is needy, he is permitted to take a wage from his ward's wealth for managing it, and if he is not, then he is to refrain. An orphan should have his money handed over to him as soon as he is old enough to be able to manage his own affairs.

18.5 Freedoms and Obligations

In every walk of life Islam gives a man or woman freedom of choice. He is responsible, however, for the consequences of his beliefs and actions. A man or woman is given the status of a free, adult, thinking being. They are liberated but their liberties go hand in hand with obligations. A Muslim is committed to follow the Qur'an and is responsible before Allah for every thought, word, or act. He is not only responsible for himself but also for those placed under his care. The Messenger used to say, 'Each of you is a shepherd, and each shepherd is responsible for his sheep.' A man is responsible for his family and dependents, a woman is responsible for her home and children. This system which allows freedom of thought, freedom of belief and action, makes each individual reach the highest potential he is capable of and live up to the trust placed in him.

18.6 The Influence of Muhammad ﷺ

Muhammad ﷺ's personal goodness played an important part in winning people to Islam. He never preached what he did not practise himself, and never allowed himself or his family any privileges that other Muslims did not enjoy. He was modest and helpful about the house. Once he was having great difficulty in mending his sandals and 'A'isha, seeing the bother he was having, started to read a piece of poetry to him. Immediately his face brightened, and he thanked her profusely. The simple things in life gave him great pleasure.

On a journey with friends, he insisted on doing his share. Someone volunteered to cook, another to fetch the water, and Muhammad ﷺ offered to gather the wood. 'But we, can do that instead of you, Messenger of Allah,' his Companions said, but he insisted.

One day a Jew to whom he owed money came to demand it. The man was rude and aggressive in the way that he spoke to Muhammad ﷺ, implying that he had not been prompt in fulfilling his commitments. He included the whole of Muhammad ﷺ's tribe in the implication, which to the Arabs was an infuriating insult. 'Umar ibn al-Khattab could not bear this and rough handled the man.

Smiling, the Messenger asked him to release him. 'We needed something other than this from you, 'Umar. I need to be told to pay up what I owe, and he needs to be told to ask nicely. There are still three days for his bond, but go to the Muslim treasury and pay him, give him a bonus over it.'

After the Jew had received his money, he returned, swore allegiance to Muhammad ﷺ and entered into Islam. When asked why he had entered into Islam, he said, 'These are not the manners of ordinary mortals, these are the manners of the prophets.'

CHAPTER NINETEEN

19.1 Banu Qaynuqa'

Peace and quiet was not to be the lot of the Muslims, for as soon as they returned to Madina, the Jews began to plot and conspire against them, even more vigorously than before. They could not bear to see Muhammadﷺ dominate the city and they could not bear to see the Muslims victorious. Night and day their plots and injuries to the Muslims did not cease, and what was worse for the believers was that they slandered Muslim women, to the extent that Muhammadﷺ had to send a messenger to Banu Qaynuqa' to tell them to stop injuring Muslims and to observe the treaties between them. Banu Qaynuqa' were one of the three large Jewish tribes who lived in Madina. Instead of heeding this warning and observing the treaties that had given them both freedom and security, the answer they sent back was a challenge.

'Muhammadﷺ,' they said. 'Do not be deceived because you have met with people who have no knowledge of war. If we fight you, then you shall know what it means to face a warrior race.'

There was nothing that Muhammadﷺ could do but meet the challenge. The Muslims besieged the forts of Banu Qaynuqa', and after fifteen days of siege, they surrendered. Consultations were undertaken on what to do with Banu Qaynuqa'. Some suggested that they should be enslaved while others asked the Prophet to show them mercy. In the end it was decided that they should evacuate the city, leaving their weapons behind. They left Madina, heading northwards, until they reached Azriat on the border of Al-Sham and settled there.

19.2 Abu Sufyan Skirmishes the Outskirts

For a short time there was peace in Madina as potential plotters lay low after Banu Qaynuqa' were evacuated. However Abu Sufyan, hating to remain idle in Makka after the humiliation of Quraysh, went towards Madina with a group of men and on the outskirts of the city came across one of the Supporters tilling his land with the aid of a friend. They killed the man, burned some palm trees, and fled. Abu Sufyan thought this would raise the prestige of Quraysh among the

Arabs and make them realize that Quraysh did not fear the Muslims and still had power to strike at them. Muhammadﷺ with some of his Companions went after Abu Sufyan and his followers. The closer Muhammadﷺ came, the faster Abu Sufyan fled to avoid the encounter, and in order to go as fast as possible, they threw away their provisions onto the road. The pursuers picked of them up and Muhammadﷺ, seeing that Abu Sufyan would avoid them at all costs, turned back.

This raid did not raise the prestige of Quraysh as Abu Sufyan had hoped, but, on the contrary, his flight before Muhammadﷺ only proved that the Muslims had become a power to be reckoned with.

The tribes around Madina who levied protection dues on the summer journey of Quraysh to Al-Sham feared that if this trade was threatened by the Muslims, Quraysh would take another route and they would be deprived of their revenue. They resented that the Muslims, who only a few months earlier had been fugitives seeking shelter, should defeat the great Quraysh and exile the tribe of Banu Qaynuqa'. They decided to attack the Muslims in the hope that they would gain fame among the Arabs and earn the undying gratitude of the illustrious Quraysh. Accordingly they made preparations and gathered together a large war host.

Hearing of these movements, Muhammadﷺ thought it would be better to go out to meet them instead of waiting for them to raid Madina. He set out at the head of a group of his Companions, but whenever the tribes heard of his approach, they dispersed or fled to the mountains. Again and again they gathered, then fled when they saw him approaching.

The Jewish tribes of Madina took note of this and feared for themselves, especially when one of them who used to slander Muslims, particularly Muslim women, was assassinated. The Jews went to Muhammadﷺ to complain. He pointed out that had this man not kept on slandering people, no harm would have come to him. Then he called them to make a new treaty and to respect it. They accepted, for such treaties gave them all the rights given to the Muslims, but, cowed and resentful, they waited and bided their time to make mischief.

19.3 Quraysh's Trade Problem

Quraysh were in a dilemma. Their main source of income was commerce, and their main trade route was past Madina to the sea coast. Many of the coastal tribes had made pacts and treaties with Muhammad☀, so they no longer protected the trade of Quraysh from attacks by the Muslims. If they did not trade, they would eat up their capital; if they did, Muhammad☀ was sure to threaten their caravans on their way to Al-Sham. After holding council among themselves, they decided to try another route, through Najd and Iraq. So they prepared a caravan carrying gold and silver to trade with in Al- Sham.

One of them chanced to tell this to a Muslim, who went in turn and related it to Muhammad☀ who sent Zayd ibn Al-Haritha at the head of one hundred men. They intercepted the caravan and brought back the gold and silver. Muhammad☀ divided it equitably among them after allotting one fifth to the needy (the poor, orphans, widows, those in debt for Allah's sake, relatives, and in freeing slaves).

The leader of the caravan was brought to the Messenger who spoke to him of Islam. The man liked what he heard and became a Muslim.

CHAPTER TWENTY

20.1 Learning the Precepts of the Qur'an

In the more clement climate of Madina, in freedom and without secrecy or fear, the Messenger taught the Muslims the spiritual and moral meanings of the precepts and stories found in the Qur'an. He also taught them how to act and what was expected of them as slaves of Allah. They loved the Qur'an and cherished it. Whenever a verse was sent down they studied it and learnt it by heart. The verses were written down on parchment, bone, or wood. They realized that it was not enough only to cherish the Qur'an but that it was a code to live by. So they they studied the Qur'an in the full realisation that it was to be the law of their lives.

Abu Mas'ud relates that, 'When a man among us learnt ten verses of the Qur'an, he kept practising what he had learnt before learning the next ten.'

The Qur'an teaches that piety is not merely a matter of rising and bowing in prayers or turning one's face towards Makka; much more is involved. It is charity in all its aspects, in giving money, in being kind, in freeing slaves. It is to keep one's word, to be patient in sickness and adversity, and to be firm and strong at the moment of trial.

A Muslim is part of a community and it is in his daily behaviour inside the community that he can serve Allah best. A Muslim has to learn how to live with people, for it is in serving his fellow man that he serves Allah best. It is in the give and take of the relationships of everyday life that a man is really tested. He has to learn how to be truthful without hurting other people's feelings, to be good without being weak and submissive, to be unselfish and charitable without being prodigal, to be learned or gifted without being conceited, and to be granted more than other men without being proud.

20.2 Example of the Prophet

The Messenger living among them day by day showed by his shining example that it was possible for a man to rise to great heights. He was so intelligent, granted so much, and yet was so modest, so considerate and tactful. The Muslims loved him dearly and studied his every word and act in order to emulate him. The Messenger did not rush them but taught with kind, patient care, teaching each man according to his ability to learn. With beginners he was most lenient and ordered those he sent to teach other tribes to be lenient and to make things easy for them.

20.3 'Ali's Wisdom

But with his cousin, 'Ali Ibn Abu Talib, whom he had brought up since he was a little boy, he went into deep and great matters and expected 'Ali to be able to answer his highly learned questions. 'Ali had the makings of a great scholar in him, and the Messenger saw to it that he became the greatest of the scholars of Islam.

One day 'Ali who was yet young in years was unable to answer one of the Messenger's difficult suppositions, for he consulted him about legistlative and jurisdical matters. When he was unable to answer the Messenger then placed his hand over 'Ali's breast and prayed for him. From that day 'Ali was able to answer any question concerning Islam and was of deep and sound judgment.

After the Messenger passed away each of the three Khalifs who preceeded Ali used to send for him whenever they had a difficult case. Both Abu Bakr and 'Umar made him their counsellor. And Abu Bakr, the first Khalif who was one of the two wisest men in Quraysh used to say, "I seek the aid of Allah against a question that Abu'l Hassan (a reverential way of referring to 'Ali) would be unable to answer."

CHAPTER TWENTY-ONE

21.1 Quraysh Prepares An Army

Quraysh who had suffered defeat and humiliation before all the Arabs could not rest or allow the Muslims to rest. Their trade had been threatened and was in constant danger. They had to revenge themselves, retrieve their prestige, and consequently regain their hold upon the coastal tribes and make safe their main trade route. The very next day after Badr, they had allotted all the money gained by Abu Sufyan's trade in Al-Sham to arm and equip an army capable of regaining for them all they had lost of influence and honour.

The great army they prepared was divided into three groups of one thousand men each. They were all Makkans, except one hundred men who came from Ta'if, and all were well-equipped and fully armed. They had two hundred horses and three thousand camels, and they had seven hundred armour bearers.

The women of Quraysh, led by Hind, the wife of Abu Sufyan, whose father, brother, and loved ones had been killed at Badr, insisted, against the men's protests on attending the battle. 'If you fail,' the women threatened their near ones, 'we will be taken as slaves by the enemy.' Thus each man was placed in the position of having to fight for his wife, sister, or daughter. His honour was at stake.

Al-'Abbas, the Prophet's uncle, was with Quraysh as they prepared this great army. He knew every detail about it, and in spite of being a loyal Qurayshi, something prompted him to write a letter to his nephew, warning him of the approach of the army and giving him all the details about it. He gave the letter to an Arab to deliver and the man reached Madina three days later and gave the letter to Muhammadﷺ. Muhammadﷺ confided its contents to his intimates, then sent two brothers as scouts to find out what they could. They came back, bringing information that confirmed Al-'Abbas' letter.

21.2 Muslims Debate Matter of Defence

Quraysh marched on until they were only five miles from Madina. The Muslims slept in the mosque that night in a state of alert for they feared that Quraysh would strike during the night. When morning came, the Prophet called the nobles of Madina together and held a council. Muhammadﷺ was of the opinion that they should remain in the city and fortify and defend it. 'Abdullah ibn Ubayy, who had been one of the chiefs of Yathrib, and who had much experience in war and many followers, was of the same opinion. He said, 'Prophet of Allah, we have fought in this manner before. We used to fortify the city, then place the women and children within forts from which they threw stones at the enemy while we met them with our swords. Our city, Prophet of Allah, is a virgin city. No enemy has ever set foot upon its soil without being defeated.

The words of 'Abdullah ibn Ubayy found favour with the Prophet's counsellors as well as the Prophet himself, but some fiery-hearted youths, who had not fought at Badr and longed to engage the enemy, and some of the men, whom Allah had granted victory against seemingly impossible obstacles at Badr, said that if they remained inside Madina, Quraysh would say, 'We have besieged Muhammadﷺ and his associates inside the walls of Yathrib and none dared come out to us. Moreover these men would burn the fields and come to raid us again and again.' They had witnessed the victory at Badr when they were less numerous, less experienced, poorly armed, and away from their city and people. Would He who gave them victory then not grant them victory now when they were in more favourable circumstances? Surely Allah was capable of that. The deep faith and courage that prompted them to speak moved all who heard them and now many were in favour of going out to meet Quraysh, even though Quraysh had come to them with an army they had never seen the like of before. The Messenger accepted the opinion of the majority. Ever careful to follow the precepts of the Qur'an, he settled affairs after taking counsel. He told them to get ready for battle, and promised them that if they were patient and persevering, victory would be theirs. Then he entered his house to dress for battle.

After the Prophet went in, Sa'd ibn Mu'adh, the chief of Al-Aws, who was in favour of staying in Madina, spoke to the youths whose fiery speeches had induced Muhammadﷺ to decide to fight the enemy outside the city. He said that they had pressed the Prophet to do what he did not like and perhaps it was not a good thing. The youths reflected on this and as soon as the Prophet came out to them, dressed in armour, they went to him and said, 'Prophet of Allah, we should not have differed from you. Do what you think best. We should not have pressed you; the decision belongs to Allah and you.'

Muhammad៉ said, 'I did suggest it, but you refused. No prophet, once he wears armour, shall take it off again until Allah decides between him and his enemy. So listen to what I command, and obey, and if you are patient and persevere, victory shall be yours.'

We perceive in Muhammad៉'s refusal to go back on his decision strict adherence to the teaching of the Qur'an,
'Once you take a decision, then trust in Allah.'
A Muslim should not be panicky and hesitant but should trust in Allah
who rules over all. He should take his time to decide, but once he has decided, he does not waver but marches forward in the firm belief that the conclusion of all issues rests with Him who rules all.

21.3 'Abdullah ibn Ubayy Deserts

While placing the army groups in positions of combat, the Messenger saw a battalion whose people he could not recognize. He asked who they were and on being informed that they were the Jewish allies of 'Abdullah ibn Ubayy ibn Salul, he said, 'One does not seek the aid of the polytheists against the polytheists.' Then he commanded that they return. (Many Jews then believed that 'Uzayr was the son of Allah; they did not worship Allah alone.) Muhammad៉ needed men and weapons, he needed the support of Ibn Ubayy, but what was more important to him than men and materials was to keep the principles of Islam uncompromised. At the darkest moment he would refuse aid if it meant the least compromise.

The allies of 'Abdullah ibn Ubayy considered this an affront and went to him and said, 'Look, Muhammad៉ did not listen to your advice but to his boys, and now he drives your allies away.'

'Abdullah ibn Ubayy was so offended that immediately before the battle he withdrew with his followers, diminishing substantially the Muslim ranks. There remained only the true Muslims. They were only seven hundred in number and they had to face three thousand Qurayshis, well-prepared and burning for revenge.

21.4 Battle of Uhud

In the evening, the Muslims marched out until they reached the mountain of Uhud. They crossed it and kept it as a shield behind them. Muhammad៉ placed fifty archers on the mountainside and said to them, 'Protect our rear. We fear they will come from behind us. Keep to your places. Do not leave them. If you see us defeating them, do not leave your places until we enter their camp. If you see us getting killed, do not try to aid us or defend us. Your job is to pelt the horses with arrows. Horses do not come forward where there are arrows.' Then he gave the orders that, apart from the archers, no-one should start fighting until he gave the signal.

Quraysh also had placed themselves in positions of combat. On the right wing was Khalid ibn Al-Walid, at the head of the cavalry. On the left wing was 'Ikrima ibn Abi Jahl and the banner was carried by Talha in the centre. The women of the Quraysh kept walking up and down the rows of fighters to fire their zeal. Thus they sang, 'If you charge forward, we embrace and spread the cushions, if you flee, we part, parting forevermore.' They were adorned in jewelry and dressed in gay, alluring clothes. The Muslim women were inconspicuously dressed and carried jugs of water to quench the warriors' thirst in the burning desert heat. Each side was emotionally charged - Quraysh by the memory of humiliation, the desire for revenge, and the desire to appear brave before their women, the Muslims by the desire to spread the word of Allah in freedom, without fear, and to place it high above the word of men. After speaking words full of faith and wisdom to his men, Muhammadﷺ produced a sword and said, 'Who will take this sword and give it its due?'

Some of the youths jumped up to take it, but he kept hold of it until Abu Dujana asked, 'What is its due, Messenger of Allah?' Muhammadﷺ said, 'To strike the enemy with it until it is bent.'

Abu Dujana was a fearless warrior, a man of rare courage. He rose and put on a red turban that he never wore except in war and that those who knew him called the turban of death. Then he took the sword from the Prophet and went forward.

Now the battle began. Quraysh tried to unbalance the Muslim ranks on the left, but could not. Hamza, the lion of the battle as well as the hunt, gave the battle-cry of Uhud and then thrust himself amid the ranks of Quraysh. Talha of Quraysh challenged, 'Who will fight me?' and 'Ali ibn Abi Talib made his way out of the ranks to meet the challenge. He was able to dispatch his adversary in no time, while Abu Dujana with the Prophet's sword in his hand met none without killing him. He saw a masked figure who was slashing and harassing Muslim soldiers. He raised his sword to kill him, but the strange person whimpered in a thin voice and was revealed to be a woman, Hind, the wife of Abu Sufyan, who had led the women, but was not content to wait with the women for the outcome of the battle. Abu Dujana refrained from touching her. Later he explained, 'I did not want the Prophet's sword sullied by a woman's blood.'

Hamza ibn 'Abdu'l-Muttalib was one of the finest huntsmen and greatest warriors of the Arabs. In the battle of Badr, he had killed many of the Qurayshi nobles, and now he cut his way through their ranks like a mighty wave sweeping all before it. One of the Qurayshi nobles had a black slave from Abyssinia. These people could use the javelin with great skill. Hind, the wife of Abu Sufyan, had said to this slave called Wahshi, 'Wahshi, if you kill Hamza, you are a free man.' His master promised him the same thing. Wahshi prowled among the fighters until he saw Hamza. He said, 'I held my spear and balanced it well, then I aimed it. It entered into his abdomen and went out the other side. I waited until he was dead, then I took my spear and went to wait in the camp. I had no quarrel with anyone. I killed him only to be set free.'

The Muslims continued to fight against overwhelming numbers for the sake of their Lord, not caring whether they lived or died. To die for His sake was the highest attainment; to die a martyr was an honour unsurpassed and a promise of paradise. Before such faith and courage Quraysh began to waver, to weaken, to retreat, then to flee the field. With all their numbers and arms, with all their might and experience, once again they fled. They were defeated and scattered in disorder left and right, away from their camp.

21.5 Victory then Defeat

Seeing how weak their enemy was before them, and how far they had fled, the Muslims entered the camp and began to collect the loot and captives. This occupied them and prevented them from pursuing the enemy. The archers, seeing what was happening,wanted to go down to collect their share of the booty and captives. One of them reminded them that the Prophet had commanded them to remain upon the mountain under any circumstances, but many of them did not listen. They thought the battle was over and they said, 'The Prophet did not say we should remain after Allah had humiliated the polytheists.' Their leader spoke to them but in vain. Down they all went except a few who remained with him.

Seeing what was happening, Khalid ibn Al-Walid, a brilliant

strategist, took the opportunity to collect his cavalry and charged the few archers who now held the mountain and easily broke through. He then gave the battle-cry of Quraysh to signal that they had been able to penetrate to the Muslim rear. The scattered Qurayshis rallied to the cry from every direction. The Muslims, few and in disorder, found themselves caught in the talons of the Qurayshi hawk. Quickly they threw down the booty and picked up their swords to fight, but alas! What a vast difference there was between fighting firm in faith for Allah's sake as one man, and fighting with the dross of this world in their hands, each trying to save his own life. They fought in confusion and disorder; they fought each other unknowingly. They were driven to the left and right and knew not where to turn. To break their morale completely, a voice from Quraysh cried out that Muhammadﷺ was dead. Now the Muslims fought with weeping hearts, for they loved Muhammadﷺ dearly. Some laid down their weapons out of sheer despair.

On hearing of Muhammadﷺ's death, all Quraysh charged forward in the direction where he was. Each wanted to take something of him as a relic to show to his children and grandchildren. The Muslims around him fought with surpassing courage to protect him. Abu Dujana used his own back as a shield to protect Muhammadﷺ from the arrows of Quraysh, while the others shot arrows like rain to drive Quraysh off. Umm Ayman, one of the women who had come out at the beginning of the day with a jug of water for the fighters, threw down the jug and picked up a sword, fighting a rearguard action with the men to protect him until she fell. At last the Muslims were able to drive them off and make a retreat up towards the mountain. On the way, Muhammadﷺ fell in one of the pits that Quraysh had built and wounded his face, but 'Ali ibn Abi Talib supported him up the mountainside.

Some of the Muslims were stunned by the rumour and sat bewildered on the mountainside. A young warrior, called Anas ibn Al-Nadr, saw them and said, 'Why are you sitting here?'

'The Messenger of Allah is dead,' they said.

'And of what use is life after him? Rise and fight for what he has died for.' He returned to the battle and kept fighting on until he had received seventy blows. After the battle, only his sister could recognize his body, and she only recognised him by his fingertips.

As Muhammadﷺ and those around him climbed the mountain of Uhud, people began to realize that he was still alive and rallied round him. At the same time Khalid ibn Al-Waid, the head of the cavalry forces of the Quraysh, also heard and came after them. Wounded, defeated, through no fault of his own, Muhammadﷺ continued to give instructions to those around him, continued to direct the battle. He said to them, 'They should not attain a higher position than us.' Whereupon 'Umar ibn Al-Khattab and a group of other Muslims blocked the way of the Qurayshi cavalry and by dint of sheer courage and perseverance were able to drive them back.

Abu Sufyan, the head of the Qurayshi forces, also pursued them and cried, 'Is Muhammadﷺ alive?'When no one answered, for the Messenger had given instructions that they answer him not, he assumed that Messenger had been killed. He then asked about the man who was of the greatest importance after the Messenger and said, 'Is Abu Quhafa (meaning Abu Bakr) alive?'Again no one answered and he assumed that Abu Bakr had been killed. So he asked, 'Is Ibn Al-Khattab alive?'

On hearing his own name, 'Umar could contain himself no longer and said, 'You lie, you enemy of Allah!'

Then Abu Sufyan realized that they were alive, but he was only too happy with the sudden and unexpected victory he had attained, so he did not recall his forces or press home his advantage while the Muslims were still weak, but he could not help crying out in satisfaction, 'A day for a day and our appointment is next year at Badr.'

21.6 The Lesson

To be defeated is a painful experience, but to be defeated when victory is within one's grasp is bitter indeed. To some of the Muslims it was a double grief and a double woe, for they felt they were responsible for their comrades being slaughtered, they felt they were at fault for not obeying the Messenger's orders. They had been warned after Badr by the Qur'an not to care for the wealth of this world but some had not heeded the warning. So at Uhud they had to learn by painful experience. They had attained an easy victory at Badr in spite of inferiority in men and weapons. After the battle the holy verses had reminded them that they had chosen the dross of this world while Allah had desired something better for them. He desired the eternal life. Nevertheless they were forgiven their desire for ransom and allowed to keep the ransom and loot they had taken. The Prophet had told them that victory would be theirs if they were patient and persevering. They had not been patient but had sought booty. He had ordered the archers to remain on the mountainside but they had disobeyed. The result was disaster.

21.7 Quraysh Mutilate the Dead

Quraysh were clamourous and exultant in their triumph, having snatched a great victory after a moment of certain defeat. They buried their dead, then the Qurayshi women, led by Hind, the wife of Abu Sufyan whose brother, uncle, and loved ones had been killed at Badr, began to mutilate the Muslim dead. Hind went to the body of Hamza whom she had hired Wahshi, the black slave, to kill and vented all her vicious fury on it. She cut open the abdomen and chewed Hamza's liver.

When Quraysh left, the Muslims went to the battlefield. The Messenger seeing Hamza, his uncle and foster brother, lying dead and mutiliated, was deeply moved. Hamza, the greatest of warriors, the greatest of huntsmen. Hamza, who had struggled for fourteen years to establish the word of Allah. Hamza, who had stood all those years like a mighty shield to protect him from the wrath of Quraysh. Muhammadﷺ was furious to see him so horribly mutilated. He took off his own cloak and covered him with it, then said, 'If ever Allah gives me victory over them, I shall mutilate them as the Arabs have never done before.'

Mutilating the dead was something alien to the Arabs. It was something that their nature shunned, and Abu Sufyan himself had declared before all that he was innocent of what Hind had done.

On this occasion the holy verses address the Messenger, saying:

If you chastise, chastise as you have been chastised,
and if you are patient it is better for the patient.
And be patient and your patience comes only from Allah.
And do not grieve for them or be distressed by their cunning.
Allah is with those who fear Him, those who are gracious. (16:127-129)

As soon as these verses were revealed, Muhammadﷺ decided to forgive Quraysh and forbade the Muslims from mutilating the dead.

Years later, when Makka lay open at his feet, he gave all its inhabitants, including this same Hind, a free pardon.

21.8 Error and Forgiveness

It is difficult to accept defeat when it is one's own fault, but even more difficult to accept it when it is not one's own fault, but the fault of others. To be cheated of victory over Quraysh when it was within his grasp, to be defeated after the long years of patient perseverance and sacrifice, and all because of man's love for the things of this world. He had done all he could and victory would have been his had not some of the archers disobeyed and some of the soldiers failed to pursue the enemy. This must have been very difficult for the Messenger to accept. What does a general do when he loses the battle because of the insubordination of some of his soldiers? For Muhammad܀ this was not just a battle for a city but a struggle for the survival of Islam. The years of struggle and sacrifice might have all been in vain.

At this bitter moment, the holy verses came down to console and guide him with the following words:

By the mercy of Allah you have softened towards them.
Had you been rough, hard-hearted,
they would have dispersed away from you.
So pardon them, ask forgiveness for them and consult them in affairs.
Once you make a decision, then trust in Allah.
Allah loves those who trust in Him. (2:159)

The Qur'an ordered him to forgive them, as Allah in His mercy forgives the erring, and not only was he to forgive them, but to call them to him and consult them in affairs, thus restoring their self-respect.

Allah taught His slaves a lesson that was hard and bitter, but once it was over, He restored to them their self esteem by making the Messenger, whom they all loved and revered, forgive them and consult with them. As we shall see, immediately after, they were commanded to carry arms again in the name of Allah and their self-confidence was restored. They were still the soldiers of Allah even after this terrible trespass that had plunged many of them in deep despair. To save those who err unwittingly one does not crush them or make them despair, but opens the way to them to redeem themselves by renewed effort.

The Messenger - and indirectly all Muslims - were made to perceive new heights of forgiveness, new horizons in understanding.

21.9 Pursuing the Enemy

The next morning a herald went around the streets of Madina, calling all those who had fought with the Prophet the day before to get ready to pursue the enemy again. No one who had not fought at

Uhud the day before had a right to join this army. The Muslims took up their swords and rose to fight, eager to redeem themselves. They were now less than seven hundred and many were wounded, tired, and weary, and they had to pursue an enemy over four times their number - an enemy with high morale and hopes, fresh from victory. But with their wounds and in their grief, the Muslims still rallied to the call. Not a single one of them stayed behind.

Abu Sufyan, learning of their approach, and fearing they had brought reinforcements from Madina and were hungry for revenge, sought information about them. A man who had seen them confirmed his fears, saying he had never seen such numbers or such readiness, all burning for revenge. In order to weaken their morale, Abu Sufyan sent a message to them at Hamra' Al-Asad where they had dismounted, threatening that he was coming to finish them off. So every night Muhammadﷺ lit a great bonfire as a signal that he had received the message and was waiting for Quraysh. For three nights in succession he waited, but Abu Sufyan never came. Quraysh saw the fire, as all the Arabs saw the fire, but the Quraysh did not move. Then on the third day, deciding that they had seen enough of war for the moment, they headed towards Makka.

Muhammadﷺ's dauntless spirit and his firm belief that Allah would grant them victory against all odds, provided they did not trespass, mitigated the defeat at Uhud. The Muslims felt that they had answered the call of duty, which attenuated their feelings of remorse; while those who wished them ill realized that they were still a power to be reckoned with.

In spite of their courage and perseverance in pursuing the enemy, some of the tribes, who were biding their time, thought this was the moment to attack the Muslims while they were still weak after Uhud. Some two months after Uhud, news came that Banu Asad, stirred by some of its leaders, were coming to raid Madina. The Prophet prepared an army group of one hundred and fifty men and put Abu Salama in charge. He commanded them to travel by night and hide by day and to take an unfrequented route in order to surprise the enemy which was far greater in numbers.

They fell upon the enemy in the fog of an early dawn. Surprised, the tribesmen did not resist. Abu Salama sent one group of men to pursue the enemy and another to bring in the booty while he remained with a third group until they returned.

Abu Salama did not live long after that, for he was suffering from a wound he had received at Uhud. It had not healed completely and this new exertion re-opened it. The Messenger sat by his deathbed until the last moment for he had been one of the first Muslims.

21.10 Banu Lihyan

Banu Lihyan, a branch of the large Hudhayl tribe, were making preparations to attack the Muslims. Muhammadﷺ sent a man to find out the facts. This man, 'Abdullah ibn Unays, travelled until he reached the lands of Banu Lihyan. There he asked to speak to their chief, pretending to be a man seeking to join the fighting against Muhammadﷺ. When he became certain that this chief was collecting warriors to attack Madina, he managed to lure him away from his men and kill him. His women raised the alarm, but he managed to escape before the rest of the tribe arrived. Banu Lihyan were quiet for a while after this blow, but they were planning to seek revenge for their chief.

21.11 The Three Martyrs

One day a delegation from two smaller tribes went to Madina, saying that they wanted to enter into Islam, and needed teachers to instruct them in religion.

The Messenger often sent some of his Companions to instruct people in religion, for his aim was to spread the words of Allah as far as possible and eradicate the evil of idolatry. So he sent with them six men learned in the teaching of Islam.

The small party of travellers passed near to the lands of Hudhayl, who learning of their presence, took the opportunity to avenge the assassination of the Chief of Banu Lihyan. The six men found themselves being attacked by thousands of armed men. They raised their swords to defend themselves, but Hudhayl said to them that they had no wish to kill them, but only to deliver them to Quraysh for money. To the Muslims this was worse than death so they fought a desperate battle against the whole tribe. Three of them died fighting and three were overpowered and taken captive.

One of these three who died of their wounds used to do a most remarkable and noble service. He used to go under cover of night, slip into Makka and free the weak and helpless Muslims from Quraysh's captivity.

On the way to Makka one of the captives was able to free his hands and tried to escape. The tribesmen could not catch him, but they kept throwing rocks at him until he was stoned to death.

They travelled on with the other two. Quraysh wanted to buy them to kill in revenge for their relatives who had fallen at the Battle of Badr. The first, called Zayd, was a devout soldier of Allah. Like most of these early Muslims he would use a sword when necessary, otherwise he spent the nights in prayer and many days in fasting. He was delivered to Quraysh and as he was about to be killed, Abu Sufyan said to him, 'Zayd, would you not have preferred to have Muhammadﷺ in your place being crucified and you safe with your family?'

'No, by Allah,' answered Zayd, 'I would not like a thorn to prick Muhammadﷺ's finger in exchange for my being safe with my family.' From such incidents, Abu Sufyan used to say in exasperation, 'I have never seen a man whose followers love him as the followers of Muhammadﷺ love him.'

The other captive was Khubayb. He was imprisoned for some time before he was killed at a certain woman's house. In prison he asked for a knife or blade to shave with. The woman at whose house he was imprisoned almost forgot that he was the enemy because of his devotion and goodness.

She sent her little son to him with the blade. He held the blade in one hand and the boy in the other and said, 'Does your held not fear treachery?' Then he let him go.

When they brought him out to be executed, he asked permission to pray first. After praying two rak'ats (prostrations in prayer), he said, 'I would have liked to pray more, but I feared lest you said I prayed in fear of death.'

As they tied him to the stake, he suddenly looked down upon them in anger and said, 'My Lord, record their numbers, devastate them completely, leave not a single one of them on earth.'

Somehow they felt that his cry was like a curse on them. They shied away for a moment, then they returned and killed him.

The two men died martyrs. They could have saved themselves by a single word, by rejecting Islam and returning to the worship of idols. But they were true to the end, to the last moment and the last breath.

Of such men the Qur'an says:

Of those who believe are men true to what they have promised Allah.
Some have fulfilled their vows by death and some await.
They have altered nothing. (33:23)

Muhammadﷺ and the Muslims grieved for these men who died martyrs while on the call of duty, and continued to pray for them every evening for a whole year. Others also went on the same errand and were taken and killed by treacherous tribes. This did not prevent Islam from spreading further and further, nor Muslims from risking their lives to teach people the words of Allah.

CHAPTER TWENTY-TWO

22.1 Banu Nadir's Plot

During these years the Jews had never ceased plotting and trying to create misunderstanding between Muslims, between Emigrants and Supporters, between Al-Aws and Al-Khazraj. Here the wisdom of making the Emigrants and Supporters brethren in Islam appears, for it forestalled many a misunderstanding. The Jews together with the Hypocrites (people who pretended to be Muslims but who had entered into Islam for political reasons only) were constantly creating trouble. Perhaps they thought that if they could not defeat Muhammadﷺ in open warfare, they could assassinate him by treachery.

An opportunity presented itself when the Messenger with only a handful of men went to the Jewish tribe of Banu Nadir to discuss with them the blood money that had to be paid for two men who had been killed by mistake. These men were from Banu 'Amir, allies of Banu Nadir.

Banu Nadir met the Prophet with great welcoming and rejoicing, but planned to throw a large rock from above while he sat with them discussing the blood money. He sat with them for a moment and then got up suddenly without a word and left. Everyone thought he would be back in a moment and waited for him but he did not return.

Banu Nadir did not know what to think. If Muhammadﷺ by supernatural means had found out their design what were they to do with his friends? If they killed them, he was sure to retaliate. The best thing was to pretend that nothing had happened and hope that they had not been found out. So they remained hospitable to his friends until the latter could wait no longer, took leave of them, and went out to look for Muhammadﷺ.

On the way a man met them and said that the Prophet requested their presence in the mosque. In answer to their questions, he replied that Muhammadﷺ had come back and headed straight to the mosque. So they went there where all important meetings took place. The Messenger related to them what had been happening behind the scenes while they sat there. Then he sent an emissary to Banu Nadir to say, 'Get out of my city for you have broken the covenant between you and us when you plotted to kill me by treachery. You have ten days to leave the city. Whoever of you is found in it after the ten day period expires shall die.'

Banu Nadir were shocked to find out that Muhammadﷺ knew all their designs to the last detail. All they said to the messenger, a man who had been their ally before Islam, was, 'We never thought it would be you who would carry these words to us.'

'Hearts have changed,' he answered.

While they were yet undecided as to what to do, a messenger came to them from the head of the Hypocrites, 'Abdullah ibn Ubayy ibn Salul, saying that he had two thousand warriors ready to withdraw into their forts with them to defend them. Many of them had no confidence in Ibn Salul. Had he not previously made promises to Banu Qaynuqa', then at the crucial moment deserted them? But their chief, Huyayy ibn Akhtab, said, 'I shall send to Muhammadﷺ saying that we will not leave our houses and our possessions. Let him do what he will. All we have to do is to strengthen our forts, then get in all we need. We have food that will last for a year and our water is perennial. Muhammadﷺ will not besiege us for a year.

So the ten day period expired and Banu Nadir did not leave the city, thinking that their forts and the armed warriors of 'Abdullah ibn Ubayy would defend them. On this occasion the holy verses say:

Have you seen the hypocrites telling their companions,
from those who deny of the people of the Book,
'If you are driven out, we shall go out with you,
and we obey no order from anyone against you,
and if you are fought with, we shall support you,
and Allah witnesses that they are liars.
If they are driven out, they will not go out with them;
if they are fought with, they will not support them,
and if they do, they will turn in flight,
then they shall not be delivered. (59:11-12)

When the ten days expired and Banu Nadir showed no signs of leaving, the Muslims went and besieged them. Whenever the Muslims took a fort or house, the Jews destroyed it and climbed to the one behind it. In vain did they wait for 'Abdullah ibn Ubayy to fulfill his promise. All he wanted was to create more trouble for Muhammadﷺ by their resistance; he had never intended to help them in earnest. This the Qur'an had pointed out.

At last they realized that they would be defeated, so they asked for a truce and permission to leave. This was granted. For each individual there was granted a camel's load of whatever he desired to carry with him: money, clothes, articles, etc. They departed leaving to the Muslims many weapons and shields and also their lands. They went to Khaybar where many Jewish tribes lived and where some of them owned land, while some of them went to Azriat, near Al-Sham, as Banu Qaynuqa' had done before them.

Muhammadﷺ distributed the lands of Banu Nadir among the Emigrants, those who had left their lands and money for Allah's sake, so they became independent of the Supporters, the native inhabitants of Madina. He allotted the revenue of one fifth of this land to the poor.

22.2 Going Out to Meet Quraysh

The Supporters agreed to give their share of this land to the poor of the Emigrants, those who had left, their money and possessions in Makka. About the Supporters the Qur'an says,

And those settled in the home and in faith before them,
love those who emigrated to them,
and fmd no envy in their hearts
because of what the latter are given.
They prefer them to themselves even if they are in need of it.
Those spared their own niggardliness, those are the successful. (59:9)

Just as it teaches the Muslims everything by degrees, the Qur'an teaches them charity by degrees. They are first taught that to give of what you have been given is a sacred duty. Give what you do not need. Then they are taught that you do not give things in poor condition but in a condition that you yourself would accept. The third stage is to give what you like and cherish. The holy verses say:

You do not attain benevolence, until you give of what you love. (3:92)

The fourth and finest stage is to give what you need. Few people are able to reach that stage, but those early Muslims whose faith was new and pure, who had the example of Muhammadﷺ before them, were able to attain it. The Supporters were happy to give the Emigrants land that they themselves needed and desired, as the verses above point out.

Muhammadﷺ was continually giving. One of those who knew him said that he gave way as if he could never become poor.

Once a woman gave him as a present some material that he

needed to make a garment. A little later someone came and asked if he had anything to wrap the dead in and immediately he produced the new material. He could not bear to see anyone need something that he had without giving it to him, preferring him to his own family. When he came to die, his armour was pawned with a Jew to provide food for his own family. He used to take much in loot and ransom, but all went to the poor.

One day 'Umar ibn Al-Khattab found him sleeping on a hard mat which left marks on his side. 'Umar had tears in his eyes for he loved Muhammad☀. The Messenger said, 'Whatever makes you cry, Ibn Al-Khattab?'

'Caesar and Chosroes of Persia sleep on soft feathers while you, who are the Messenger of Allah, sleep on this hard mat.'

Muhammad☀ said, 'Wouldn't you like them to possess this world and have us possess the eternal world.'

'Certainly,' said 'Umar.

'Then so shall it be,' answered Muhammad☀.

Abu Bakr also lived and behaved in the same manner. Though he was a rich merchant, most of his money went to the poor or in freeing slaves. When asked why he did not live more leniently, he said, 'I would hate to allow myself what the Messenger of Allah does not allow himself.'

Years later, when 'Umar had become the Khalif and his realm had expanded into a vast empire, he was asked why he would not be less severe with himself and he said, 'I have two friends who have taken this road before me. I fear that should I deviate from them I would lose the way.

22.3 Return to Badr

For a while Madina could breathe in quiet. The Emigrants were happy to have land of their own again while the Supporters were relieved of the burden of helping their Emigrant brethren. They studied the Qur'an, they spent the nights in prayer when they chose, and many could recite the Qur'an by heart for they had grown to understand and cherish it. However the months passed quickly by and it was time to meet the challenge of Abu Sufyan for he had said, 'A day for a day, and our appointment is next year at Badr.' He meant that the Battle of Uhud made Quraysh even with the Muslims for the Battle of Badr, but it still had to be decided who would have the upper hand.

It was a year of scarcity in Makka and Abu Sufyan hoped to postpone the appointment till the year after, so he sent word to Madina to say that he was coming with a great army to annihilate the Muslims completely. Some people panicked at this and hoped they would not have to fight, but Muhammadﷺ was angry and said that he was going to Badr even if he had to go all alone. After this remark the Muslims who loved him dearly prepared to go out to war. They went to Badr and waited for the enemy.

Abu Sufyan marched with his army out of Makka, then after two days' march he thought better of the matter and said to Quraysh, 'Quraysh, this is a year of scarcity, and only a year of plenty is suitable for war. So turn back, I am returning to Makka.'

For eight days Muhammadﷺ waited at Badr. During that time the Muslims were able to trade and make profit, for Badr was a market-place as well as a watering place. They then returned to Madina with shining honour and in good spirits.

On this occasion the Qur'an says:

Those whom people told,
'Hosts have gathered against you, so fear them.'
This increased their faith and they said,
'Allah suffices for us. He is the best Guardian.'
So they returned with the blessing of Allah and His bounty.
No harm touched them, and they pursued the approval of Allah,
and Allah is of very great bounty. (3:173 -174)

Now all the Arabs could see that it was Quraysh who feared an encounter and not the Messenger. The Muslims had become a power. Instead of trying to come to terms with them, many of these idolatrous tribes made preparations to come and fight them. They had their reasons: economically their welfare was tied up with that of Quraysh, politically they resented the power of the Muslims over vast tracts of Arab land, socially they feared for the idols around which all their social and religious life revolved. If Muhammadﷺ was allowed to eradicate idol worship from the Arabian peninsula, it meant that their customs and social life would be disrupted.

Whenever Muhammadﷺ heard of such gatherings he used to send out an army headed by one of his Companions or lead an army himself to meet them before they could march upon Madina. No sooner did these tribes hear of his approach than they fled to the mountains, for they were not moved by faith or a righteous cause, only the desire to dominate and plunder. They knew that the Muslims did not retreat, but fought until they attained either the honour of dying for Allah's sake or victory. These tribes were not ready to die for the sake of plunder and they knew that victory could not be attained except at an exorbitant price, so they plotted, they gathered, but whenever they heard Muhammad was approaching, they fled. To be safe from these tribes the Muslims had to travel far and wide in the Arabian peninsula right up to the borders of Syria. They suffered much from heat, hunger, and thirst. They waged battles with numbers four or five times their own, but they marched on with hearts full of faith and joy to be soldiers of Allah.

22.4 The Greater Struggle

One day when returning from battle, Muhammad said to his Companions, 'We have left the lesser struggle to return to the greater struggle.'

'What is the greater struggle, Messenger of Allah?' his Companions asked.

'It is the struggle of a man with himself,' he said.

Muhammad believed that each individual should struggle to attain the highest potential his soul could reach. Thus he taught his Companions:

'My Lord has recommended nine traits to me which I recommend to you. He has commanded me sincerity, openly and in secret, justice in contentment and in anger, thrift in opulence and in penury, to pardon him who has wronged me, to give to him who has deprived me, to connect him who has cut me off, to let my silence be meditation, to let my speech be prayer, to let my perception bring a moral to me.'

CHAPTER TWENTY-THREE

23.1 The Jews Conspire with Polytheist Tribes

Islam continued to spread to more remote parts, and the enemies of Islam grew more desperate and frantic. The most bitter of all were the Jews. Immediately before Muhammad☾'s advent, all the signs had pointed that a prophet was about to appear. They believed that this prophet would appear amongst themselves as they were the chosen people. They were aware through all the questions they asked and all the tests they made on Muhammad☾ that he spoke the truth. They were aware through an accurate description they had of him in their books that he was the chosen prophet, but they were not going to follow an illiterate Arab. The spread of Islam gave Muhammad☾ the temporal power that they coveted and they resented his authority. They put their heads together, plotted, conspired, and finally came up with the idea that all the tribes of Arabia, all the polytheists, should unite to exterminate the Muslims.

The elders of the tribe of Banu Nadir, headed by their chief, Huyayy ibn Akhtab, went to see Quraysh, taking with them some of the leaders of the polytheist tribes that lived near Quraysh. The leaders of Quraysh asked them how they fared, and they replied that they were waiting for Quraysh to come to Madina so that they could march with them to meet Muhammad☾. Quraysh then asked them about Banu Qurayza, the only Jewish tribe that had not broken its covenant with the Messenger and was still living in Madina. They answered that Banu Qurayza too were waiting for Quraysh to come, so that they could show their true colours and fight on their side. These words were tempting to Quraysh, but still they hesitated.

Day by day it had become clearer and clearer that Muhammad☾ was neither an impostor nor a madman. Those of them who had been present at Badr or Uhud had seen strange and inexplicable phenomena. They felt that behind Muhammad☾ there stood a mighty power. They were not sure anymore that to fight him was the right thing. In doubt, they consulted the nobles of Banu Nadir, for they had great respect for the Jews' knowledge of these things, which were obscure to them. They said to them, 'You are the people of the first book, and you are the people who know most about what we and

Muhammad🕮 differ. Is our religion better or his?'
The Jews assured them that their religion, idol worship, was better than the worship of Allah alone. Concerning these words the holy verses say:

Have you seen those given a part of the Book[1]
belive in Al-Jabt[2] and the godless and those who deny
that they follow a more true way than those who beliive?
Those are the ones Allah curses.
He whom Allah curses will find none to support him. (4:51-52)

Alas, the hatred and envy in the Jews' hearts was so great, it made tnem betray the truth and betray Allah whom they worshipped. They kept pressing Quraysh and did not leave Makka until extracting a promise from Quraysh to come and fight the Muslims in Madina.

With this promise in their pocket, the Jews went to seven other tribes. They promised them a swift victory and much loot, assuring them that Quraysh would lead the battle. Now every tribe that had a grudge against the Muslims got ready to march upon Madina, tempted by the promise of a quick kill and easy spoils.

23.2 The Tribes Prepare for War

Quraysh went out to war, led by Abu Sufyan. They had four thousand warriors, three hundred horsemen, and one thousand five hundred men on war camels. The banner had been given in the House of Debate to 'Uthman ibn Talha whose father had been killed at Uhud. They were joined by Banu Fazara who came out to war with thousands of warriors including one thousand camel men. Two lesser tribes came with four hundred warriors each, and Banu Asad joined the march, so that in total they were ten thousand warriors. Abu Sufyan was made head of all these armies.

23.3 Digging the Trench

The Muslims were alarmed by news of these hosts converging upon them. After consultation it was decided that it would be best to fight such a large force inside their city, after fortifying it. Among the Muslims was a Persian, a man who had travelled much in search of the truth until he found it in the words of Muhammad🕮. He knew of arts and wisdom that the Arabs knew nothing about. His name was

---

[1]. The expression 'The Book' as used in the Qur'an refers to the Torah, the Gospel, and the Qur'an, all together. That is why the Jews are referred to as 'those given a part of the Book'.
[2]. The name of an idol the Makkans used to worship.

Salman the Persian and he knew of war tactics unheard of among the Arabs. Now he suggested that they should dig a trench around the city. The Muslims quickly took up this novel idea. By toil and diligence the trench was dug in six days. Muhammad☙ himself helped in the work. Once when striking a large rock with his pick, there was a great flash of light. His Companions asked him the significance of this phenomenon, this light spreading out, and he smiled and told them to be of good cheer, for one day the light of Islam would shine over lands which at that time belonged to Chosroes of Persia and Caesar of Byzantium. The Muslims raised their voices in praise of Allah, the Greatest. The Persian and the Roman empires were the two great powers that dominated the world at that time. They were feared neighbours to the Arabs and their lands stretched out east and west, two giants encircling Arab land.

Hearing of this, the Hypocrites, the Jews, and the polytheists laughed in glee. They made fun of these words and propagated them far and wide, little knowing that they were being made witnesses to the truth of Muhammad☙'s prediction. 'There,'they said, 'the Muslims are about to be exterminated, wiped of the face of the earth, and Muhammad☙ tells them that the lands of Caesar and Chosroes of Persia will be theirs, and the fools believe him.'

Less than three years after Muhammad☙'s death, these prophetic words were no longer a joke, but historic fact. The holy verses say in answer to the polytheists' jibes:

Say, 'O Allah!, King of Dominion.
Thou givest kingdoms to whom Thou wilt
and seizest kingdoms from whom Thou wilt.
Thou givest power to whom Thou wilt,
and humiliation to whom Thou wilt.
All good is in Thy hands, Thou art able to do anything. (3:26)

23.4 The Women and Children

The women and children were placed in fortified houses behind the trenches, and piles of stones were placed beside these houses for defence. Then the men, with Muhammad☙ at their head, came out and placed the mountain of Sal' as a shield between them and the enemy.

The converging hosts expected to attack Madina immediately, to kill, loot, pillage, and return victorious, laden with spoils. They were amazed to find a trench around the city. What curious thing was this?

They did not know how to send missiles across it. Baffled and furious, they accused the Muslims of being cowards to hide so behind a trench, a thing the Arabs had never heard of before. They exchanged a few arrows with the Muslims, then, in frustration, set up camp to watch.

23.5 Huyayy Persuades Banu Qurayza

Huyayy ibn Akhtab, the Jewish chief, feared that the tribes would be disillusioned by their long wait and turn back. It would then be difficult, if not impossible, to bring them all together again. Already Ghatafan, the second biggest tribe after Quraysh, was getting restless. So he went to them and said that he was convinced that Banu Qurayza, the last Jewish "tribe that had not broken its covenant with the Messenger and had its forts inside the city walls, were ready to be on their side, to cut the Muslims' food and water supply (the Muslims were besieged from all sides, except that of Banu Qurayza) and open the gates to the enemy, then they would exterminate the Muslims in a matter of hours.

Then he went to work on Banu Qurayza. At first its chief, Ka'b ibn Asad, would not let him in or listen to him. He knew how fair the Messenger was, and what great advantages and security this treaty was giving them. Muhammadﷺ would never go back on any part of it as long as they did not break it themselves. The tribes were not so trustworthy. But Huyayy kept pressing him, promising him power and glory for the whole Jewish nation, appealing to his feelings as a Jew. Finally he gave in.

On top of all that they had to face, the Muslims received news of Banu Qurayza's treachery. Muhammadﷺ sent three men to them to find out if the rumour was true. These three men were the head of Al-Aws, who had been the allies of Banu Qurayza before Islam, the head of Al-Khazraj, the second most important tribe in Madina, and one of the great men of the Emigrants.

On entering the forts of Banu Qurayza, they found them in a vindictive and evil mood. Sa'd ibn Mu'adh, the head of Al-Aws and their former ally, tried to warn them of the consequences of breaking the covenant that protected them and of becoming traitors to the city that sheltered them, but his efforts were in vain. They were certain the Muslims would be annihilated and let all the bitter envy and hatred in their heart appear. Like the polytheist tribes, they were roused and wanted Muslim blood. They used vile language and nearly came to blows with their distinguished visitors. The three men returned to report the treachery of Banu Qurayza to the Prophet.

Banu Qurayza asked the tribes to give them ten days to get ready. During those ten days the tribes were to begin the fighting, entering into heavy fighting by the time the Banu Qurayza were ready. The tribes divided themselves into strategic positions. One contingent was to enter Madina from the side, another from above it, while Abu Sufyan with the main force was to engage Muhammad☀ and his army, and stood facing the trench ready for action.

23.6 Moment of Trial

Muhammad☀ was serene and full of courage and hope. He went about his work, placing the Muslims in positions of combat with a sure and tranquil heart. Those of true faith realized that this was the moment of trial and prepared themselves to die fighting for what they believed in, happy to attain the honour of dying for His sake. But those of little faith, the hypocrites, who had entered into Islam to gain worldly profits were in a state of sheer panic. Entering into Islam to gain worldly profits had not been such a good idea after all! The Qur'an describes their condition in these perspicacious words:

Niggardly with you, when fear comes, you see them look at you
with eyes rolling like one about to faint from death.
When fear goes, they scald you with sharp tongues.
Niggardly in doing good.
These do not believe, so Allah has vitiated their deeds,
and this is always easy for Allah. (33:19)

Some of the warriors of the tribes, in high spirits after they had heard of the treachery of Banu Qurayza, and impatient for the kill, found a part of the trench narrower the rest of it and leaped their horses over it. Among them was that famous warrior of Quraysh, Ibn Wudd.

Ibn Wudd cried in a loud voice, for he knew no man was a match for him, 'Who will fight me?'

Among the Muslims none was considered a match for Ibn Wudd. No one moved. But 'Ali ibn Abi Talib, fearless and of infinite faith, rose to meet the challenge. 'Ali was very young and had not Ibn Wudd's experience or mastery of arms, nevertheless he would not let the challenge of the enemies of Allah go unanswered. Muhammad☀ looked at his cousin, the young man he had brought up as a son, but did not forbid him, for his faith in Allah ruled all his actions. The

Muslims held their breath in trepidation for 'Ali.

When Ibn Wudd saw who was meeting the challenge, he said, 'Nephew (a term used to address youngers by the Arabs), I have no wish to kill you. Your father was always good to me.'

'Ali did not answer this remark but spoke to the man as Islam decreed enemies should be addressed. He offered him the worship of Allah and the rejection of idol worship. When Ibn Wudd refused, 'Ali said, 'Then I shall have to kill you.'

'I have no wish to kill you,' said Ibn Wudd.

'But I wish to kill you,' said 'Ali, and without wasting more words, he walked to Ibn Wudd's horse, pulled him down and with one blow finished him. The Muslims cried in wonder, 'Allah is the Greatest!' Obviously 'Ali could not have done this without the aid of Allah. The other Qurayshi warriors were taken aback. Was there among the Muslims someone as great, even greater than Ibn Wudd? They wheeled round their horses and leaped back over the trench.

In the evening another Qurayshi warrior, testing his luck, tried to leap over the trench but fell into it and broke his neck. Abu Sufyan sent emissaries to Muhammadﷺ to ransom his corpse by a hundred camels.

Muhammadﷺ said, 'Take him, he is base and of base ransom.' He meant that the man deserved no ransom and they could take him free.

At night the tribes stoked their campfires high to strike terror in the Muslims' hearts. Everywhere they looked, they could see the tribes' fires spreading endlessly out into the desert. Meanwhile the zealots of Banu Qurayza, not satisfied with breaking the covenant, used to come out of their forts and prowl in the city around the houses where the women and children were, knowing that the men were by the mountain of Sal' facing Quraysh.

In order to lessen the pressure upon the Muslims, Muhammadﷺ tried to negotiate with the tribe of Ghatafan. He offered them one-third of the harvests of Madina if they would turn back and not fight. These negotiations failed, however, for some of the Muslims he consulted said that before Islam they had never done such a thing, so now that Allah had honoured them with Islam, they felt too secure under His protection to do so.

23.7 Nu'aym's Plot

Nu'aym, a man newly entered into Islam, thought of fighting Jewish cunning by cunning. So after getting permission from the

Prophet, he went to speak to Banu Qurayza. He had been their ally before entering Islam and they did not yet know that he had become a Muslim. He told them that the tribes were restive, unhappy about this long wait. What would their fate be if the tribes were to debunk after they had broken their covenant with Muhammad ﷺ? Pretending to be concerned about their welfare, he counselled them not to fight on the side of the tribes until the latter gave them a collateral of their good will. 'Let them give you hostages,' he said, 'so that they do not depart and leave you to Muhammad ﷺ.'

Then he went to Quraysh, who also did not know that he had entered into Islam. Telling them that he was speaking confidentially, he told them that Banu Qurayza regretted breaking faith with Muhammad ﷺ and would do anything to appease him. 'They are going to ask you to give them hostages, and they plan to kill them to appease Muhammad ﷺ. So if they ask for hostages, you will know what to think.' Then he went to the tribe of Ghatafan and told them the same thing.

To test Nu'aym's words, Abu Sufyan sent a messenger to Ka'b ibn Asad, the head of Banu Qurayza, telling him that they would attack immediately after KaWs answer came. Ka'b told the messenger that the next day was a Saturday and that they could do nothing on a Saturday. This offended Abu Sufyan and he sent a reply, 'Make another Saturday a holiday and fight tomorrow with us. If you go back on your agreement with us, we shall start attacking you.' The answer of Banu Qurayza was that they did not fight on Saturdays and that Elohim had cursed some of them because they worked on a Saturday. Then they demanded hostages. Abu Sufyan now had no doubts about Nu'aym's warnings. Ghatafan also thoroughly believed him and an atmosphere of doubt and suspicion began to spread between the tribes and their Jewish allies. Nevertheless Abu Sufyan and the heads of the tribes decided that the time to attack was the early morning as they felt they could not delay any longer.

23.8 The Storm

Night fell and with it came an unexpected guest, a ferocious wind, ruthless in its fury. It pulled down their tents and killed their horses and camels. In the dark, amid the howling winds, a nameless terror struck in their hearts. Unseen hands battered and buffetted them from all sides. Then voices screamed out that the Muslims had come to assassinate them. Some were attacked by their own animals who had been driven wild by the storm. Talha ibn Khuwaylid said, 'Quraysh, Muhammadﷺ has fallen upon you with evil, so save yourselves, save yourselves!'

They ran bewildered, stumbling in the dark. Then in a moment of stillness, at the break of dawn, Abu Sufyan rose and said, 'Quraysh, we are in a hostile and uninhabitable place. Our horses and camels are dead, Banu Qurayza have altered their agreement with us, and we have heard from them words we do not like. You have seen what we have suffered from the storm, so let us turn back. I am for returning to Makka.

Quraysh took only the light things they could carry, and walked towards Makka on foot, while the winds continued to harass them. Ghatafan followed the example of Quraysh and the lesser tribes did the same. Thus dispersed the greatest army that the idol worshippers had ever gathered against the Muslims. The Muslims spent a quiet night, mostly in prayer, then gathered together to pray the dawn prayer, unaware of what the day would bring.

Morning came and the Muslims found the desert before them still and lifeless. Where had the formidable army vanished as if it had never been? At first they went out tentatively to find out whether this was a ruse, but soon reports verified what they could see with their own eyes - Abu Sufyan and remnants of his army were seen walking towards Makka. On this occasion the holy verses say:

When they came to you from above and from below you,
when eyes rolled in fear and hearts leaped to the throat.
and you thought different thoughts about Allah.
That moment believers were being tried and severely shaken.
When the Hypocrites and those with disease in their hearts said,
Allah and His Messenger have promised us only deceptions. (33:10-12)

The verses continue to describe how Allah sent the winds to save those who believed and torture the polytheists. Allah does not charge a soul with more than it can do. He tested the Muslims, but at the end He saved them from an unfair and uneven battle. The Muslim camp was only three miles from the polytheists' camp, but the storm neither frightened or harmed them.

23.9 Siege of the Banu Qurayza

On the afternoon of the same day, a herald walked through the streets of Madina calling all those who believed to meet at the forts of Banu Qurayza - Banu Qurayza who had broken their covenant, agreed to open the gates to the enemy, and to cut the Muslims' food and water supply. They had prowled in the city threatening the women and children when the men were away. These Banu Qurayza were traitors who could not be trusted nor allowed to remain inside the city walls.

'Ali ibn Abi Talib preceded the Muslim banner, and others followed. As if all that they had heard was not enough, when 'Ali approached their forts he heard them insulting the Prophet and slandering Muslim women. A little later, he saw Muhammadﷺ coming and asked him not to approach near their forts. 'Why,' smiled Muhammadﷺ, 'perhaps you have heard what they say about me. When they see me, they will stop it.'

According to the ancient books of the Jews, a group of them who had transgressed on the Sabbath had been changed into monkeys and pigs. Now Muhammadﷺ called out to them, 'Brothers of monkeys and pigs, has Allah humiliated you and let His curse fall upon you?'

The Muslims continued to arrive until a large number had gathered, then Muhammadﷺ asked them to besiege the forts of Banu Qurayza. The siege lasted for twenty-five days, until Banu Qurayza realized they had to come to an agreement with the Messenger. They sent word that they wanted to go to Azriat as other Jewish tribes had done before them, but he refused saying that they had to submit to his decision. This they refused, and they asked their former allies, the tribe of Al-Aws, to intercede between them and Muhammadﷺ.

23.10 Arbitration in the Case of Banu Qurayza

By nature Muhammadﷺ was generous and tolerant, he never bore a grudge, but did his best to mitigate the after-effects of what people did to wrong themselves. The Jewish tribes who had plotted to assassinate him were allowed to leave Madina and to take whatever they would with them except weapons. What he did was for protection rather than revenge. To all the Qurayshi nobles who had persecuted him and the Muslims for years, he was to give a free pardon after the liberation of Makka. The Qur'an says to him:

We have not sent you, except out of mercy to mankind. (21:107)

By refusing the decision of Muhammadﷺ, Banu Qurayza were rejecting the mercy of Allah for the arbitration of man at a time when what they needed was mercy and not justice. Justice in the case of a traitor, according to the rules of men, was death. What they needed was the mercy of Allah, and that only the Messenger of Allah would give, but they appealed to their former allies, Al-Aws, to intercede for them as the tribe of Banu Qaynuqa' had appealed to Al-Khazraj after they had been defeated.

Accordingly, Al-Aws went to Muhammadﷺ and said, 'Messenger of Allah, would you not allow us what you have allowed Al-Khazraj and their allies?'

'Certainly,' said Muhammadﷺ, 'Would you like one of you to be arbiter between Banu Qurayza and me?'

'Yes,' answered Al-Aws.

'Then let them choose one of you to be arbiter between them and me,' said Muhammadﷺ

He gave up his right as the wronged party, his authority as the victor, and allowed Banu Qurayza to choose whom they would. But as if fate insisted on making Banu Qurayza sign their own doom, it let them choose the one man they should not have chosen, Sa'd ibn Mu'adh. They forgot it was Sa'd who had come to warn them not to break their covenant; they forgot it was Sa'd who had heard them revile the Prophet and wish the Muslims an evil fate. They forgot that it was before him that they had revealed that they respected neither oath nor treaty, city or land, but only their Jewish race.

Before accepting to be arbiter between Muhammadﷺ and Banu Qurayza, Sa'd made both parties sign and swear to accept his decision, then he asked Banu Qurayza to step down from their forts and lay down their weapons. His decision was read out to them.

All the men of Banu Qurayza were to be put to death and all the women and children were to be taken as slaves. Had they accepted Muhammadﷺ's decision, they would not have come to this fate, but they trusted more in their allies among men than in the mercy of. Allah

Muhammadﷺ did not revoke the decision of Sa'd since he had sworn to abide by it, but he made one request. He stipulated that families should not be separated, and thus he taught his Companions: 'He who separates mother and child shau be separated from those he loves in the eternal life.'

Before being put to death, the men of Banu Qurayza were offered Islam. Islam wipes clean what was before it, and whatever a man has done in ignorance before Islam is not held against him. He is accepted as a brother, new-born, by the rest of the Muslims. Only four men accepted, saving themselves, their families, and their possessions. All the rest refused, while one of the elders of Banu

Qurayza declared it was an epic that Elohim had written for the tribes of Banu Israel.

In principles and basic tenets there is no difference between Judaism and Islam, in ritual there is much difference, but how often men adhere to the form rather than the core.

Sa'd ibn Mu'adh, the head of Al-Aws, who was the arbiter in the case of Banu Qurayza, had received a fatal arrow wound in the fighting with Quraysh immediately before the siege of Banu Qurayza. He said, 'My Lord, if there still remains war with Quraysh, let me live for it for I would struggle against none more willingly than those who have injured the Messenger, driven him out, and insulted him. My Lord, let this be martyrdom for me (in case there is no war) and do not let me die until I have had satisfaction from Banu Qurayza.'

After Quraysh returned to Makka in frustration, they were never to raise a sword against the Messenger again, and Sa'd died of his wounds.

CHAPTER TWENTY-FOUR

24.1 Banu Al-Mustaliq

For some time the Muslims enjoyed peace, except for a few raids by envious or covetous tribes. When news came that Banu Al-Mustaliq were making preparations for war, Muhammad☙ took the initiative and went to meet the enemy before they were ready.

It was a minor battle in which the Muslims were victorious, but on the return journey a hired man of 'Umar ibn Al-Khattab's quarrelled over precedence to the water with a man from Al-Khazraj.

The man cried, 'Help, help, people of Al-Khazraj!'

In answer, 'Umar's man cried, 'Help, help, Emigrants!'

24.2 'Abdullah ibn Ubayy ibn Salul

The quarrel was stopped immediately, but 'Abdullah ibn Ubayy, the chief of the Hypocrites, who professed Islam yet plotted against the Muslims whenever he found an opportunity, heard these cries and began to stir up trouble.

He said, 'We have let the Emigrants into our city and our homes and now they want to drive us out. Fatten your dog and it will eat you. By Allah, when we return to Madina, the noble will drive out the base.' He meant that the native inhabitants of Madina would drive out the Emigrants. This would have broken the strength of Muslim unity and power.

People began to repeat his words, which spread like an evil wind throughout the camp. They started taking sides; old feuds and old jealousies were fanned. These words went round until they reached the Messenger.

'Umar ibn Al-Khattab who was with him and who hated anything mean or underhanded said, 'Tell Bilal to cut off his head.'

The Messenger rebuked him gently saying, 'Would you have it said that Muhammad☙ kills his confederates?' It was true, to all appearances, that 'Abdullah ibn Ubayy was Muhammad☙'s ally and counsellor.

The Prophet taught his Companions not to be suspicious, but to accept of men what they declared about themselves and to leave the rest to Allah. Of unshakeable faith, all the plots and conspiracies against him left him unruffled, for he knew they would not harm him unless it was the will of Allah.

In order to cool the flames of sedition and make people stop talking, for talking ill of others is a sin in Islam, he ordered them to rise and march even though they had not had time to rest - a rest was less important than stopping the evil rumours that were spreading amongst them. They marched on and on, and he did not give the order to stop until at the end of the day when they were too tired to think of 'Abdullah ibn Ubayy and what he had said, or the original cause of the quarrel. All was forgotten in the long, forced march.

24.3 Father and Son

After arrival in Madina, a rumour spread that 'Abdullah ibn Ubayy would be beheaded. This was not the first or second time that he had created trouble. He was always up to some mischief. 'Abdullah ibn Ubayy had a son, also called 'Abdullah, who was a true Muslim and who now found himself in a terrible dilemma. If the Prophet gave the order to have his father beheaded, he would be honour-bound, according to the customs of the Arabs, to kill the man who had killed his father. If he did not, he would not be able to raise his head among his tribe for the neglect of his filial duty. He knew he would not be able to endure seeing the man who had killed his father sit, eat, and pray side by side with him; and he knew that if he killed that man, he would suffer eternal torture for it - Allah has made the soul sacred and it shall not be killed without just cause. He was completely bewildered, then it occurred to him in a moment of terrible despair that he should be the man to kill his father. He would not then have to kill an innocent soul.

He went to the Messenger in a pitiable plight and begged to be given permission to kill his father. 'Abdullah ibn Ubayy was a most dangerous man to keep alive, but Muhammadﷺ looked at the youth before him and then said, 'We shall not kill him; we shall be good to him and companion to him so long as he remains among us.' He granted the father a complete pardon out of compassion for the son.

'Abdullah ibn Ubayy did not stop plotting and conspiring against the Messenger. That he owed his life to Muhammadﷺ seemed to make him more bitter and resentful. He gathered all the Hypocrites and opportunists around him until his own people were ashamed of him and used to rebuke him for his lack of gratitude. When speaking of the Hypocrites, whose leader he was, the Qur'an says to the

Messenger:

**Plead forgiveness for them or do not plead for them.
If you plead for them seventy times, Allah will not forgive them.
This is because they have denied Allah and His Messenger,
and Allah does not guide trespassers. (9:80)**

When 'Abdullah ibn Ubayy was dying, the Messenger was called to pray over him. 'Umar ibn Al-Khattab, who was with him, later recalled, 'I said, Messenger of Allah, will you pray over one of the enemies of Allah?"

And I kept enumerating his evil deeds while the Messenger continued to smile until I pressed him. Then he said, "Leave me alone, 'Umar, I was given a choice. I was told to plead forgiveness for them or not. If you plead for them seventy times, Allah will not forgive them. If I knew that if I exceeded seventy times, He would forgive them, I would do so." Then he prayed over him and walked in the funeral procession, and sat by his grave until it was over.'

'Umar, the epitomy of stern justice, continues, 'I was amazed at my boldness with the Messenger of Allah, but soon after verses of the Qur'an were revealed that stated, **"And do not pray over any of them ever or stand upon his grave."** (9:84) So after that the Prophet never prayed over a Hypocrite until he was gathered to his Lord.'

24.4 The Slander

Often when the Prophet went to war, he took one of his wives with him. He did not choose but drew lots and took the wife whose name appeared. When he went to fight Banu Al-Mustaliq, the lot fell to 'A'isha, the daughter of Abu Bakr. 'A'isha was small, slim, and graceful, so that the men who carried her litter could not tell by any perceptible change in weight, whether she was in it or not. When the Prophet ordered the abrupt, long march towards Madina, 'A'isha had left her litter for a moment. On her way back, she missed her necklace and so retraced her steps in order to find it. She searched and searched until at last she found it and returned to the Muslim camp. When she came back, she found there was no one left. Thinking she was still in her litter, they had picked it up and marched on.

'A'isha, brought up by Abu Bakr and taught by Muhammad☙, trusted in Allah; she knew that He forgets no one. So she sat in the empty camp and waited, hoping that they would miss her and come back for her, or that someone would pass by. She did not have to wait long, for Safwan ibn al-Mu'attal, a young Muslim man, passed by a short time later. He was amazed to see her sitting there and said, 'To Allah we belong and to Him we shall return.' These are the words Muslims say in the face of disaster. Then without more words, for he revered the wife of the Prophet, he brought his camel nearer to her, so that she could ride. He walked beside it as quickly as he could in order to catch up with the army, but it arrived in Madina before them. He arrived with 'A'isha on his camel a little later, delivered her at her house and went on his way.

'A'isha was the Prophet's favourite. Ever since she had come to his house as a little girl, he had cared for her and was kind and affectionate to her. He taught her much and was delighted by her intelligence and quick learning, her eloquence and wit.

The wicked in Madina, seeing her return on Safwan's camel instead of in her litter, began to whisper, 'Whatever made her leave her litter? Where and how did she meet Safwan?' From tongue to tongue the story spread and grew until it became a slander discussed in the whole city. People began to take sides. There were those who absolutely refused to believe such gross lies, those who doubted and wavered in between, and those who propagated the evil lie. Some were ready to fight for 'A'isha while others were ready to believe the worst. 'Abdullah ibn Ubayy found this a fertile field to sow. In the end the story reached the Prophet. He could not believe this of the little girl he had cared for almost from childhood until she had become a woman of such intelligence, refinement, and charm. but as a man and a husband the story upset him.

'A'isha noticed that he was rather preoccupied, a little cold in his treatment of her, and she did not know how to account for this sudden change. Was the cause the presence of Juwayriya among the captives? Had Juwayriya taken her place in his affections? It is true that he had married her to save the face of Banu Al-Mustaliq, but who can tell what changes occur in the human heart? 'A'isha was not used to this cold treatment, she who had always been so tenderly treated. Muhammadﷺ was the soul of courtesy to everyone, but to her he had been more, so much more. It broke her heart; she fell ill from grief.

Her mother came to nurse her in her illness, and whenever Muhammadﷺ came to ask about her, he spoke rather formally, asking about her and her mother at the same time. This hurt her terribly. She asked permission to go to her father's house in order to be better nursed by her mother, and permission was readily granted. 'A'isha nearly died of grief. Was she no longer indispensable? She who had been his beloved child bride?

People continued to talk to the extent that the Prophet had to speak to them in the mosque, saying that they were injuring him and his family and a man he knew only good of.

A man from Al-Aws said, 'Messenger of Allah, if those that speak against you are of our brethren, Al-Aws, we shall rid you of them. If they are of our brethren, Al-Khazraj, then command us and we shall obey, for they deserve to have their heads cut off.'

The old, old feud between Al-Aws and Al-Khazraj was about to raise its head again, for a man from Al-Khazraj said, 'Yes, you say this because you know those who spoke to be from Al-Khazraj and not from Al-Aws.'

People began to quarrel and it took all Muhammadﷺ's tact and intelligence to stop a civil war from breaking out in Madina. A revelation from Allah would have gladdened his heart and cleared his perception, but not a word came on the subject. He had to act according to his own judgment. This was a trial for him, for 'A'isha, and for all the Muslims, but at that moment they did not realize it.

At last the story reached 'A'isha. She was so shocked. Ill and weak, she nearly fainted from horror at the idea, then all the suffering she had gone through in silence began to find an outlet. She began to sob and sob as if her heart would break.

She could not control herself and still sobbing, said to her mother, 'May Allah forgive you, mother, you heard people talk so and did not tell me?'

Her mother tried to comfort her, -telling her that every lovely woman who had rivals was talked about, but this was no comfort to 'A'isha. Muhammadﷺ was unhappy, could he possibly doubt her? She sat crying in her room when Muhammadﷺ entered. Her father and mother were also present.

Muhammadﷺ said, 'A'isha, fear Allah, if you have committed what people say, return to Allah, penitent, for Allah out of His mercy accepts the penitent.'

She was shocked. Did he really doubt her? She looked at her parents and said, 'Will you answer?'

They said, 'We do not know what to say.'

She burst into tears again. Did her parents also doubt her? Then she was furious with them all. How could he? How could they? Those who knew her so well. She turned upon them saying, 'No, I will not repent of what I have not committed. Allah knows I am innocent. I will not say what has not been. But when I deny it, you do not believe me.' She was quiet for a moment, then said, 'I will only say what the father of Joseph said, 'Good patience, and Allah is my aid against what you depict.'

Here she did what older and wiser people sometimes fail to do. She sought the aid of Him who answers the call of the distressed. Immediately after, Muhammad鸞 began to tremble and feel cold which always preceded a revelation from Allah. They covered him and left him to receive the message.

'A'isha says, 'I was not afraid. I knew myself to be innocent and I knew Allah would not wrong me, but as to my parents, I felt their souls were about to leave their bodies out of fear lest the message from Allah verified what people said.'

Muhammad鸞 rose wiping the sweat from his forehead. (Communication with the unseen, tremendous and difficult to bear, always left him exhausted). He said, 'Be of good cheer, 'A'isha, for Allah has sent down proof of your innocence.' Then he went to the mosque and read to the people what had been sent down:

Those who have fabricated the lie are a group among you.
Do not think it is an evil, but a good thing for you.
For each of them has his share of sin,
and for him who has undertaken the greater part of it,
there is great torture. (24:11)

The holy verses continue to point out that Muslims should think only good of each other, and should not speak ill of anyone. Slander is an ugly and an evil sin.

Since you receive it with your tongues,
and utter with your mouth what you have no knowledge of,
and think nothing of it,
when to Allah it is very grave. (24:15)

24.5 The Case of Tu'ma

Muhammad鸞 was asked to decide in all sorts of cases, great and small. Sometimes the Qur'an would discuss a minor case and leave a great one unmentioned. The reason is the principle involved in each case. If a minor case teaches the Arabs something they did not know, or had neglected, then it is discussed in the Qur'an and used as a precedent for further reference.

Once a man called Tu'ma stole a breast-plate that was hidden in a sack of wheat. He took it and hid it in the house of a Jew. The sack had a hole in it, and kept dripping wheat all the way to the Jew's house. When the owner of the breast-plate missed it, he was able to trace it to the Jew's house, and he reported the incident to Muhammad. The Jew said that Tu'ma had brought it to his house, while Tu'ma denied that he had stolen the breast- plate and accused the Jew of stealing it. Then Tu'ma's people went to Muhammad and swore that it was the Jew who had stolen it and begged him to defend Tu'ma. Muhammad who was very truthful himself suspected no one of telling lies. Moreover the breast-plate had been found in the Jew's house. He was about to defend Tu'ma when these holy verses were revealed:

We have sent down the Book to you with the truth
that you may decide between men as Allah has shown you
and not to be the defender of the treacherous. (4:105)
Had it not been for the goodness of Allah to you and His mercy,
a group of them would have attempted to deceive you,
but they deceive only themselves, they do not harm you in the least.
And Allah has sent down the Book and wisdom to you,
and taught you what you did not know.
The goodness of Allah to you is very great. (4:113)

Then the holy verses point out that if a man does wrong, then asks forgiveness, he will find that Allah is the Merciful, the Forgiving. But if he does wrong then charges an innocent person with it, he has committed a grievous sin. The principle involved in each case is pointed out.

Before Islam when a man of noble birth did wrong his fault was overlooked, but when a commoner did wrong he was punished. Muhammad strove to break this pernicious attitude, applying the decrees of the Qur'an to the noble and commoner alike. He taught his followers, 'Allah has destroyed a people because if the honoured among them did wrong they did not punish him, but if the common man did wrong they punished him.'

CHAPTER TWENTY-FIVE

25.1 Muhammadﷺ as a Worshipper

In the preceding chapters we have described the personality of Muhammadﷺ as the Messenger between Allah and man, the leader of men, the ruler, the judge, and the commander of an army. There is a very important side of Muhammadﷺ's nature that we have so far paid very little attention, and one that is very difficult to describe because Muhammadﷺ himself kept it private and screened. Before becoming Messenger of Allah, before becoming a leader of men, Muhammadﷺ was first and foremost a worshipper. A very long time before he became the Messenger, he forsook the roads frequented by men and sought refuge in the austere seclusion of the desert. He had a refined and sensitive soul that longed to worship. He was a worshipper seeking eternal truth, a slave who longed for contact with his Master.

The trait may be hereditary, we find it in all the line of his descent as far back as his ancient grandfathers, Ibrahim and Isma'il. Ibrahim was prepared to sacrifice his son to Allah and Isma'il went willingly to be sacrificed since this was the will of Allah. The offering sacrificed at the end of the Haaj is symbolic of this memorable occasion, when Allah in His mercy ordered Ibrahim to sacrifice it instead of Isma'il. We know that Muhammadﷺ's fifth grandfather Qusayy ibn Kilab was a pious sheikh who ordered that the guests of Allah should be attended to and served more than all others. His grandfather, 'Abdu'1-Muttalib, after finding the gold swords and struggling with the Quraysh for them, placed them as an ornament at the door of the Ka'ba. When Abraha came with a great army to destroy it, and he knew that they were no match for him, he said, 'The Ka'ba has Allah who protects it.' Although Muhammadﷺ's father died young, this spiritual tendency already showed in him and his slave, later Muhammadﷺ's nurse, used to say to him, 'I see in you the piety of your father.'

Muhammadﷺ had in him this same spiritual transcendence, this piety that shielded his character from anything unworthy or unseemly. He was made on the grand scale of his ancient grandfather Ibrahim. When we first encounter him as a mature man, we find him shunning the amusements, the honours, and the busy social life of Makka, deserting worldly gain and the trade he was successful in to flee to the seclusion of the cave of Hira'. Year after year he would remain there, particularly in the month of Ramadan. He would spend long days in the cave oblivious of time and place, in worship. He cared neither for food or drink, and if left to himself would not think of them, and it was the lady of Khadija, seeing how emaciated he became after these periods of worship, who insisted on sending food to him.

With the years, as his relationship to his Creator who guided him grew closer and deeper, he spoke little about Him who was closer to him than life itself. He said only what he was ordered to say, no more and no less. He spoke in his capacity as a messenger but his own relationship to Allah he kept private, although we do get significant information from those who lived with him and from his Companions who asked him about everything he did in order to emulate him. He was keenly sensitive to what others could not see, deeply aware of the truth behind the thick screens of matter, conscious of the presence of Allah more than the presence of those around him, and he told his Companions, 'Worship Allah as if you saw Him, because even if you do not see Him, He sees you.

One day when on pilgrimage with his Companions, he saw them calling upon Allah with upraised voices and he said to them, 'Softly, He you are addressing is neither deaf nor dumb.'

The lady 'A'isha told of how he used to spend long hours of the night in prayer. Standing he would read the Qur'an, prostrating he would call upon his Lord.

Sometimes he would exhaust himself in prayers, oblivious of time and place but keenly aware of the goodness of Allah to him and of the magnanimity of the gift of the Qur'an, relayed to mankind through him. He felt that no matter how long he prayed, it would not pay his debt of gratitude or express his feelings of thanks. He exhausted himself to the extent that one day verses were revealed to him which say:

Taha, We have not sent down the Qur'an upon you to exhaust you. It is only a reminder to those who fear Him. (20: 1-3)

25.2 Some Prayers of the Prophet

Below are some of the prayers he used to say and that he taught some of his Companions. He taught each man according to his ability to assimilate and according to his particular need:

'O Allah, forgive me what I have done, and what I may do; what I profess and what I conceal; forgive me in what I have done to trespass and in what Thou hast more knowledge about than me. Thou bringest forward, and Thou takest backwards. There is no deity but Thee.'

He was fully aware of the power of Allah to grant anything and therefore he prayed and taught his followers to pray for all their needs, both in this world and the next:

Abu Umama said, 'I heard the Messenger pray for so many things I could recall none of them, so I said to him, "You have prayed for so many things that I have been able to recall none of them.

He said, 'Shall I tell you what would collect for you all that I have prayed for? "O Allah, I ask you for the best of what Your Prophet Muhammadﷺ has asked, and I seek Your aid against the worst that Your Prophet Muhammadﷺ has sought aid against. You are the support and Yours is the communication. There is no ability and no power without You.'

Shahr ibn Hawshab says, 'I asked Umm Salama (the Prophet's wife) what were the most frequent prayers the Prophet repeated when he was at her house and she said, "Thou who art able to alter hearts, keep my heart steadfast in Thy faith."'

And also, 'O Allah, make good my religion for me, it is the strength of my being, and make good my world for me, it is the place where I live, and make good the eternal world for me, it is the place of my appointment, Make life an increase for me in all good, and death a rest for me from all evil.'

When Abu Bakr, who was very close to Muhammadﷺ, asked him for a prayer, he gave him the following words, 'O Allah, I have wronged myself greatly and no one can pardon wrong except Thee, so grant me Thy forgiveness and have mercy on me. Thou art the Merciful, the Forgiving.'

Abu Bakr was a devout Muslim of sublime faith, but the Messenger knew that no man, even the very best, was infallible. All should ask forgiveness, for man is always liable to wrong himself, and he used to tell his Companions, 'I ask forgiveness from Allah over seventy times a day.'

He taught his followers that Allah is near and that prayers are granted so long as they are not reprehensible, that is for something religion forbids, and so long as the person praying has not committed a sin that prevents his prayers from being heard. But patience is required. Patience is a virtue held in very high esteem in the Qur'an. It is the mark of true faith. The Messenger said, 'A slave's prayers are answered so long as he does not pray for a sin or the rejection of kin, so long as he does not precipitate matters.'

When he was asked what was meant by precipitation, he said, 'That the man should say, "I have prayed and prayed and my prayers have not been answered," so he becomes bitter and stops praying.'

Sometimes a man's prayers are not answered directly (they may not be for his own good), but he may attain something good or even better than what he prayed for because of the purity of his intention.

'No Muslim on earth prays for something without getting it, or having its equal of evil diverted from him, unless he is praying for a sin or the rejection of kin.'

'My Lord, 'I plead protection from Thy wrath in Thy approval, and in Thy pardon against Thy punishment. I plead for Thy aid. I can recount no praise sufficient for Thee. Thou art as Thou hast described Thyself.'

One of his Companions asked, 'Prophet of Allah, what shall I say?' And he answered, 'Say, "My Lord, forgive me, have mercy upon me, pardon me, and provide for me." These would combine for you this world and the eternal.'

He also used to say, 'My Lord, I beg for the causes of Thy mercy, the potential of Thy forgiveness, safety from all sin, abundance in all good, the attainment of paradise, and salvation from the fire.'

And also, 'O Allah, I seek Thy aid against the reprehensible in behaviour, deed, and desire.'

'O Allah, grant me righteousness and help me against evil from myself.'

25.3 Fasting

It is decreed that Muslims shall fast the month of Ramadan, unless they are ill or travelling. In Ramadan, the month of the fast, the Messenger used to expend himself to the utmost in worship of all forms - in charity, in reciting the Qur'an, and in prayers. The last ten days he used to spend in seclusion to be able to give all his time to his Lord. The year he was collected to his Lord he spent the last twenty days in seclusion.

Once in Ramadan his Companions noticed that he ate only after sunset and would not eat again until the same time the next day, so some of them began to do the same, but found it difficult to continue. When the Messenger learnt of what they were doing, he forbade them, saying, 'No, I am not like you, I continue to be fed and given to drink while fasting.'

He was most diligent in prayers during Ramadan and encouraged his Companions to be so. He used to pray additional prayers after the evening prayer in the mosque. When the Muslims heard of them, they used to flock towards the mosque in the evening to pray with him.

He feared lest it became custom and many would not be able to maintain these additional prayers after a long day of fasting, so he stoppedpraying them in the mosque and used to pray them at home. The Muslims, realizing that he did this out of compassion for the old and very young, began to pray these additional prayers in their homes as he did. It is said that at this hour in Madina, the hum of human voices praying was heard emanating from every house.

Apart from Ramadan, he used to fast regularly on unspecified days so as not to make others feel they were obliged to do the same. The lady 'A'isha says he used to fast for so long that she would think he was never going to break his fast, and then he remained for long periods without fasting. He is known to have fasted three days of every lunar month, the three first days, and also the three days when the moon is full, which are called 'the three white days' (the twelfth, thirteenth and fourteenth). He also used to fast on Mondays and Thursdays.

He used to say that while the month of Ramadan was obligatory for those who were physically fit, additional days of fasting were entirely optional. Those who cannot fast because of illness in Ramadan may feed a poor man for one day for each day of the fast instead. On days when the Muslims faced heavy tasks he made a point of showing them that he was not fasting.

CHAPTER TWENTV-SIX

26.1 Words of the Prophet

Six years had passed since time the Muslims of Makka had emigrated to Madina and much had occurred in these years. Islam had grown and spread throughout all the peninsula up to the borders of Syria and Iraq. Revelations from Allah continued to reach men and teach them how to live, and the Muslims cherished these verses. Some studied them by heart and some wrote them on parchment, bone, or wood. There were men who knew by heart every single verse of the Qur'an, men who sat with the Messenger daily and discussed with him every topic that they could think of. Muhammadﷺ explained and gave examples in his own words of the teachings of the Qur'an.

26.2 Visit to the Ancient House

About one year after the Muslims had emigrated to Madina, they made their orientation the Ancient House, the first house erected for the worship of Allah on earth. It had been reconstructed by Ibrahim and Isma'il, the grandfathers of the Arabs. When it needed reconstruction at the time of Muhammadﷺ, it was he who put the sacred Black Stone in its place. To this house the Arabs from every quarter of the peninsula made a pilgrimage each year in certain appointed months. In these months the Arabs refrained from fighting. The Qur'an stated that this house was for all men, every man had the right to enter the House of his Lord, every man had the right to be secure in it, and every man had the right to visit it on a pilgrimage of peace. It was an ancient custom, as ancient as the House itself.

After remaining for six years in Madina, Muhammadﷺ announced his intention of visiting the Ancient House as a pilgrim and he invited anyone who wished to join him. He wanted to reassure Quraysh that he came in peace as a pilgrim and had no intention to fight.

When those on pilgrimage reached Dhu'l-Hulayfa, they all put on the same simple garb of the pilgrim, symbolic of the equality of status before Allah and of their submission and humility before Him. They marked out the animals to be sacrificed as offerings at the

Ka'ba and took no weapons with them except what a pilgrim might need. Umm Salama, the wife of the Prophet, was to travel with him on this occasion.

When Quraysh learnt that Muhammadﷺ was coming, they were not sure whether or not he was coming in peace, and their hatred and arrogance was such that they wanted no Muslim in Makka, even as a pilgrim. They assembled an army to meet them and stop their approach. 'Ikrima ibn Abi Jahl was at its head and Khalid ibn Al-Walid lead the cavalry. The Messenger and the pilgrims marched on until they reached 'Usfan, near Makka, where they met a man from Banu Kalb who informed them that Quraysh were adamant in their resolution to refuse him entry. They had donned their war gear and swore by Allah that Muhammadﷺ should not enter.

Muhammadﷺ said, 'Woe unto Quraysh, war has exhausted them. What do they lose if they leave me to the rest of the Arabs. If they defeat me, then this is what Quraysh wants. If they do not, then Quraysh would enter Islam with honour. If they defeat me, then Quraysh will fight me with the upper hand. What do these Qurayshis think? By Allah, I shall continue to struggle for what I was sent until Allah makes it prevail or until this collar-bone is severed.' He meant until death.

Although Quraysh hated Muhammadﷺ and were mean and bitter in their hostility, Muhammadﷺ, as the above speech shows, worried about Quraysh and their condition. He would continue to struggle against them as they were in the wrong; he would guide them to the right whatever the cost, but he felt great pity for them. He knew that Allah would give him victory sooner or later, and he wanted to spare them this bitter dragging, costly, and futile war against the Almighty.

The Messenger continued his peaceful march towards Makka, insisting on not fighting for he came as a pilgrim. Quraysh sent people to him from the tribe of Khuza'a to find out what his intentions were and they, after speaking with Muhammadﷺ, were convinced he came in peace. They reported this to Quraysh, but Quraysh were furious and said that even if Muhammadﷺ had not come to fight, but as a pilgrim, he should not enter the House, for what would the Arabs think? That he had compelled them to allow him entry?

26.3 Emissaries

Next they sent to Muhammadﷺ the head of the Abyssinian

mercenaries whom they had engaged for the defence of Makka. Before speaking to the man, the Messenger told his followers to place the camels decked out as offerings in front of them. Seeing these camels walking towards him convinced the man of their intention for pilgrimage and he returned without speaking to Muhammad☺ for he could see that Quraysh were in the wrong as they had no right to prevent the Muslims or any man from entering the House of Allah. He returned to Quraysh and related what he had seen and they told him that he was a simple Arab and knew nothing. He became angry and said that his people had not made a treaty with Quraysh to drive pilgrims from the House of Allah. If they did not allowMuhammad☺ to observe his religious rites, the Abyssinians would leave Makka. They tried to soothe and appease him, asking him to wait until they had considered the matter.

They then decided to send a man of judgment, a man known for his keen perception, called 'Urwa ibn Mas'ud, but he apologized, for he had seen how they treated those who differed from them. Quraysh kept pressing him, assuring him that they would submit to his decision until in the end he accepted.

26.4 'Urwa ibn Mas'ud as Emissary

When he went to Muhammad☺, he informed him that the army had gone to intercept him far from Makka. (Muhammad☺ in an effort to avoid any skirmish with the Qurayshi army, had taken an unfrequented route while the army of the Quraysh had left by the usual route.) So the road to Makka was open, and the city lay unprotected before him. 'Urwa said, 'Makka is an egg peeled in your hand.'

By nature and by the teaching of Allah, Muhammad☺ was upright and truthful so when he had announced that he came as a pilgrim, he meant exactly that. Before him was an opportunity to dominate Makka and humiliate his enemies without much effort or bloodshed, but he would not take it. He would not go back on his word that he came in peace, even if the Makkans had come out to fight him. His answer to 'Urwa was that he had come as a pilgrim and as a pilgrim, he was asking permission to enter.

'Urwa, much impressed, returned to the Quraysh and said, 'I have seen Chosroes of Persia in his realm, Caesar in his domains, the Negus in his kingdom, but I have never seen a people who love their leader as these Muslims love Muhammad☺. Not a hair falls from his head that they do not cherish. They would never give him up, so think of what you are going to do.'

Muhammad⬥ sent a messenger to Quraysh, hoping he could convince them, but they killed the man's camel and would have killed the man had not the Abyssinians interfered. Then the rabble of Quraysh went out under cover of darkness and threw stones at the Muslims. One night about fifty of them were caught and brought before Muhammad⬥ who set them free and returned them to their people. He had not come to fight or to take captives.

26.5 The Mission of 'Uthman

Once more Muhammad⬥ tried to come to an understanding with Quraysh. This time he sent them a noble messenger whom they knew and liked well, 'Uthman ibn 'Affan. Before his entering Islam he had been one of the great men of Quraysh, after it he became a devout Muslim and

Muhammad⬥'s son-in-law. He was a man loved and respected by all- extremely generous and open-handed.

The first man 'Uthman found on entering Makka was Aban ibn Said. He asked him to be responsible for his life and safety. The man agreed to protect him for the duration of his negotiations with Quraysh. Then 'Uthman went to see the Qurayshi chiefs.

They said to him, "Uthman, if you would like to visit the Sacred House, you may do so.'

He replied, 'It is not for me to visit the House of Allah before the Messenger of Allah.'

Then Quraysh informed him that they had sworn a solemn oath that Muhammad⬥ should not enter Makka.

Now long and laborious negotiations began, so long that a rumour came to the Muslim camp that Quraysh had killed 'Uthman who was the most kindly and generous of men and a man who had gone to them on a peaceful errand in the Sacred Months inside the Sacred Precincts. This was too much even for Muhammad⬥. He said, 'We shall not leave without fighting them.'

The Muslims had come as pilgrims, they had no weapons, no shields, no war camels or horses. They had come to answer the call of Allah, unarmed and in the garb of humility. However, in sheer indignation, they all gathered around Muhammad⬥ who was standing under a tree and one by one they swore allegiance to fight to the death. When they had all sworn, the Prophet held both his hands together and said, 'And this is the oath of 'Uthman,'so that 'Uthman, dead or alive, would not be left out of this oath of faith.

A little while later, they heard that 'Uthman was alive, but carrying on lengthy negotiations. And when after some time 'Uthman appeared in person, they were overjoyed.

The rumour about 'Uthman's death had been a test to them. Would they fight without weapons and put their trust in Allah, or were they still trammelled by material considerations? The Qur'an says:

Allah has approved of those who believe,
when they swore allegiance to you under the tree
He knew what was in their hearts,
so He sent down His tranquility upon them,
and granted them a conquest soon. (48:18)

'Uthman returned to say that, although Quraysh were now sure that Muhammadﷺ had not come to fight, they would not allow him, for the sake of their pride and prestige, to enter Makka since they had sworn he would not enter it that year. They feared the Arabs would say that they had let him enter out of fear.

26.6 Treaty of Al-Hudaybiya

More complicated and laborious negotiations now followed. Quraysh sent one of their leaders, Suhayl ibn 'Amr, to undertake these negotiations and he was aggressive and discourteous in addressing Muhammadﷺ, who bore it all with great forbearance and tolerance. He kept demanding one concession after another and Muhammadﷺ acquiesced, and had not the Muslims had great faith, they would not have agreed to these terms.

Among the terms of the treaty was that the Muslims should not enter Makka that year, but could come as pilgrims the year after. The Muslims were heartbroken. Had they travelled hundreds of miles to be turned away when they were within sight of the holy city? This was their motherland, the centre of all their hopes, and they considered their surrendering to Suhayl a great humiliation.

Normally Muhammadﷺ consulted his Companions, but when he received a command from Allah he followed it meticulously to the last detail, consulting neither their opinions nor his own, neither their feelings nor his own.

After the treaty, 'Umar, who gave quarter to no one, went to Abu Bakr and said, 'Are these not polytheists?'

Abu Bakr answered, 'Indeed they are, 'Umar.'
'Are we not Muslims?' continued 'Umar.
'Indeed, we are,' said Abu Bakr.
'Then why do we make compromises about our religion?'
'Hold your tongue, 'Umar, for I swear he is the Messenger of Allah,' said Abu Bakr.
'I also swear it,' said 'Umar.

Then still furious, he went to Muhammadﷺ and spoke similarly to him.

Muhammadﷺ answered calmly, 'I am the slave of Allah and His Messenger. I do not disobey His orders and He will not let me perish.'

Looking back at this treaty from the cool distance of fourteen hundred years, one cannot help being impressed by its wisdom. Quraysh were, as Muhammadﷺ had expressed earlier, exhausted by war and growing weaker every day while the Muslims were getting stronger and growing more numerous. This treaty was the only thing that would have saved the face of Quraysh and mitigated their feelings of bitter inferiority. To the Muslims, to wait one year seemed a dreadful humiliation, but one year is not much in the history of a nation, and one year was not much to pay for a peaceful entry to the Sacred Precincts. Nor was it a great price to pay for stopping the endless war of vengeance between Quraysh and the Muslims. Had they insisted on fighting, it would have meant that they would have kept on fighting until one party annihilated the other. The Muslims were the stronger, but what would they have gained by exterminating their own kin and devastating their motherland? What seemed to them a great humiliation proved to be an outlet, the only means of reconciliation.

Dominion by the force of arms can dominate the bodies of men, but it cannot dominate their souls, and what Allah wanted was the hearts and souls of these stubborn Qurayshis.

The Qur'an explained to the Muslims that in Makka there were many men and women who believed like them in Allah, but were unable to proclaim their faith. Had the Muslims been given permission to fight in Makka, these people would have suffered with the polytheists at the hands of the Muslims, which would in turn have had evil repercussions, since to injure the innocent incurs His wrath.

26.7 Rites of Pilgrimage on that Occasion

Muhammadﷺ asked the pilgrims to perform the rites of
pilgrimage where they were, outside the Sacred Precincts, and to
sacrifice in the same place. But they were so miserable that they sat
gloomily and did nothing. Muhammadﷺ was appalled and entered
his tent with horror in his eyes. Other peoples had disobeyed the
command of Allah in ancient times and were annihilated. He said to
his wife, 'Umm Salama, the Muslims will perish. They have refused
to obey the command of Allah.'

This mature and experienced lady said, 'No, Messenger of Allah,
they are only grieved. You go and perform the rites of pilgrimage and
they will obey.'

So Muhammadﷺ sacrificed the offerings he had brought, then
shaved his head according to the rituals of pilgrimage. Seeing this,
all the Muslims rose to follow the example of their beloved prophet,
and the situation was saved by the judicious advice of this kind lady.

As if to make the Muslims as unhappy as possible about this
treaty, one of the people who believed in Allah and lived in Makka
hurried to join the Muslims as they were leaving. But according to
the treaty Muhammadﷺ had just signed, those of Quraysh who
wanted to join the Muslims were to be returned to Quraysh while any
Muslim who wanted to defect was to be allowed to go back to
Quraysh. The man's relations came to take him by force, and he cried
to the Muslims, 'Help, help, Muslims! Will you leave me to the
polytheists?'

The Muslims could hardly control themselves. Muhammadﷺ,
whose faith in the wisdom of Allah could move mountains and who
possibly knew what would happen soon after, said, 'Abu Jandal, be
patient. Allah will make an opening for you and for the downtrodden.
We have made a treaty with these people, swearing by Allah, and we
shall not break it.' In theory the terms of the treaty seem untenable,
but what happened in fact was that Muslims did not defect or go back
to Quraysh. Supposing some had gone back, they would have been
of no use to Allah. Keeping them in Madina would have been only
hypocrisy. Far better to let them go where their hearts belonged.
Then the Makkans who believed in Allah did find an opening, as
Muhammadﷺ had promised, by creating new groups and growing
only stronger in the faith they felt they were deprived of. Moreover
only two years later, the whole of Makka entered into Islam and this
treaty became an obsolete document. At the moment, though, the

Muslims could not see the future even if it was so near, all they could see was a fellow Muslim being beaten because he believed in Allah. It was only faith in Allah and His Messenger that made them endure this ordeal.

26.8 The Breakthrough

The Muslims travelled towards Madina with pain in their hearts, and on the way between Makka and Madina, like a ray of the light of heaven, these holy verses came down:

We have opened a clear breakthrough for you,
so that Allah forgives your sin, in the past and in the future,
completes His blessing upon you, and guides you to the straight way,
and gives you a triumphant victory. (48:1-3)

To the Muslims words more cheering than these there never were. They combined forgiveness, hope, assurance, and gracious bounty, everything that could gladden their hearts.

This treaty of Al-Hudaybiya was indeed a breakthrough. What they had considered to be a shameful defeat turned out to be victory with honour, attained without bloodshed or destruction.

Soon after this treaty it became apparent that the whole of the Arabian peninsula would be lit up by the words of Allah, the merciful rule of Islam.

The portent of these verses is of very great significance. The Messenger to whom they are addressed was overjoyed by the graciousness of his Lord - to have all one's sins, throughout the whole of one's life, forgiven and to be granted a breakthrough as well, was magnanimity indeed, beyond his greatest hopes. He felt so grateful that he kept standing in prayer in thanks for so long that his feet became swollen. The lady 'A'isha said to him in awe, 'But Messenger of Allah, Allah has forgiven you your sins, so why do you pray so long?'

'Then should I not be a grateful slave,' he answered gently in explanation.

CHAPTER TWENTY-SEVEN

27.1 Islam after Twenty Years

After nearly twenty years of struggle, Muhammadﷺ was now ordered to proclaim his religion to all men. 'And we have not sent you, except out of mercy to mankind,' the Qur'an states. During those twenty years he had constant communications from Allah, and the noble precepts of Islam had taken definite form. With meticulous planning and perfect timing each of the abhorrent customs of the Arabs was dealt with and replaced by what was more sane and more true, beginning with the main issue, the unswerving worship of Allah alone and the rejection of false deities. Gradually, step by step, year after year, the Muslims were led to the straight path as no new lesson was taught before the preceding one had been thoroughly digested.

After the sole worship of Allah, the basic principles of Islam were introduced; the principle that neither money, power, lineage or tribe was of any consequence to Allah and that purity of heart alone elevated one man above the other. Hand-in-hand with this precept that shattered the Arab class system came the idea that man was on earth to be tested and that his status in the eternal world depended on his deeds in this world.

Once this broad outline was accepted, the Muslims were daily inspired by Muhammadﷺ's example and by the teaching of Islam which covered everything from the great and noble principles of religion to the minor details of social etiquette. For example, a Muslim does not enter a house without permission and he does not depart without taking leave. If he is greeted he answers the greeting or says a better one. There is not a field of life that Islam does not tackle with judgment, fairness, and precision. There is no relationship between people that is not regulated with justice and mercy and with special care given to the weaker party, that is women, children, and subordinates.

To discuss all the precepts of Islam is outside the scope of this work. Suffice it here to note that it changed the Arabs from being a people who lived amid rigid customs and superstitions on the one hand and great licentiousness and corruption on the other, to being a people who worshipped Allah with a clear perception and high morals. They were transformed from a people who used to bury their daughters alive, sacrifice their sons to stone idols, and torture their slaves to death, to a people who cherished their daughters as precious jewels, smashed idols, and set their slaves free. Instead of spending their nights in revels and drink they became a people who spent the night in prayer or looking after the needs of the poor. From people whose pride and joy was their children and their wealth they became a people whose greatest pleasure was to arrive one step closer towards pleasing their Maker.

27.2 Proclaiming Islam to the Rulers of the World: the Negus, Cyrus, Heraclius, Chosroes

One day Muhammadﷺ went out to his Companions and said, 'Allah has sent me out of mercy to all peoples. So do not differ about me as the disciples have differed about Jesus, son of Maryam.'

His Companions said, 'How did the disciples differ, Messenger of Allah?'

'He called them to what I am calling you to. He who was sent on a nearby mission accepted and submitted. He who was sent on a far-off mission hated it and tarried behind.'

Then he told his Companions that he was sending them with letters to Heraclius, the Roman Emperor, to Chosroes of Persia, to Cyrus of Egypt, to Al-Harith, the Ghassanid king of Al-Hira and to Al-Harith, the Himyarite king of Yemen, as well as the Negus of Abyssinia, calling them to Islam.

His Companions accepted these missions and the Prophet had a silver seal made for him with the inscription, 'Muhammadﷺ, the Messenger of Allah.' Each sovereign was called to the worship of Allah alone and the rejection of all else and informed that in Islam (which means in Arabic submission to Allah) he would find salvation and reminded that he was responsible for those he ruled. Each answered according to his nature and knowledge of true religion.

The Negus of Abyssinia answered Muhammadﷺ's letter warmly and graciously for he already knew much about Islam from the Muslims who had emigrated to Abyssinia in the days of persecution. Muhammadﷺ sent him another letter, asking him to allow the Muslims who had emigrated to Abyssinia to return to their homeland, and they were permitted to return with Ja'far ibn Abi Talib at their head.

Cyrus, the head of the Copts of Egypt, answered Muhammadﷺ's

letter in friendly words, saying that he had known that a prophet was to appear and had been looking towards Al-Sham where prophets had appeared in olden times. He feared the Copts of Egypt would not accept this new message, and he feared for his position among them if he accepted it personally. He sent Muhammadﷺ many presents, among them two sisters, Maria and Serene, and also a white mule, which was something novel to the Arabs.

When Heraclius, the Roman Emperor, received Muhammadﷺ's letter, he did not question Muhammadﷺ's messenger about him, but sought out the Arabs in his land. He found a delegation that had come for commercial purposes and was headed by Abu Sufyan, Muhammadﷺ's implacable enemy.

Heraclius brought this delegation before him, seated them amid his nobles and asked them, 'Which of you is the most closely connected to him?'

Abu Sufyan, whose daughter Muhammadﷺ had married when she was forsaken and in need in Abyssinia, answered, 'I am the most closely related to him.'

Heraclius, observant and judicious, said, 'Come forward and let the rest of the delegation stand behind you.' Then he told the rest of the delegation, 'If he tells me a lie, raise your hand.'

After careful questioning of Abu Sufyan, Heraclius said, 'I asked you about his descent, and you said he was of noble birth; so are prophets, they are chosen from the best among their people. I asked you if any of you had said what he says before, and you said no one had. Had you said others had spoken such words before, I would have said he was emulating others. I asked you if any of his fathers were kings and you said none of his fathers were kings. If you had said his fathers were kings, I would have said he had come to claim the throne of his fathers. I asked you if you knew him to be a liar, and you said he had never told lies before. So I say, if he does not tell lies about men, he would not tell lies about God. I asked you if the leaders of his people follow him and you said that only the weak, women, and children do. So are prophets always followed by the weak. I asked you if his followers were increasing or diminishing, and you said they were increasing in numbers. I asked you if any of them wanted to defect from his religion after entering into it, and you said no. Such is the greatness of faith, none can forsake it after feeling its power. I asked you if he betrayed and you said he did not. Such are prophets, they do not betray. I asked you if you have fought against him, and you said yes, war has been waged between you for years. You have injured him, and he has injured you. Such are prophets, they are always opposed. I asked you what he commands you, and you said he commands you to worship Allah alone and forbids you to worship idols and that he commands for you prayers, charity works, and purity. If what you have told me is the truth, then he will possess this land where I put my feet now and if he were here, I would have hastened to meet him and I would have washed his feet.'

When Heraclius read Muhammad ﷺ's letter to his court, a stormy moment of confusion and outrage followed. Abu Sufyan and his delegation were asked to leave the court. Heraclius sent Muhammad ﷺ a most cordial reply, so that some historians believe that he entered into Islam while others state that he did not, but that he would have if he had not met great opposition inside his own court.

The reaction of the Persian emperor was very different when he read Muhammad ﷺ's letter, calling him to Islam. He had just been defeated by the Roman emperor and in a very bad humour. He tore up the letter and ordered his agent, the king of Yemen, to go and bring him the head of that man in the Hijaz.

When Muhammad ﷺ heard of how his letter had been received by the Persian emperor he said, 'May Allah tear his kingdom apart!' A few days later the emperor died and was succeeded by another and yet another in a matter of months. The Persian throne was rent apart by strife, one prince ascending the throne only to be overthrown and beheaded by his successor. Hundreds were assassinated or beheaded and the Persian empire continued weak and torn by strife until the Muslims conquered Persia and its dominions during the khaliphate of 'Umar ibn Al-Khattab.

When the emissaries of Badhan, the king of Yemen and agent of the Persian emperor, went to Muhammad ﷺ, he informed them that their emperor was dead and asked them to return with a message to Badhan. Muhammad ﷺ invited Badhan to enter into Islam and be his agent over Yemen, Badhan accepted and Yemen became one of the lands of Islam.

When the Ghassanid king, who was the vassal of Heraclius, informed him that he had received a letter from a man who alleged to be a prophet and asked permission to cross the border with an army to fight him, Heraclius answered that he had received a similar letter and that the Ghassanid king would do far better to come and attend the victory celebrations of Heraclius in Jerusalem.

27.3 Jewish State within State

The treaty of Al-Hudaybiya made the south of Arabia safe for Muslims, but in the north lived the most powerful and numerous of the Jewish tribes who had such great influence inside the peninsula as well as influence and connections outside it that they formed a separate entity within the Arab polity.

Some of the Jewish tribes evacuated from Madina had joined the tribes of Khaybar making them more powerful and numerous. It was no use making pacts with these tribes for it was they, with Huyayy ibn Akhtab at their head, who had gathered the polytheist Arab tribes to come and exterminate the Muslims at Madina. Every Jewish tribe Muhammad變 had made a covenant with had broken it at the convenient moment, therefore the only thing to do was to fight these tribes and subjugate them.

Muhammad變 had received the command to proclaim his religion to all men and to fight the Jews of Khaybar at the same time, and he proceeded with both actions simultaneously. Some historians state that it was an error to do so, for the Jews who had great influence outside the peninsula could have combined militarily with Chosroes of Persia and Caesar, both of whom had received Muhammad變's letters calling them to Islam, and with their huge resources could have overwhelmed the Muslims. The Messenger was not a politician - Allah's Messenger obeyed His orders and trusted in Him.

The Jews of Khaybar did not ask for outside help for they thought themselves more than a match for Muhammad變 and his men. They had everything in their favour - men, money, power, and experience in war. All the Arabian peninsula held its breath for no one knew how the issue would end. Those who trusted in Allah knew that Allah would let His Messenger prevail; those who did not felt that the Jews with their great forts and large numbers had the advantage. Quraysh even made bets as to who would be victorious.

Muhammad變 marched out at the head of one thousand five hundred men. Meanwhile the Jews, in preparation for the battle, placed their women and children in two forts, their treasures in a third fort, and the warriors occupied the fourth fort. Unlike the Jews who went to harass the women and children in the fortified houses when Madina was besieged, the Muslims would not approach the women and children or the fort that contained the treasures, but sought the men in the fourth fort, as Islam decrees that women, children, and elderly men are not to be injured, and houses and fields are not to be burnt unless they are occupied by fighters.

The battle raged fierce and long for the fourth fort, and fifty Muslims were killed on the first day. On the Jewish side a great number were killed, including their leader, who was immediately replaced by another and battle raged on.

The Prophet had asked. Abu Bakr to lead an attempt to force the gate, and both he and those with him fought bravely, but so did the Jews and the gate was not breached. The next day the Prophet sent 'Umar ibn Al-Khattab to make a breach. 'Umar was fierce and brave, nevertheless he failed in the attempt. On the third day the Prophet sent 'Ali ibn Abi Talib and, giving him a banner, dispatched him with these words, 'Take this banner and keep fighting until Allah opens the fort to you.'

'Ali, powerfully built and absolutely fearless, kept fighting until one of the Jews struck his shield away. 'Ali wrenched out a door and, using it as a shield, kept on fighting until the fort was breached.

Thus the most powerful Jewish tribes in the peninsula were subjugated. The lands of the Jewish tribe came under the Muslims' control. Muhammad ﷺ, not caring for material possessions, allotted the revenue of much of these lands to the poor, for the heritage of prophets is not in this world but in the next.

27.4 The End of Jewish Power in the Peninsula

After the capture of Khaybar the Jews offered to remain in the land and cultivate the palms for the Muslims, saying that they knew more about trees. So the Messenger made a treaty with them enabling them to remain and to take half of the harvest on condition that he could have them leave their lands if this proved to be necessary. The Jews of Fadak did not attempt to fight the Messenger but sought a similar treaty and this was granted to them. He had to fight the Jews of Wadi'l-Qura and then came to a similar agreement with them. The people of Tihama made an agreement with the Messenger to pay defence tax (jizya) and remained on their land.

This was the end of Jewish power in the peninsula and although they still remained on the land they ceased to be of importance politically or to form an independent entity within the Arab polity. They had used all their cunning and all their power, all the brute force and all the credulity of the idol worshippers to destroy the Messenger, but Allah had willed otherwise. In the end they were defeated and subjugated to Muhammad☀'s will.

The Messenger spent the revenue that came from the lands of the Jews upon the poor, in freeing slaves, and on the furtherance of religion generally. For himself he took nothing at all and he taught his followers that whatever prophets left was for charity, their heritage being not of this world but in the eternal.

Although Muhammad☀'s Companions were not prophets, they too cared for nothing except the religion that had made them see beyond the limitations of this world. One day 'Umar ibn Al-Khattab went to consult the Messenger. He had received a piece of land from the wars and wanted to give it to the poor. Should he sell it and distribute the money upon the poor? The Messenger advised him to keep it, thus preserving the capital, but to give away the income he got from it every year. So 'Umar assigned it to the poor and this was the first gift of its type in the history of Islam.

CHAPTER TWENTY-EIGHT

28.1 The Pilgrimage

The year passed and in accord with the treaty of Al-Hudaybiya it was the Muslims' right to enter Makka as pilgrims. Muhammadﷺ announced his intention of going as a pilgrim and thousands flocked around him, even more that the previous year. They all went unarmed, except for swords in their scabbards, observing the terms of the treaty of Al-Hudaybiya. Muhammadﷺ, feeling he could not trust Quraysh, sent a hundred horsemen before them as scouts and gave them strict orders not to enter the Sacred Precincts.

Hearing of Muhammadﷺ's approach, Quraysh decided to leave the Sacred Precincts to the Muslims and took refuge in the mountains where they erected their tents and awaited the arrival and eventual departure of this strange man who, although one of them, would fight the whole world, if need be, for what he believed.

The Muslims approached from the north and as soon as they could see the Ancient House, they called out, 'I come in answer to Thee, my Lord, I come in answer to Thee.' In awe, hope, and fear, they approached the Ancient House of Ibrahim and Isma'il with Muhammadﷺ leading the way on his white camel. When he reached the mosque he went down and baring his right arm he went to the Ka'ba and said, 'My Lord, have mercy upon a man who has let them see strength in him today.' Then he went to the corner where the Black Stone lay and began the rites of pilgrimage and all those who were with him followed his example and as they circled the Ka'ba, their bared right arms faced outwards towards the onlooking Quraysh.

'Abdullah ibn Rawaha, the poet, saw Quraysh staring awestruck at them, and out of sheer joy and excitement he wanted to hurl the battle-cry at them, but 'Umar restrained him. This was not the moment.

Muhammadﷺ said to him, 'Patience, Ibn Rawaha, rather say this: "There is no deity but Allah. He gave victory to His slave and power to His soldiers and alone defeated the tribes."' Ibn Rawaha repeated these words and all the Muslims repeated them after him, and they were carried by the winds and echoed by the mountains until they encircled all Makka.

After going round the Ka'ba seven times, Muhammad ﷺ went to Al-Safa and Al- Marwa, as the Arabs since the time of Ibrahim had done, and the Muslims followed his example. Next he sacrificed the offerings at Al-Marwa, then shaved his head, according to the rites of pilgrimage. They remained for three days in Makka, the three days allowed them in the treaty of Al-Hudaybia. The Emigrants visited their homes and their relations, and took the Supporters along with them as honoured guests. There was an atmosphere of rejoicing and reunion, tender memories, and cherished hopes.

The Makkans were much impressed by this stately yet simple faith, and by the noble change that had come over the Muslims. In Makka there lived among Quraysh four lovely sisters who, although Muslims, could not leave their home city. Muhammad ﷺ called them the four devout sisters, the oldest of them being the wife of his uncle, Al-'Abbas. Her youngest sister, Maymuna, longed to be with the Muslims, and to be near the Messenger. She confided to her sister who spoke to her husband who approached his nephew. Maymuna came from one of the noblest families of Quraysh, and she was the aunt of Khalid ibn Al-Walid. When Al-'Abbas asked Muhammad ﷺ to marry her, and to refuse would have been considered an insult to the family, Muhammad ﷺ thought this a good opportunity to soothe the hurt pride of Quraysh by accepting to be connected to them. He hoped it would promote the atmosphere of friendship and good-will.

During these three short days the Muslims tried to satisfy their longing for the Ancient House and the Holy Precincts by offering prayers of thanks, and took the opportunity to walk upon the soil of their beloved Makka to visit those too old to emigrate and to console the weak who were shackled to the polytheists by unbreakable ties. At the end of the prescribed period, two representatives of the eminent Qurayshis went to Muhammad ﷺ and asked him to leave with the Muslims according to the treaty. Muhammad ﷺ, in an effort to open Makka to the Muslims by amiable means, suggested that he marry Maymuna in Makka and celebrate his honeymoon among them with banquets and feasting. The Makkan nobles bluntly refused; they had seen how much all the Makkans longed to be with the Muslims, and if they accepted to sit at table with him, then Makka would be forever open to the Muslims.

Muhammad ﷺ did not tarry long in Makka after that. He gave his followers the order for departure and asked that Maymuna be escorted to Sarif and there they were married. She was the last of the wives of the Prophet and lived fifty years after him. When she came to die, she asked to be buried in Sarif where she had spent her honeymoon with him.

28.2 Khalid ibn Al-Waid

Khalid ibn Al-Walid was a man of keen perception and sharp intellect. He came from the powerful tribe of Banu Makhzum who had been entrusted for generation after generation with the defence of Makka. They had a hereditary knowledge of war tactics and excelled in these. It was he who changed the defeat of Quraysh into victory at Uhud.

All during the years of his youth Khalid had lived in an atmosphere hostile to the Messenger, for his father, one of the greatest and most influential men in Quraysh, was a bitter enemy to Muhammad. Khalid, however, had an observant mind of his own, and as he fought with surpassing courage in one battle after another, he could see that the laws of nature were being broken for the sake of a few, poor, ill-equipped, and inexperienced Muslims. He began to study Muhammad's words, as indeed all his enemies did, in the hope of finding something absurd or incongruous in them that they could use to divert people from him.

Khalid studied his words to find out the truth, whatever it may be. Then one day he stood in a council of Quraysh and with moral courage, equal to his physical courage in battle, said, 'It has become clear to any who has a brain that Muhammad is no sorcerer and no poet, that his words are the words of the Lord of creation. It is the duty of all who have intelligence to follow him.'

His words created a storm of confusion in the meeting and he was accused of defecting from the religion of his forefathers.

Khalid replied, 'Nay, I have submitted myself to the Lord of All after the truth has been revealed to me.' Then he left for Madina to swear allegiance to Muhammad and enter into Islam.

Two more of the Qurayshi nobles entered into Islam after the pilgrimage of the Muslims to Makka. One of them, 'Amr ibn Al 'As, was to be the general who conquered Egypt.

CHAPTER TWENTY-NINE

29.1 The Battle of Mu'ta

Muhammadﷺ sent an army to the borders of the Roman territories in Al-Sham to chastise the tribes there for killing the emissaries he had sent to call them to Islam. The army was three thousand strong, the banner of command being given to Zayd ibn Al-Haritha. If he fell, it was to go to Ja'far ibn Abi Talib, and if he fell, it was to be given to 'Abdullah ibn Rawaha. Khalid went out with this army. He had just entered into Islam and wanted to prove his valour in the service of the religion that had convinced him of its truth.

Before they left, Muhammadﷺ did something he had not done with the armies he had sent out before. He seemed afraid for them and prayed for them, and ordered all the Muslims to pray that they would return safely to their homes, then he went out to bid them farewell and walked with them to the outskirts of the city. He charged them not to kill women, children, boys, or blind men, not to destroy a house or cut down a tree.

They had hoped to take the tribes who had killed their brethren by surprise, but when they arrived in Mu'ta in Al-Sham, they found the tribes had heard of their approach and were prepared for them, having collected all the neighbouring tribes. They had also alerted the agent of Heraclius in the area and asked for his assistance and Heraclius had sent some battalions to strengthen their own numerous forces.

When the three thousand Muslims learnt of what was awaiting them, some counselled that it would be better to inform the Prophet of the numbers of their enemy, then wait for his orders. Many approved and this counsel would have prevailed had not 'Abdullah ibn Rawaha, who besides being a passionate poet was also an indomitable warrior, spoken fiery words to them, saying that they were evading what they had come for, the honour of dying for Allah's sake. 'We do not fight by weapons and numbers, but by the great religion that Allah had bestowed upon us,' he reasoned.

They were all moved by these words and decided to march forwards. So on marched the three thousand to face an army of, some say, two hundred thousand in all.

On the borders of Al-Balga', they met the Roman legions and the tribesmen in a village called Masharif where a fierce battle took place. Zayd ibn Al- Haritha charged forward with the banner, knowing very well that it meant death, and fought bravely until he was killed. Ja'far ibn Abi Talib took the banner from his hand and led the battle until he fell. The enemy killed his horse and he fought on foot until they cut off his right arm, so he held the banner with the left. When they cut it off, he held it by the upper arms until he was killed. Now it was the turn of 'Abdullah ibn Rawaha to lead the battle. He hesitated a moment and uttered this poem:

'I swear, my heart, thou shalt charge in,
I swear I shall compel thee.'

Then he charged in and continued to fight until he too was killed. Who would take the banner after that, knowing full well that he would be cut to pieces? Khalid ibn Al-Walid accepted it. Khalid was a military genius of rare ability and he could see that the Muslims were beginning to lose control over their movements and were being driven right and left by the two great hosts. So he turned the army round and fought a rearguard action. It is said nine swords were broken in his hand that day. Fighting continued until it was dark and the Muslim and Roman armies separated for the night.

In the cool of the night, Khalid made his plans. Before dawn he changed the positions of his men. He placed the right wing in place of the left and the centre in place of the rear and vice versa. In the rear he ordered a long line of men to march, making such noise and din as to give the impression that a great army was on its way to reinforce the Muslims.

When morning came, the Romans saw faces they had not seen the day before (due to the change of position) and heard great noise from afar. They feared that a great army was coming as reinforcements from Madina. If three thousand had been able to stand against them and almost win, what would this great army do to them? They drew back and would not fight the Muslims anymore. Khalid was then able to withdraw and turn with the army towards Madina, saving it from odds far beyond its powers to tackle.

The Romans were relieved that the Muslims had left their territory, but the Arab tribes of these parts had watched with great admiration how the Muslims had fought. These were Arabs like them, yet they surpassed the feared Roman legions in courage and ability. What was it that gave them this tremendous power and endurance? Surely there must be something in this new religion that liberated the souls of men. One of their leaders, who was at the same time the head of a Roman detachment, entered into Islam and would not be deterred by the threats or temptations of Heraclius. He was beheaded, but Islam began to be studied and loved by these northern tribes. Many from the tribes of Ghatafan, Salaman, Ashja', Abbasa, Zabyan and Kazan entered into Islam.

29.2 Muhammad Visits Ja'far's Family

When news reached Madina that Zayd ibn Haritha and JaTar ibn Abi Talib had been killed in battle, Muhammad went to JaTar's house. Ja'far was his cousin, one of the first to enter into Islam. He had led the Muslims to Abyssinia to attain freedom of worship, and then come to live in Madina when Muhammad asked them to return to their homeland. He was a man of both courage and faith.

The Messenger found Asma', Ja'far's wife, who had just baked bread and bathed her two little sons.

He said to her, 'Bring me the sons of Ja'far.' He put them on his knee and tears began to stream down his face.

Asma' said, 'My mother and father be your ransom, Messenger of Allah. Has anything happened to JaTar and those with him?T

'Yes, said Muhammad, 'he was killed today.' Then he left JaTar's house, telling those with him to prepare food for Ja'far's family for they could not think of themselves that day.

People were amazed to see the tears in his eyes. He said to them, 'It is the expression of grief that a friend feels when he loses his friend.'

On the way back he met the daughter of Zayd and patted her on the shoulder.

29.3 Quraysh Revoke the Treaty

At a distance things can be misrepresented, and the Muslims in Madina met their returning army with words of derision, because for them to turn round and not defeat the army of polytheists was a great shame. That the polytheist army was a hundred thousand and the Muslim army three thousand seems to have made no impression upon them. They met the army with the words, 'Did you flee for Allah's sake?' as well as many other such remarks.

The only person who gave the army a hearty welcome and

encouragement was Muhammadﷺ. He congratulated them on their courage in facing two hundred thousand and called Khalid 'the Sword of Allah.' People wondered at the title, thinking that Khalid had hardly earned it, but a few years later after Muhammadﷺ had passed away and Khalid had defeated both the Persian and Roman empires in the name of Allah, this title was heard on every tongue and in every land.

Quraysh heard rumours that the Muslims were finished, and that this battle of Mu'ta had annihilated their fighting power. So they decided it would be quite safe to break the Treaty of Al-Hudaybiya without fear of retaliation. They went to the aid of their allies, Banu Bakr, in the old feud the latter had with Banu Khuza'a, who were the allies of Muhammadﷺ, and they killed some of them. This was a flagrant violation of the treaty of Al-Hudaybiya. In this treaty Muhammadﷺ had conceded so much to Quraysh to the extent that the Muslims felt it was a humiliation. Nevertheless the moment they felt that the Muslims were no longer as strong as they used to be, Quraysh broke it. A delegation from Khuza'a went to seek Muhammadﷺ's assistance and he assured them, 'Khuza'a, you will be aided.' He hated war and bloodshed and had done everything to avoid it, but he hated even more aggression and treachery. There was nothing left now but to conquer Makka, the city he loved and had tried so hard to spare. He began to collect troops without informing them what their destination would be.

Quraysh began to realize the enormity of what they had done. They had miscalculated - the Muslims were not as weak as they had estimated, and they had broken their treaty and attacked the Muslims' allies without just cause. Muhammadﷺ was sure to retaliate. He was a man who never went back on any pact or treaty he had made or on any word he had given. If he had given his word to support Khuza'a against aggression, he was sure to do so no matter what price he had to pay.

29.4 Abu Sufyan as Emissary

They sent Abu Sufyan, the greatest of their nobles, as a herald of peace. Abu Sufyan feared going directly to Muhammadﷺ for he knew they were in the wrong. So he went first to the house of his daughter, Umm Habiba, who was the Prophet's wife. His reception was ominous. She asked him not to sit on Muhammadﷺ's bed.

Hearing this, the respected Abu Sufyan did not know what to think, so he asked her whether she considered him too great for the bed or the bed too good for him. She answered, 'You are an unclean polytheist, and this is the Prophet's bed.'

'Woe, woe, child, evil has befallen you after me,' he said in spleen.

Angry and indignant, he now went to Muhammad&. He offered peace and the extension of the treaty of Al-Hudaybiya for another ten years. Muhammad& was very truthful, he would not attempt to mislead an enemy as many would in war today, but at the same time he could not declare war openly, for he hoped and prayed to enter Makka without bloodshed, and this would not happen unless he could take it by surprise. So he rose and left Abu Sufyan without a word, good or bad.

Next Abu Sufyan tried to seek Abu Bakr's help in conciliation - the kind- hearted, gentle, conciliatory Abu Bakr, but he had misjudged Abu Bakr. All his life Abu Bakr was gentle and mild, except when it was a matter of principle. Now Abu Bakr was as firm as Muhammad& himself.

Almost in despair, Abu Sufyan tried 'Umar. 'Umar, forthright as always, said, 'I speak for you! If I had only my bare hands, I would still fight you with them!'

Abu Sufyan went to 'Ali ibn Abi Talib next, but 'Ali told him that he could do nothing for him. He tried lesser men, men who before Islam would have been only too happy to speak for the great Abu Sufyan, but it was of no avail. Then at last he took his weary, humiliated, undesirable person out of Madina.

29.5 The March Towards Makka

Muhammad& ordered the troops he had been collecting on a quick march towards Makka. He hoped he could take Makka by surprise and avoid a long and protracted struggle, and he prayed and prayed that there would be no fighting inside the Sacred Precincts which had been for centuries immemorial a sanctuary to all men.

The army marched quickly forwards. It was an army so large that the Arabs had never seen one like it, and on its march many of the tribes who had entered into Islam joined it, so that it grew greater and greater as it approached Makka.

Quraysh were yet unaware of what was approaching. They still sat arguing and bickering on what was to be done about

Muhammad嶸. Al-'Abbas, the Prophet's uncle, left them in their endless talk and went out of Makka to meet Muhammad嶸. Two others, who were Muhammad嶸's cousins from Banu Hashim also came, each separately. They had been too proud to listen to the truth before, now they begged permission to meet the Prophet. At first Muhammad嶸 refused, for they had spoken ill of him and persecuted Muslims for years. When one of them threatened to lose himself in the desert to die of hunger and thirst, Muhammad嶸, always kind-hearted, relented and let them in. They professed their belief in him and entered into Islam.

Although Al-'Abbas, the Prophet's uncle, was now a Muslim, he was appalled by the great armies that accompanied his nephew. Makka was his city and he feared for it. He spoke of this to Muhammad嶸 who was glad to make Al-Abbas a means of entering Makka in peace. It was agreed that Al-'Abbas would go to Quraysh and relate what he had seen and convince them to accept the Muslims' entry into Makka without resistance. So he rode the Prophet's white mule in order to pass unmolested amid the great hosts and headed towards Makka.

As he got nearer to Makka he heard two familiar voices speaking in the dark. They were the voices of Abu Sufyan and Budayl ibn Waraqa whom the Quraysh had sent to see if they could find out anything. Abu Sufyan was saying, 'I have never seen so many fires as I see today nor such a great camp.'

'I think it is Khuza'a excited by war,' said Budayl.

'Khuza'a are far too few and too humble to have such a camp.'

Al-'Abbas called out to them by the names they were known by inside their tribe so that they would realize he was not an enemy. In order to bring home to them what he had to say, he offered to take them and show them Muhammad嶸's camp.

As they passed amid the ranks, the soldiers once again recognised Muhammad嶸's mule and let them pass. They walked until they reached the Prophet's tent, and Muhammad嶸 asked Al -'Abbas to bring them to him in the morning. They slept in the camp and in the morning Al-'Abbas brought them before the Messenger. Abu Sufyan, the proud and powerful, declared his belief without reservation, saying that though he had believed in gods other than Allah he could see that they were of no use now. Then Al -'Abbas asked a favour of the Prophet. He said, 'Abu Sufyan is a man who likes to boast, give him something to boast of.'

'Certainly,' said Muhammadﷺ. 'He who enters the house of Abu Sufyan is safe, he who enters his own house and shuts the door is safe, and he who enters the area of the Ka'ba is safe.'

In spite of all the years of persecution and injuries, the Messenger was willing to save the lives and the honour of his enemies. He bore no grudges, remembered no wrongs.

Muhammadﷺ divided the army into four contingents. Each was to enter Makka from a different direction. They were given strict orders to march peacefully and not to fight unless it was forced upon them.

29.6 The Conquest of Makka

As they approached Makka, Muhammadﷺ noticed that there were no preparations for resistance and he stopped to pray and thank Allah, for his heart's desire was to enter the Ancient House inside the Holy City without bloodshed. News came to him that Sa'd ibn 'Ubada, one of the group commanders, had been saying, 'Today is the day of the epic when the inviolate is no longer inviolate.' He immediately deposed him and replaced him by his son, a man larger in stature, but milder in temper.

Three of the four groups found no resistance and were able to enter the Holy City in peace. The fourth group, led by Khalid ibis Al-Walid, was forced by men who were implacable enemies of the Messenger to fight. It was only a minor skirmish and Khalid was able to disperse them quickly. Only two of his men who had been cut off from the group were killed while fifteen of the enemy were killed.

At last peace reigned in Makka, and a calm followed that it had not known for years. The Muslims at last could return to their own homes, and at last the House of Allah was to be returned to His worship alone.

A tent was erected for the Prophet by the grave of his grandfather and that of his beloved wife, Khadija. He was asked if would like to rest in his own house and he replied, 'No, they have left no home for me in Makka.' He remained in his tent for some time to pray in thanks to Allah, then he went to the Ka'ba. He went round it seven times. People began to gather around him, so he read to them these verses of the Qur'an:

Mankind, We have created you males and females,
and made you nations and tribes to become acquainted.

To Allah the most honoured among you is the most devout.
Allah is the All-Knowing, the All-Aware. (49:13)

29.7 The General Pardon, the Trust, More on Pardon

Quraysh came to find out what their fate would be. They had
harassed, injured, persecuted, killed and imprisoned Muslims for
years and now they were in the hands of the Muslims, in the hands
of Muhammad☺, the man they had done everything in their power
to destroy.

He looked at them smiling and said, 'People of Quraysh, what do
you think I shall do to you?'

'You are a gracious brother and an honourable kinsman,' they
said.

'Go, you are all free men,' he said.

Then he entered the Ka'ba. Inside, on the walls there were
pictures of the prophets and the angels. He looked at the painting of
Ibrahim and said, 'May Allah forgive them. Is this how they paint an
old, venerable man?' The angels were painted as beautiful women,
and he explained that angels were neither male nor female but
something quite different. He asked to have all these paintings erased
and the walls made a pure white. Then he took a chain and went with
it to idol after idol and broke them to pieces while reciting these
verses from the Qur'an:

And say, 'The truth has come and the false has perished away.
The false always perishes.' (17:81)

Thus the Ancient House of Ibrahim was purified from idolatry
and returned to being the House of Allah alone as it had been in the
days of Muhammad☺'s ancient grandfathers, Isma'il and Ibrahim.
Then Muhammad☺ went to pray by Al-Safa.

In order to allow the Messenger to enter the Ka'ba, 'Ali ibn Abi
Talib had gone to the custodian of the Ka'ba who was a polytheist
and taken the keys by force. The man protested, saying that if he
knew Muhammad☺ to be the Messenger of Allah he would have
given him the keys himself.

After performing the rites of visiting the Ancient House,
Muhammad☺ returned the keys to the polytheist custodian.
Completely amazed, the man asked why he was giving him the keys
again. The Muslims were in power and the city was completely
under their dominion. Whereupon Muhammad☺ read to him these
words from the Qur'an:

**Allah commands you to restore trusts to their owners,
and if you decide between people, decide fairly. (4:58)**

Talha, the polytheist custodian, entered into Islam in awe of Him
who made men submit to the right, even when might and victory was
theirs. The keys of the Ka'ba returned to him by the Prophet
remained a sacred trust inherited from father to son until today.

When the Supporters, the native inhabitants of Madina, saw the
simple, yet majestic and awe-inspiring Ka'ba, the curious position of
Makka surrounded by fort-like hills, its atmosphere of strange,
spiritual beauty, and how well this background suited Muhammad,
they said to each other, 'Makka has the Sacred House, Makka has Al-
Safa and Al-Marwa, Makka has the Place of Ibrahim, it was
Muhammad's homeland where he lived and grew up, surely he is
not going to leave all this to go back to Madina with us.'

The Muslims of Madina feared he was lost to them now that he
had recovered his own. After finishing prayers, for Muhammad
had been praying while they conversed, he rose and asked them what
they had been discussing. Hesitant and shy, they explained their
fears.

'Allah forbid,' he said. 'My life is with you and my death will be
among you.' As always Muhammad was true. He would not go
back on his word to them nearly ten years earlier when they swore
the   oath   of
Al-'Agaba. These were the people who had opened their city and
their homes to him when all else had rejected him, and no matter
what sanctity or love for Makka he had in his heart, he would not
prefer it to them.

The Makkans looked in awed wonder at the Prophet and at the
Muslims, these people who had become so mellowed, so refined, so
benevolent. They saw how his followers loved Muhammad, and
how they loved and trusted each other, and how kind and good they
were to all mankind and to all creation. They looked at the serene
security, the tranquility these people enjoyed - a tranquility that had
nothing to do with material circumstances, but was a spiritual
content, the feeling that the truth, the secret of the whole universe
was within one's grasp.

In spite of the general pardon, some of the Makkans feared lest
Muhammad remembered what they had done. There were those
who had tortured Muslims, and there was Hind, who had mutilated
the body of Hamza, the Prophet's uncle and foster brother who had

been so dear to him. Hamza was perhaps the greatest warrior and huntsman the Arabs had ever known, but Hind had cut open his body and chewed his liver. Muhammad ﷺ did not have it in his nature to bear a grudge or hurt those who had become the weaker party. He forgave all, pardoned all. In his goodness of heart he told the Makkans that he loved them dearly and that he would have never have made another people their equals if they had not driven him out. Muhammad ﷺ sent guarantees of peace and safe conduct to the people who had fled from Makka when he arrived. They could return to their homes and families unmolested. Of all the people in Makka only four men were put to death. These were men who had committed murder for personal reasons and so were put to death according to the decrees of Islam.

Now most of Quraysh entered into Islam - men, women, and children. They swore allegiance to Muhammad ﷺ and began to be instructed in the religion that would be their refuge, hope, and pride for all the generations to come. Muhammad ﷺ remained in Makka for fifteen days. Every day Bilal would give the call to prayer and all the Muslims, Emigrants, Supporters, Makkans, and tribesmen would respond, leaving everything and heading towards the Ka'ba to pray. Then Muhammad ﷺ would lead prayers. No more strife, no more discord, all were brothers in Islam.

CHAPTER THIRTY

30.1 The Battle of Hunayn

In the midst of peace and rejoicing news came that the tribes of Hawazin and Thaqif were making preparations to attack the Muslims. So once again they had to leave their families to answer the call of duty. In this battle their situation was different from all the preceding battles. In previous battles the Muslims had been inferior in number and weapons to their enemies, often overwhelmingly so. In this battle they had all the means at their disposal in terms of men, weapons, and experience, to expect a resounding victory. They were twelve thousand strong, consisting of the ten thousand who had conquered Makka reinforced by two thousand from Quraysh, while the enemy numbered around four thousand.

Each tribe marched in splendid array preceded by its banner. Khalid ibn Al- Walid lead the procession at the head of the tribe of Sulaym. They marched forward until they reached the valleys at the pass of Hunayn where they camped for the night. Well pleased with their numbers, they said to each other, 'Today we are invincible, today none is a match for us.

At first light they began to move with Khalid always in the forefront and Muhammadﷺ in the rear. Suddenly like a furious avalanche, thousands of warriors rushed upon them from the mountain heights, attacking like one man. They were nonplussed by the suddenness of the attack and confusion reigned. Something unnameable seemed to terrify them in the dim light, and they began to flee the field.

Muhammadﷺ saw one tribe after another flee in confusion. 'Where to? Where .to?' he asked, riding on his little white mule.

When Abu Sufyan saw the tribes running, he said gleefully, 'Now they will continue to run until they reach the sea.' He meant that their defeat would be without limits.

The charging enemy were led by a man riding a black war camel and carrying a black banner on the point of a long spear. As the tribes fled past him, Muhammadﷺ could see the man, and went forward on his little white mule to face this formidable enemy. However one of his Companions, knowing it would be suicide, held tight the reins of the mule to prevent it from moving, and Al-'Abbas, Muhammadﷺ's uncle who had strong lungs, cried, 'You Supporters who have given shelter and help! You Emigrants who have sworn the oath under the tree! Muhammadﷺ is alive, so come to him!'

These words were carried by the winds and echoed by the mountains. Those of true faith heard them and began to flock around the Messenger. They came from every direction crying, 'I come, I come in answer to thee.' They came, knowing they would face certain death. And they came to die with Muhammadﷺ. The enemy were four thousand, fighting in perfect order while those who answered the call were six hundred.

30.2 The Change of Tide

Then the wondrous happened. Those six hundred, by Allah's will, were able to drive back the four thousand and change the tide of defeat to victory. Slowly the others began to return and by the end of the day it was a complete victory for the Muslims. The Qur'an says:

Allah has given you victory in many situations,
but on the day of Hunayn, when you were pleased with your numbers,
they were of no use to you.
And the earth in spite of its spaciousness seemed narrow to you,
and you turned round in flight. (9: 25)

It was a similar lesson to that of Uhud - a hard, clear lesson they had to learn. Victory comes from Allah, and from Him alone. It was not a matter of arms or numbers, for when they had neither arms nor men and trusted in Him, He gave them victory, but the moment they relied on their numbers, He withdrew His support, and they ran as if they had never seen a battlefield before. When six hundred trusted Him and were ready to die for His sake and the sake of His Prophet, Allah supported them again and victory became theirs. This lesson served the Muslims through all the years of fighting and empire-building that lay ahead of them, when they had to face armies of Romans, Persians, and Berber tribesmen of far greater numbers in distant lands.

The Muslims were able to take many captives and collect much loot, but they learnt that the leaders of Hawazin and Thaqif who had instigated their tribes' action had taken refuge in Al-Ta'if, the home of Thaqif.

30.3 The Siege of Al-Ta'if

Al-Ta'if was a fortified city of great wealth and strong defences. The Muslims marched on the city only to be met by showers of arrows, so withdrawing out of range they set up camp. Muhammad⁕ began to think of what would be the best way to take this city with such formidable fortifications. He came to the conclusion that the only way to make them surrender the city without needless bloodshed was to burn the palms in the fertile fields around Al-Ta'if. He hated to do what he had always ordered his followers to refrain from (a palm tree takes over ten years to grow and yield fruit) but realized that it would quickly bring pressure to bear, and, as he had calculated, as soon as he began burning their palm trees the inhabitants of Al-Ta'if asked what his terms were. The Holy Months, when fighting was forbidden to the Arabs, were approaching, so Muhammad⁕ let this temporary siege be a reminder to them that if they attacked others they were liable to be attacked themselves. He then withdrew his forces and marched towards Makka.

30.4 Hawazin Asks for Booty Back

A group of the defeated tribe of Hawazin went to the Prophet and asked him to return their money and children to them because of the connection between him and them. They reminded him that his foster mother had been one of them. The Messenger always tried to comfort and soothe the pride of the defeated. His duty was to break up their idols, but once the job was done he was magnanimous and obliging. Muhammad⁕ who had been very considerate to his foster mother until the day of her death now declared that his portion of the spoils and that of his tribe, Banu Hashim, would be returned to them and he suggested to them a way to retrieve all their property. He told them to stand up after the prayer in congregation and say that they had asked the Prophet to intercede for them with the Muslims and then they should ask the Muslims to intercede for them with the Prophet. So after prayers, they did so, and Muhammad⁕ said that he would return his share of the booty to them. The Emigrants, following his example, said that they would give their share to the Prophet to dispose of, that is return it to its owners, and then the Supporters did the same. The Prophet then asked them about their leader, Malik ibn 'Awf, who had fled to Thaqif and asked them to deliver this message to him: if he should go the Prophet, his money and children would be returned to him.

Muhammadﷺ had given booty most generously to the nobles of Quraysh, newly entered into Islam. Even though he knew that the declaration of faith of some of them had been a matter of noblesse oblige, nevertheless he gave them hundreds of camels and heads f cattle - may more than he had given the Emigrants and Supporters. He had done this to wipe away the bitterness in their hearts and to let them enter into Islam willingly instead of feeling compelled.

30.5 Distribution of the Booty

Seeing how generously he had given to those newly entered into Islam, who had once been his bitter enemies, the Supporters said to each other, 'The Prophet has found his tribe and his people indeed.'

These words reached Muhammadﷺ, so he called the Supporters and said to them, 'Supporters, did I not find you astray and Allah has guided you to the Way? Were you not in need and Allah has made you opulent? Were you not enemies and Allah has created harmony between your hearts?'

'All good and bounty comes from Allah and His Messenger,' they replied.

'Nay, answer me, Supporters.'

'But what can we say, Messenger of Allah, when Allah and His Messenger are the best, the most gracious.'

'If you wish,' said Muhammadﷺ, 'you could say, "You have come to us despised and we believed in you; a fugitive and we gave you shelter; defeated and we gave you victory; needy and we gave you help." Supporters, do you resent that the dross of this world is given to some to soothe their hearts and make them enter into Islam?

'Supporters, would you not prefer to have people take goats and camels and that you take the Messenger of Allah with you?'

There were tears in his eyes for he loved these men who had stood at his side in the darkest hour. The Supporters were very much moved, many to tears, and they called out, 'We are happy and content to have the Messenger of Allah as our share and our destiny.'

214

CHAPTER THIRTY-ONE

31.1 The Wives of the Prophet

Each of the women who entered the life of the Messenger, and in consequence into the life and customs of all Muslims, was of well-known and noble lineage. Each of them in her own way was exemplary as an individual, and each had special characteristics or circumstances that make it imperative for Muslims to study her life and emulate it. The women in the Messenger's life were exceptional women, just as the men who helped him were very great indeed, but besides the overpowering light of the Messenger they seem no different from the common run of men. It is when each is studied apart and individually that one discovers how truly great these early Muslims were.

31.2 The Lady Khadija

We shall begin in chronological order with the life of the lady Khadija. Khadija, the daughter of Khuwaylid, was of noble birth. She was beautiful and intelligent and had inherited much wealth from her father and from a previous marriage. She was independent and had a prosperous trading business that she preferred to manage herself in an age when most women could do nothing for themselves. Several Qurayshi nobles sought the honour of her hand but were graciously and firmly refused - the lady Khadij a was gracious in all her ways. The day she met Muhammad, however, it was love at first sight. He was of such noble character and from the most honoured family of Quraysh and was indeed a suitable consort for this great lady. She, in turn, was the only woman who could have understood and helped him in the trials that lay ahead.

At first he took over her trade and was successful in performing his duties as a husband and agent, but Khadija, perspicacious and understanding, could see that his heart was not in business, so she relieved him of it in order to enable him to spend long months of contemplation and solitary worship in the mountains, in the Cave of Hira', which he felt a terrible urgency to do, and which Khadija recognized and understood. Muhammad used to forget himself and not think of food or drink during those periods of worship, so thoughtfully Khadija would send him food to the cave.

One day he returned from the mountain trembling in fear and wonder, to relate his vision to her. With a wisdom beyond most women's, she understood the nature of Muhammad's visions and assured him that Allah would never visit someone so good with madness. As soon as he was ordered to proclaim the Message, Khadija professed her belief in Allah and in Muhammad as His Messenger. She became, after the Messenger, the first Muslim on earth.

The Qur'an says that between man and wife is affection and mercy. Khadija was the soul of mercy and tenderness, and when the years of struggle against the idol worshippers began, she stood firm and steadfast by her persecuted husband. She saw him risk his life and hers, she saw him spend all his money and hers for 'the sake of religion, and she accepted it all, always encouraging, comforting, and helping him. She made his heavy responsibilities seem light and the injuries of Quraysh seem trivial.

She suffered patiently with him during the three years of severe privation in the mountains and, being a lady unused to such rough conditions, her health suffered and she died with a word of encouragement to her husband and complete trust in her Lord.

Muhammad felt the loss of Khadija as he felt no other loss and he grieved for her as he grieved for no one else. Theirs was love on a grand scale, not of this world but of the eternal, and in all his life after he cherished her memory and revered anything or anyone connected with her. No one was ever able to take her place in his affections. What the lady 'A'isha says is significant, 'I am jealous of no woman as I am of the memory of Khadija.'

The marriage of Muhammad and Khadija lasted for twenty-seven years. It was an ideal marriage of mutual love and respect. During those twenty-seven years Muhammad grew from a very young man, for he was only twenty-three when he first married, to a mature and gifted prophet. He lived in many ways like the people of his age and class, but two things marked him out: his long months of worship in the mountains, and his never marrying or even desiring a woman other than Khadija. This was extraordinary in an age when most men had several wives and many slavegirls.

In the following pages we shall discuss the marriages of the Messenger after the lady Khadija died, but first a word about the background of these marriages. Marriage to the Arabs did not mean the union of two individuals, but the union of two tribes. What each man sought in marriage were powerful in-laws who could be an honour to him in peace and a support to him in war. Very often it was the woman's family that sought union with such-and-such a man because he was worthy of being their in-law and came from such-and-such a tribe. It was a social and political matter, and love and beauty were a side issue.

The three years after Khadija had passed away were the three saddest years in Muhammad's life, for with the death of Khadija he had no comfort and no understanding at home, and with the death of Abu Talib immediately before it he had no support outside his house. Just when Quraysh were augmenting their campaign against him and increasing their pressure upon him, he was alone without comfort or aid to uphold the word of Allah against the most vicious forces of evil and brute cupidity.

31.3 The Lady 'A'isha and Sawda

After three years of this constant struggle when Muhammad was fifty-three years old, a relative called Khawla went to him and pointed out that his house was sadly neglected and that his daughters needed a mother to look after them. Muhammad was aware of that, but he had never thought of re-marriage.

'But who can take the place of Khadija?' he asked in wonder. "A'isha, the daughter of Abu Bakr,' she answered.

Abu Bakr was Muhammad's dearest friend, and more than once he had risked his life to save Muhammad's, and more than once he had risked his livelihood and possessions for the sake of Islam. He had dedicated his whole life to the service of Allah and his Messenger. Honour was Abu Bakr's due, Muhammad felt, and to bring him and his tribe closer to him was a service to Islam, but Abu Bakr's daughter was a pretty little girl of seven years old, hardly the person to take care of his daughters. 'But she is very young,' he said.

Khawla had a solution for everything. He was to marry at the same time Sawda, the widow of Al-Sakran ibn 'Amr. She had been the first woman to emigrate to Abyssinia for the sake of her religion and had endured much for the sake of Islam and was then living with her aged father, her husband having died. She was middle-aged, rather plump, with a jolly, kindly disposition, just the right person to take care of growing little girls. So Muhammad gave permission to Khawla to speak to Abu Bakr and to Sawda on the subject.

Both parties accepted, feeling that it was a great honour. Sawda went to live in Muhammadﷺ's house and immediately took over the care of his daughters and household, while 'A'isha became betrothed to him and remained in her father's house playing with her dolls.

Some years later after Muhammadﷺ and Abu Bakr emigrated to Madina, 'A'isha became Muhammadﷺ's bride at the request of Abu Bakr. Abu Bakr was a man with broad vision who travelled and studied much, and who had a wide knowledge of the wisdom of the Arabs and was the authority on Arab genealogy. He was very fond of poetry and taught 'A'isha and her older sister, Asma', the best of Arab verse and Arab proverbs.

When she was removed to Muhammadﷺ's house, he found in her an apt and avid pupil, quick to learn, with a quick and accurate memory. Very intelligent, she soon became a keen scholar and would sit and argue with others. Whenever she beat someone else in argument, Muhammadﷺ used to smile and say, 'She is the daughter of Abu Bakr.'

She became so learned that one of her contemporaries used to say that if the knowledge of 'A'isha were placed on one side of the scale and that of all other women in the other, 'A'isha's would win. She used to sit with the women and teach them about the precepts and rituals of Islam which the Messenger had taught her, and long after the Messenger and Abu Bakr passed away she was a source of reference on the practice of Islam and the words of the Messenger as applied to both men and women. It is an example of Divine wisdom that she went to Muhammadﷺ's house so young, absorbed so much, and was able to transmit it to another generation intact.

Besides being a scholar, 'A'isha was a very graceful young woman with comely features. A friendship grew up between her and Sawda when she was removed to Muhammadﷺ's house as a little girl and Sawda took care of her with the rest of the household. When 'A'isha grew up, Sawda passed up her share of the Prophet's time in favour of 'A'isha and was content to manage his household and be 'the Mother of the Believers'.

Being the daughter of Abu Bakr, who on one occasion had given away all his capital for the sake of religion, and the wife of Muhammadﷺ, who kept nothing for himself, she was very generous. One day the Messenger had an offering killed. According to Islam, the giver of an offering is entitled to retain a part, one third, and the rest is to go to the poor. It was 'A'isha's job to distribute the meat to the poor. And when she had finished giving to all the poor, she found that she had left nothing for the Messenger's large household except the neck of the animal. Distressed, she went to Muhammad and said, 'I have been able to save nothing but this.'

That is the only part you have not saved,' said the Messenger smiling. For what goes to Allah is saved indeed.

'A'isha had charming ways and the Messenger grew very fond of the young woman who was brought to his house as a little girl and grew up under his care.

One day an elderly lady came to visit them and Muhammad was most attentive to her. After she left, 'A'isha asked who she was and Muhammad said, 'She used to visit us in the days of Khadija.' Anything that reminded him of his beloved Khadija was dear to him.

On another occasion he heard the voice of Hala, Khadija's sister, in the courtyard outside and hurried out to meet her. Annoyed, 'A'isha later said to him, 'Khadija was an old woman, and Allah has given you better than her.'

'By Allah,' he said, 'my Lord has not given me better than her. She trusted me when people scorned, she believed in me when people denied, she comforted me with her money when people deprived me, and Allah has given me issue from her to the exception of other women.'

'A'isha says, 'I learnt to hold my tongue where Khadija was concerned.'

Muhammad was most kind to all people, and gallant as well as kind to women, but he had loyalties that he allowed no one to approach. He never forgot someone who did him a good turn, and Khadija's memory he held very dear.

31.4 Umm Habiba (Abu Sufyan's Daughter)

Umm Habiba was the daughter of Abu Sufyan, one of the most tenacious enemies of Muhammad and Islam, and a man who led armies against him on many fields. She had entered into Islam with her husband and emigrated to Abyssinia with him. There her husband, finding the whole land Christian, defected from Islam and entered into Christianity. She found herself in a most painful position as she could not remain with her husband nor could she return to her father. Islam decrees that a Muslim woman shall not marry a man unless he is a Muslim, and her father was not only a polytheist but one of the chiefs of denial and wrong. This lady, used to every comfort before Islam as she came from the proud and wealthy house of Banu Umayya (the Umayyads of history), shut herself and her little daughter away from the eyes of all men. Forgotten and forsaken, she lived in very frugal circumstances but adhered steadfastly to Islam.

She may have been forgotten by men, but Allah in His mercy forgets no one. One day as she sat in her solitary room in this alien land, a slave called Abraha knocked on her door and said that she had been sent for by the King of Abyssinia to receive a message. The message was that Muhammadﷺ had requested her hand, and the king said that if she accepted the match she was to name one of the Muslims in Abyssinia as her deputy. Umm Habiba was overjoyed; she was not forgotten. This was the highest honour and, moreover, Muhammadﷺ had sent her four hundred dinars as a dowry. (A very large sum of money at that time, of which she was badly in need.) Muhammadﷺ knew that he could not meet this wife in distant Abyssinia, but the fact that he had thought of her, the financial support he sent to her, and the honour and protection that his name gave her, cheered the poor lady's heart.

Six years later, when the emigrant Muslims could finally return from Abyssinia, she came to Madina and Muhammadﷺ, who had just returned victorious from Khaybar, gave her a most cordial welcome.

31.5 'Umar's Daughter, Hafsa

'Umar ibn Al-Khattab was a man who had influence both among the Muslims and among Quraysh. He had endured much and struggled much for the sake of Islam. Next to Abu Bakr he was the man who had done most for the new religion. He was a constant companion to the Messenger and discussed with him every issue. In fact he and Abu Bakr, as previously stated, were Muhammadﷺ's two closest counsellors.

'Umar had a daughter called Hafsa whose husband had died and left her a widow when she was still very young. It was an age when no woman could live alone or unmarried, so 'Umar decided to look for a suitable husband for her. At first he thought of Abu Bakr, the head of Banu Taym, and very close to the Messenger.

'Umar went to Abu Bakr who listened sympathetically as he spoke of Hafsa, but when 'Umar offered marriage he excused himself. 'Umar was hurt, but he tried to approach 'Uthman ibn

'Affan on the subject. Next to Abu Bakr, 'Uthman, so very wealthy, devout, and generous, would be the most suitable husband, but 'Uthman also excused himself. This was too much for 'Umar, for such refusal was an affront to the lady's family and tribe.

Smarting under the two blows, 'Umar went to Muhammad☙ to complain of the behaviour of his two companions. Muhammad☙ gallantly offered to marry her himself. He could not forget all that 'Umar had done for Islam and that it was only fair to place his two closest advisers on equal footing. When 'Umar met Abu Bakr later, the latter explained that the Messenger had mentioned his desire to ask for her hand to him, and that that had been the reason he had refused 'Umar's offer, but he had not been willing to divulge something the Messenger had told him in confidence.

Before Islam, women were not supposed to have opinions of their own or to object to anything their lords and masters chose to say. Islam decrees that a woman is an individual who has the right to think for herself and to express her beliefs as men do. She is a free, responsible being before Allah. Muhammad☙, always the good example of what a Muslim should be, encouraged his wives to study to think for themselves.

Just as 'A'isha, the daughter of Abu Bakr, loved poetry as her father loved poetry, Hafsa, the daughter of 'Umar, loved to discuss issues as her father loved to discuss every issue with the Messenger.

Hafsa loved to practise this newly-acquired privilege and would argue with the Prophet much and often. Refined and kind-hearted, he allowed her to say what she thought and this continued for some time, until one day 'Umar ibn Al-Khattab, when speaking to Hafsa's mother, said, 'I think I shall do so- and-so.' Whereupon the lady answered, 'But it would be better if you did so-and-so.'

Shocked, 'Umar said, 'Are you arguing with me, woman?'

'Why not?' she answered. 'Your daughter keeps arguing with the Messenger of Allah until she upsets him for the whole day.'

'Umar put on his cloak and went directly to his daughter's house. 'Is it true that you argue with the Messenger of Allah?' he asked. 'Indeed, I do,' said Hafsa.

He was about to chastise such ill-breeding, but Muhammad☙, entering at that moment, would not allow him to touch her.

'Umar left his daughter's house and went to the house of Sawda, who was related to him, to tell her of this shocking state of affairs. Sawda who was also a wife of the Messenger and educated and influenced by him said, 'I wonder at you, Ibn Al-Khattab. You have interfered in everything. Will you interfere now between the Messenger and his wives?'

'Umar, in relating the above incident continued, 'And she kept after me until she made me give up much of what I thought proper.'

31.6 Umm Salama and the Orphans

Umm Salama is the heroine of a sad tragedy. When Quraysh were persecuting Muslims, she decided to emigrate with her husband and her little son to Madina. On the way her tribe intercepted them and forbade her husband to take her with him. In retaliation, her husband's tribe decided to take away her little son. The two tribes pulled at the child's arm, until they dislocated it. Finally her husband's people were able to take him away, and her husband had to leave for Madina without her. She was now alone deprived of husband and child, and for more than a year she used to sit on the outskirts of Makka and cry from morning till evening. She would not give up Islam nor could she forget her husband and child.

One day a passer-by took pity on her and kept after her tribe until they agreed to allow her to join her husband. Then and only then did her husband's people return her son to her and the family was finally reunited in Madina where she bore him several more children.

Abu Salama was a brave soldier of Allah, who fought valiantly at Uhud and was given the command in the operation against Banu Asad. He was able to defeat the Banu Asad and prevent their raid on Madina, but his exertions reopened a wound received at Uhud, and he died of that wound after returning to Madina. Muhammadﷺ sat by his deathbed until the last moment and prayed over him.

Some months later, to do honour to his name according to the customs of the Arabs, Abu Bakr sent to ask for the hand of Umm Salama, but she gently refused. Next 'Umar ibn Al-Khattab, a man equally worthy of the widow of such a great man, asked for her hand, but he also was refused. She was a widow, alone, with many children and without any resources, Abu Salama having left nothing to support them. She could not be left in this plight, so Muhammadﷺ asked for her hand, and again she apologized to the emissary he had sent her, saying that she was old, of a jealous nature, and had many children.

The reply Muhammadﷺ sent was, 'As for you being old, then I am older than you; as for you having a jealous nature, then Allah will cast jealousy out of your heart; as for the children, they belong to Allah and His Messenger.' As always, he kept his word. He was so good to those fatherless children, treating them as his own, that some believe he married her for their sake. He could have sent them financial support, but to a proud people like the Arabs, it would have hurt their pride and position in the Muslim community. To make them his own by marrying their mother was the only way he could help them without seeming to be giving them charity. The Muslims emulated Muhammadﷺ in everything, and by such devices the widows and children of those who died in war were not left destitute, unprotected or fatherless.

31.7 Zaynab and Islamic Legislation

Zaynab, daughter of Jahsh, was Muhammadﷺ's cousin, her mother Umayma being the daughter of 'Abdu'l-Muttalib, the head of Quraysh and Muhammadﷺ's grandfather, who had been very good to him as a child. She came from one of the noblest houses of Quraysh. The Arabs were very proud of their lineage and very careful to marry their daughters to men of the same social status. That the daughter of a great house should marry an unknown was a rare exception, that she should marry a ex-slave, a creature bought and sold, was shocking beyond belief. Islam decrees that it is not who a man's ancestors were that mattered, but how he stands in the sight of Allah. 'To Allah the most honoured among you is the most devout,' as the holy verses state. Muhammadﷺ found it hard to make the Arabs, who studied their genealogy most carefully through generation after generation and made verses in praise of their ancestors and their deeds, realize this truth. The only way to make them realize it was by acts not words.

Zaynab was his little cousin, brought up under his care. He had watched her grow and thought that she and Zayd, the little boy whom Khadija had given him as a present and whom he had liberated and brought up as a son, would make a fine couple and be a good example that it was not who a man's ancestors were, but who he was in the sight of Allah that mattered. When he asked for her hand for his client, . Zaynab and her people were shocked, and at first both she and her brother refused. Then these holy verses were revealed:

It is not for a man or woman who believes,
when Allah and His Messenger have made a decision,
to have the choice in their affairs.

**He who disobeys Allah and His Messenger
has clearly gone astray. (33:36)**

When Zaynab and her brother who were good Muslims realized that this was the decree of Allah, they submitted. Muhammadﷺ gave Zayd a handsome dowry for the bride according to the customs of the Arabs.

The marriage was not a happy one. A class barrier can be a formidable obstacle, particularly in a society based on such distinctions. Zayd had to complain more than once to Muhammadﷺ about Zaynab, and Muhammadﷺ who was trying to prove that such a marriage was practicable charged him to be patient, saying, 'Fear Allah and hold on to your wife.' In the end Zayd could endure it no longer and divorced his wife.

Another custom of the Arabs was to buy slaves, set them free and make them inherit their name and wealth as their own sons. They tended to go to extremes - either they treated their slaves and clients as inferiors with no status or they adopted them and gave them the rights and privileges that would normally have belonged to the sons of their own blood. While Islam decrees that they are not to be treated as inferiors, it decrees that such rights belong to a son, and he should not be deprived of them for the sake of an outsider.

Before Islam, Muhammadﷺ himself had adopted Zayd as a son. It was an old Arab custom, and when Islam made the above decrees, the Arabs still had these customs. They needed an example like the marriage of Zaynab to Zayd, to shatter this custom once and for all. An adopted son was not the same as a natural son in the sight of Allah, and should not be given the rights that belong to the sons or daughters of one's blood. The Arabs considered the wife or ex-wife of an adopted son forbidden to them in marriage in the way that the wife of a natural son would be.

After Zayd divorced Zaynab, Muhammadﷺ was ordered by Allah to ask for her hand. Muhammadﷺ had looked upon Zayd as a son and upon Zaynab, the little girl brought up under his care, as a daughter. It seems he was loathe to follow this command. It had no precedent in Arab history and it would shatter the notion that adopted sons could be as natural sons in the way that the marriage of Zaynab to Zayd had shattered the Arab's notions about class. This was exactly the reason Muhammadﷺ was ordered to marry her. He had seven wives already, among them those with many children and the old, and also 'A'isha who had grown to be very attractive. He obeyed as he always did; yet it was a heavy duty and he feared people would not understand, nevertheless he obeyed.

The Qur'an says:

> **When you told him whom Allah has been gracious to,**
> **and whom you have been gracious to,**
> **'Hold on to your wife, and fear Allah,'**
> **hiding in your heart what Allah was revealing,**
> **you feared men, when it is Allah you should fear.**
> **After Zayd no longer cared for her,**
> **We let you marry her,**
> **so that believers may find no sin in marrying the women,**
> **who were their clients' wives,**
> **when the latter no longer care for them.**
> **The will of Allah is ever executed. (33: 37)**

The marriage of Muhammadﷺ to Zaynab put an end to adopting clients and allowing them to inherit to the detriment of the rightful heir. Zaynab was a very good young woman, clever with her hands, and she used this gift to make clothes and distribute them among the poor. Muhammadﷺ used to tell his wives, 'She is the most charitable among you.' Such a remark cannot be truly appreciated except when we recall that all Muhammadﷺ's wives were very generous. To be the most generous of the generous was very high charity indeed, for among them was the lady known as 'Mother of the Poor', and also 'A'isha who had been brought up by both father and husband to be exceedingly charitable.

31.8 The Prophet's Insight into Character

The Messenger had deep insight into the characters of the men and women around him. He never made a remark about someone that did not prove absolutely and accurately true either during his lifetime or after it. He called Abu Bakr 'the True', and how often this epithet proved the essence of Abu Bakr's character whether during the Prophet's lifetime or after it. He called Khalid 'the Sword of Allah' and after the Messenger passed away, Khalid did earn this title with merit, and of Zaynab he said that she was the most charitable.

Several years after the Prophet died, in the reign of 'Umar ibn Al-Khattab, great wealth accrued to the Muslims through the wars with the Persians. The treasures of Chosroes fell into their hands and when 'Umar sent Zaynab a pile of gold as her share of the treasure, she called her maid and bade her take a handful and give it to so-and-so, naming one of the poor of Madina. She named one after another of the poor, until all the poor she knew had been provided for, while her maid kept observing that she was leaving nothing for herself. The pile began to diminish quickly. When all the poor had taken a share, she ordered her to uncover the pile. All that was left was eighty dinars. She accepted this as her portion and thanked Allah for it, but believing 'Umar's distributing so much money to be a temptation, she prayed that she might never witness another such distribution. By the same time next year when 'Umar came to distribute money again to the Mothers of the Believers, she had passed away.

All the wives of the Messenger were generous, useful, and frugal. Although they came from noble houses, and were used to every luxury before Islam (the daughter of 'Abdu'l-Muttalib, Muhammadﷺ's aunt, gave forty of her slaves their freedom in a single day). After accepting Islam, when given the choice by Muhammadﷺ, they accepted living as frugally as he did. They could have had all the luxuries they desired or they could be the Messenger's wives, but they could not have both at the same time. After having been waited upon hand and foot, they vied with each other to do good, help those in need, and study the Holy Book.

The Messenger taught more by deed than by words. 'A'isha says of him, 'He used to help out his family, he milked the goat, mended his clothes, repaired his sandals, swept the floor, tied the camel, and fed the cattle. He ate with the servant and made the dough with her and he carried what he bought from the market himself.'

He used to teach his wives and Companions, 'Your servants are your brethren whom Allah has placed under your care. He who has a brother under his care, let him feed him of what he eats and dress him of what he wears. When a servant comes in with food, let him sit and eat with you. If this is not possible, then hand him some of it. Let none of you say, "My slave," for you are all the slaves of Allah, but say rather, "my boy" or "my woman".'

31.9 Banu'l-Mustaliq

While the tribe of Banu'l-Mustaliq were making preparations to raid Madina, Muhammadﷺ pre-empted them by a surprise attack. This saved lives and Madina from the carnage of war. Among the captives was Juwayriya, the daughter of Al-Harith, the head of Banu'l-Mustaliq. She had fallen to the lot of one of the Supporters, and feared since the man knew who her father was that he would ask for an exorbitant ransom. So she went to Muhammad 鸞 to solicit his assistance. He was at 'A'isha's house at that time. As Juwayriya insisted that she had to see him, they let her in and she related her problem to him.

Muhammad 鸞 thought a moment, then said, 'Shall I tell you what would be better than this?' He then asked her to marry him, and she immediately accepted. Juwayriya was a beautiful woman, but Muhammad 鸞 was thinking of how.to save her and all her tribe from an ignoble fate. A way had to be found to let them enter into Islam with honour and wipe away the humiliation of defeat which, according to Arab custom, would not be wiped away except by a war of vengeance that would continue until one of the parties concerned was exterminated, or by a marriage. Muhammad 鸞, as always, chose the more humane of the two solutions.

As soon as the marriage was announced, all the booty taken from Banu'l- Mustaliq was returned and all the captives were set free. The Muslims said, 'These are the in-laws of the Prophet.'

'A'isha says about Juwayriya, 'I know of no woman who was more of a blessing to her people than Juwayriya, the daughter of Al-Harith.'

31.10 Safiyya

After the Battle of Khaybar in which the Muslims defeated the Jews, two women were brought before Muhammad 鸞. One was screaming, shrieking, and placing dust upon her head while the other was mute with horror. The silent one was Safiyya, the daughter of Huyayy ibn Akhtab, the chief of the Banu Nadir the other was her cousin. Safiyya could trace her lineage back to Aaron, the brother of Moses. Muhammad 鸞 asked to have the screaming one attended to, then took his cloak and placed it over the silent one. It was a gesture of pity, but from that moment she was to be honoured and given the highest respect in the Muslim community.

Muhammad 鸞 spoke to Bilal who had conducted the two women to him, saying, 'Bilal, has Allah plucked mercy from your heart that you let these two women pass by the slain of their men folk?' This was considered a severe reprimand, for the Messenger very rarely criticised the behaviour of those who served him. Anas ibn Malik said, 'I served the Messenger of Allah for eight years. He never once scolded me for something I did or for something that I neglected to do.'

Like Umm Habiba, Safiyya was the daughter of a great chief. The only person who could save her from becoming a slave after having enjoyed such a high position was Muhammadﷺ. Her father had planned to assassinate Muhammadﷺ and he had conspired to exterminate all the Muslims in the Battle of the Trench, but it was characteristic that Muhammadﷺ bore no grudges. For those who did wrong, he felt pity rather than anger. He felt even more for the innocent who had to suffer in consequence. So he would not leave Safiyya after her father was killed amid a hostile people of a different religion.

'Could you care for me?' he asked her later.

'Yes, Messenger of Allah,' she said.

So Safiyya entered into Islam and entered into Muhammadﷺ's house with the honoured title, 'Mother of the Believers'. One may wonder how Safiyya could accept entering into Islam and become the wife of the Messenger when her father had been his bitter enemy, and when bloody battles had taken place between the Jews and the Muslims.

The answer may be found in what she relates of her early life as the daughter of the chief of the Banu Nadir. She said, 'I was my father's favourite, and also a favourite with my uncle Yasir. They could never see me with one of their children without picking me up. When the Messenger of Allah came to Madina, may Allah bless him him, my father and my uncle went to see him. It was very early in the morning between dawn and sunrise. They did not return until the setting of the sun. They came back worn out, depressed, walking with slow, heavy steps. I smiled to them as I was used to do, but neither of them took any notice of me for they were very miserable. I heard Abu Yasir tell my father, 'Is it he?'

'Yes, it is.'

'Can you recognise him? Can you verify it?'

'Yes, I can recognise him, all right.'

'What do you feel towards him?'

'Enmity, enmity as long as I live.'

The significance of this conversation is evident when we recall that in the ancient books of the Jews it was written that a prophet would come who would lead those who followed him to victory. The Jews used to threaten the idol worshippers of Madina that when he came they were going to exterminate them as they had exterminated other tribes before. This prophet was accurately described in their ancient texts which also contained signs by which they could recognise him. That was the reason their most learned rabbi, Ibn Salam, entered into Islam on seeing Muhammad ﷺ. Huyayy ibn Akhtab could also recognise him, but while the rabbi did not hesitate to enter into Islam and give up worldly power, Huyayy who was not a man of God resented very much that the Prophet should appear among the Arabs, and moreover he had no intention of giving up worldly power. Even from the first meeting he had decided to oppose the Messenger. At the time the Messenger was making treaties with the Jews that gave them security and rights equal to the Muslims and made them citizens of Madina, they were already planning to destroy the Prophet when they got the opportunity.

Although Safiyya had in Muhammad ﷺ a most kind and considerate husband, she was not happy, for his other wives were Qurayshi ladies of noble birth who considered her only a Jewess. One day she went to him in tears, and he said to her, 'But did you not answer them? Did you not tell them, "How can you be better than me when Muhammad ﷺ is my husband, Moses my (great) uncle and Aaron my great grandfather?"' These words were a balm to her wounded pride and from then on she felt inferior to no one.

Years later when Muhammad ﷺ died, she mourned for him deeply and sincerely. 'Messenger of Allah,' she said, 'I wish I was suffering instead of you.' And all her days after it, Safiyya served Islam with deep faith and sincerity.

31.11 Maria

Maria was from the village of Hafen in lower Egypt. Her father was a Copt and her mother was a Christian Greek. She was removed when quite young to the palace of Cyrus, the ruler of Egypt. When the Messenger sent Cyrus a letter calling him to Islam, he took the letter, placed it in an ivory casket; and gave it to one of his slave girls to put away. Then he asked Hatib, the man who brought the letter, to speak to him of Muhammad ﷺ. Cyrus thought for a long moment after it and then said, 'I was aware that a prophet was yet to appear. I thought he would appear in Al-Sham where other prophets have done, but I find he has appeared in Arabia .... but the Copts will not listen to me, and I grudge giving up my realm for it.'

He sent Muhammad ﷺ a cordial letter and many presents including two slaves, Maria and her sister Serene, and he mentioned in his letter that Maria and her sister were of high status among the Copts. Hatib returned with the letter, the presents, as well as the two sisters, both of whom were homesick and afraid. To quiet their fears, Hatib began to speak to them of Islam and the Arabian Prophet.

On arrival in Madina, they were presented to Muhammad☀ who kept Maria and gave Serene to a man he wished to honour. At first Maria was only a slave and was not called 'Mother of the Believers' as Muhammad☀'s wives were. Just as Muhammad☀ was mourning for the death of his beloved daughter, Zaynab, he received tidings of cheer - Maria was expecting a child. He was overjoyed to receive some months later a baby boy. All his sons had died in infancy and he did not expect to have a child when he was almost sixty years old. He called him Ibrahim after the grandfather of both Arabs and Jews, and sent his foster mother seven goats to help her nurse him. Then he distributed the weight of the child's hair in gold upon the poor. Maria was raised to the status of 'Mother of Believers', for she was now the mother of Ibrahim.

The marriage of Muhammad☀ to Safiyya, a Jewess, then Maria, a Copt, has tremendous importance in the history of Islam. It taught the Muslims to be tolerant. If the Messenger of Allah himself had married once a Jewess and once a Christian, then all Jews and all Christians were to be treated cordially as his in-laws. It wiped out bigotry and fanaticism from the Muslim community once and for all. The history of other religions is unfortunately full of the wrongs, persecutions, and massacres that some people have suffered because of their religion, but in the long history of Islam, no one has ever been persecuted because of his religion. The Qur'an decrees that there shall be no coercion in religion, and Muhammad☀ taught it by these two unforgettable unions.

31.12 The Effect of the Prophet's Marriages on Muslim Thought

Islam had become the most important and widespread religion in the peninsula and the Messenger adhered strictly to the principle in the Qur'an that each shall worship as his conscience dictates. He warned his followers never to try and tempt any of the People of the Book away from their religion: Idol worshippers he did try to convince of the stupidity of worshipping stone or wood, but those who had a holy book he left strictly to their conscience.

He made a pact with the monks of Sinai, granting them

protection, security, freedom of worship, and exemption from all taxes. The monks have preserved this pact, and those who visit Sinai can still see it). All this he did in the seventh century when dreadful persecutions were being undertaken by others in the name of religion. While Cyrus, the agent of Heraclius in Egypt, was torturing and mutilating the Christian Copts in order to force them to adhere to the decrees of the Council of Chaldea, the Messenger was far in advance of the rest of the world in thought and action.

Each of the stories of the Messenger's wives has contributed something of value to Islam, a precedent and a heritage. The theory is found in the Holy Qur'an, but people do not understand by theory alone, it has to be actualized - they have to have the living example before them to understand.

From the story of the lady Khadija one learns much. One learns that the person who had the honour of being the first Muslim after the Messenger was a woman. Then it shows how great, sincere, steadfast and wise a woman can be. It reveals that marriage can be an ideal relationship of mutual love and respect. Over and above all, it shows that women can and are allowed to work in Islam. For many centuries after the Messenger and those great early Muslims passed away, there came the narrow-minded who would confine women at home. To these one points out the story of the lady Khadija who managed her trade business very successfully.

To those who say that women should not learn, that their place is in the house, one could point out that the Messenger urged men to teach their wives and daughters, but more than that one could point out the shining example of the lady 'A'isha and the service she did to Islam by her learning.

To those who thirst for revenge, one could point out how the Messenger sent to far-off Abyssinia to rescue the daughter of one of his staunchest enemies. The Qur'an points out that the sins of the parents are not to be visited upon the children, and in the Messenger's behaviour to both Umm Habiba and Safiyya, the daughters of two of his worst enemies, is the living proof.

From the story of Umm Salama one learns that fatherless children are the responsibility of the whole community. They should not be ignored nor neglected nor wronged. The Qur'an gives orphans very clear rights, but it is in the application of these rights that the Messenger excelled.

If any should develop religious zeal against Christians and Jews, one could always point to the Messenger's being married, once to a Christian and once to a Jewess, and his memorable words in consequence, 'He who insults one of the people of the Book has insulted me.'

Unselfish and unworldly each of the 'Mothers of Believers'tried to do her best according to the abilities Allah had bestowed on her - such were the wives of the Messenger and such should Muslim women be.

CHAPTER THIRTY-TWO

32.1 Muhammad鑿's Tribulations

For twenty-three years, ever since he proclaimed the worship of Allah alone and the abandonment of idol worship, the Messenger had suffered severe trials and privations. He had made great sacrifices for the sake of Islam. He had sacrificed his money, his position and prestige among his people, his time, his effort, his life, everything, even food and drink during the three years of boycott in the mountains. These sacrifices he had made willingly for the sake of the deity he believed in, but there were other sacrifices that were forced upon him, trials he had to suffer and great grief to endure. Prophets are the people who have to undergo the most severe trials, and Muhammad鑿, the last and greatest of the prophets, had suffered the greatest of trials. There is hardly a grief or woe he had not experienced.

He was a very affectionate and loving father, and he lost three daughters and two sons. With each bereavement he would suffer quietly with patience and fortitude. At the age of sixty, the only son left to him was the eighteen month old Ibrahim.

32.2 The Death of Ibrahim

One day the Prophet received a message from Maria saying that Ibrahim was ailing. The baby had been growing strong and sturdy, comelier every day, and Muhammad鑿 was getting more and more attached to it. Then suddenly the child fell ill.

Muhammad鑿 sat with the baby on his knee and said, 'Ibrahim, we can do nothing for you with Allah.' And as the little one breathed his last, he said, 'The eye weeps, the heart grieves, but we say nothing except what pleases the Lord. Ibrahim, I do mourn for you. To Allah we belong and to Him we shall return.'

After the little body was prepared for burial, Muhammad鑿 and his uncle, together with other Muslims, followed the bier. They made a grave for it and Muhammad鑿 smoothed over the earth, saying, 'This action does no harm nor good, but it is pleasing to the eye of the living. When man does anything, Allah likes him to do it well.'

As the child was being buried, the sun was eclipsed and it grew dark and gloomy. The Muslims cried that it was a sign of grief for Ibrahim, but Muhammadﷺ, even at this moment of deep personal grief, thought it his duty to explain to them that this was a natural phenomenon that had natural causes created by Allah. He said, 'The sun and moon are two of the phenomena of Allah. They do not go into eclipse because of anyone's life or death. When you see such phenomena, flee to remember Allah in prayers.' It is those who truly believe and truly comprehend who can see the hand of Allah in the regulation of the laws of the universe around them.

32.3 Qurayshi Spite

The Arabs loved to have sons, they were their joy, their pride, and the source of their strength. A man who did not have many sons was considered less strong and of less consequence than a man who had many sons who could help him in peace and fight for him in war. A son was also the natural extension or continuation of the line. A man who had no son had no future. It was therefore a great trial to Muhammadﷺ to have each of his sons die before reaching manhood -he who was a father to so many, who guided and helped so many, who had brought up in his house two fine young men, 'Ali ibn Abi Talib, the most brilliant scholar in Islam, and Zayd ibn Haritha, a brave warrior and devout Muslim.

Quraysh who hated Muhammadﷺ found nothing to criticise him with except that he had no son. They nicknamed him the 'issueless', which in Arabic means figuratively the childless but literally 'the amputated'. It was a cruel joke and Muhammadﷺ felt it until one day these holy verses were sent down:

We have given you Al-Kawthar,
so pray to your Lord and offer sacrifice.
He who loathes you is the 'issueless'. (108:1-3)

In the verses above, the Qur'an transcends the petty notions of men. With all the good he was doing, the wisdom and faith he instilled into human hearts, the ideals he upheld, the majestic battles he fought with evil, corruption, superstitions, and idolatry, the immortal spiritual path he had opened to man, he was not 'issueless'. He has millions of spiritual heirs, sons and daughters in every generation who follow in the broad vistas he has opened to them.

CHAPTER THIRTY-THREE

33.1 Tribes Pay Alms Money

Islam spread from Madina in all directions, to the north, to the south, and towards the east. Most of the tribes began to embrace this new religion that was far superior to anything they had known. It spread until it reached the borders of the Roman and the Persian empires, thus covering nearly the whole peninsula. The Arabs who had been disunited warring tribes began to be, for the first time, one united nation with a central authority in Madina and one religion whose sanctuary was in Makka.

The tribes who had entered into Islam paid willingly the alms tax that was an obligation on the believers. Those who had not entered into Islam paid a defence tax in exchange for security of person and property.

33.2 Preparations for the Roman Invasion

Under the merciful rule of Islam, the peninsula attained a just peace and unified stability. It was not, however, in the interest of the Romans to have a strong and unified power on their borders. They had previously been inciting the northern tribes against the Muslims and giving them money and material support, but that year in the late summer, when the heat can be as great as mid-summer or worse, news came that the Romans were preparing a great army to come and fight the Muslims. This great army was to cross the borders into Arab land to make all the Arabs, those who were their vassals and those who were not, feel Roman military might.

So once again Muhammad☀ had to carry arms to fight for the freedom of the land of Islam and for freedom of religion. It was well-known how the Romans executed those of them who entered into Islam and tortured the Christians who differed from them in religious matters. It was also known that the Roman legions were of very great numbers. Muhammad☀ had to collect an army that could stand against these great hosts, so he summoned the tribes and explained the situation to them.

33.3 Those Who Stayed Behind

The rich were called to spend of their money for Allah's sake. All those who could provide war array for themselves were called to go and fight for His sake. Once again the Muslims were being tried. To fight the famous Roman legions was a daunting prospect at a time when the Roman Empire was the dominant power in the world. Moreover it was late summer, in a part of the world, amid burning rocks and waterless deserts, where the climate could kill without the aid of any Romans. Muhammadﷺ decided to lead this expedition himself.

Those of true faith came out of their own accord, to offer their lives to Allah. They were willing to go anywhere the Prophet went, even if it meant they would die of heat or thirst. They were willing to endure anything for the sake of their religion. Communications were very difficult in the vast tracts of the northern deserts and they knew they would have to travel for many, many days before they could reach any source of water or food.

The hypocrites, those whose hearts faith had not touched, and the mercenary, those who had entered into Islam for material considerations, began to whisper to each other, 'Do not go out to war in this heat,' whereupon the holy verses were revealed to say:

Those who stayed behind after the Messenger of Allah, rejoiced in it, and hated to struggle for Allah's sake with their money and themselves.
And they said, 'Do not go out to war in this heat.'
Say the fire of Jahannam is of greater heat,
if they could only understand.
Let them laugh a little; let them cry much,
in requital for what they used to do. (9:81-82)

Some of them did not only stay behind, but were active in persuading others to stay behind. They used to have meetings in the house of a Jew called Suwaylim. Not to answer the call of duty was bad enough, but to try to corrupt others was unforgivable. Muhammadﷺ sent Talha ibn 'Ubaydullah to burn down the house where they met and put an end to these meetings.

Many of the rich offered generously, and many of the poor went to the Messenger to beg for war gear to fight for Allah's sake. He had to apologize to some of them, saying he had no means of transport for them. They returned with tears in their eyes because they were unable to fight for their Lord.

A mighty army was finally gathered, thirty thousand men. The cavalry were ten thousand and went in front, while the rest followed on camel back. The Prophet went at the head of the army after leaving a deputy over Madina. Those who were ready to meet the worst for their faith marched forward; those who preferred a life of ease, cool shade, and safety remained in Madina.

The sight of this army going out out in manly courage to cross hundreds of miles of treacherous terrain in deadly weather to meet an enemy many times their number, not knowing whether they would ever return to their homeland again, moved many of those who had decided to stay behind.

One of them, Abu Khaythama, returned after watching the army leave the city to find that each of his wives had prepared food, water, and cool shade for him. He looked at them, appalled, and said, 'The Messenger of Allah is in the noonday heat and Abu Khaythama in cool shade with food, drink, and beautiful women. Never! Prepare provisions for me, so that I can catch up with the Messenger of Allah.'

33.4 Muhammadﷺ Marches Out

The army marched until they reached Al-Hijr where they passed by the ruins of Thamud, an ancient people who had been destroyed because they persisted in ignoring the messengers who came to them and continued in their transgressions. The Qur'an relates their story, giving details that neither Muhammadﷺ nor his people had known.

The Prophet warned his men not to drink from the wells of Thamud, nor to wash for prayers with water from them,and if they had baked any bread with the water to give it to the camels. He asked them not to go out alone at night, but in twos and threes. Only two men disobeyed the Prophet's command and went out. One was carried away by the winds and the other was buried in the sands. The next day they found the wells of Thamud had been covered by a sandstorm during the night.

They marched on in the desert, the route was long and hot and their water supply was nearly finished. They had yet a long way before them and they knew not what to do, when suddenly a cloud came drifting towards them and kept pelting rain until the whole army had had its fill. Some called out that it was a miracle; others said that it was merely a cloud passing by.

33.5 Border Treaties

The army marched to Tabuk. On arrival there, Muhammad ﷺ learnt that the Romans, hearing of his approach, had retreated into their own territory. Muhammad ﷺ, who had never fought for the sake of winning a battle, saw no reason why he should follow them and thought this to be a good opportunity to come to an understanding with the border princes. He summoned the princes who formed buffer states between him and the Romans and spoke to them of Islam, then he undertook to give them protection on sea and land in exchange for the defence tax that non-Muslims had to pay and the alms tax that Muslims had to pay. Here is the text of one of these agreements written to Yuhanna ibn Ruba:

'In the name of Allah, the Most Merciful, the Compassionate.

This is security from Allah and Muhammad ﷺ, the Prophet, the Messenger of Allah to Yuhanna ibn Ruba and the people of Iliya. Their ships and conveyances upon sea and land are under the protection of Allah and Muhammad ﷺ, the Prophet, and those with them of the people of Al-Sham or Yemen or the people of the sea. Any of them who meets disaster shall not try to retrieve his money, but shall go to Muhammad ﷺ to retrieve it for him from the people who took it. They are not to be forbidden any water they desire nor road they wish to follow upon sea or land.'

To cement this treaty Muhammad ﷺ gave Yuhanna a garment decorated with the luxurious embroidery of Yemen, as well as many other tokens of friendship, and it was agreed that Iliya should pay three hundred dinars a year.

After making these treaties to secure the borders of Arab lands, there was no need to fight anymore, but the prince of Duma, one of the border princes, was still to be feared. He might conspire with the Romans. Muhammad ﷺ set out with the bulk of army, to return to Madina, but sent Khalid ibn Al-Walid to Duma at the head of five thousand horsemen.

Khalid and his men found the prince out hunting and took him captive, forcing the city to open its gates to them to ransom its prince. They took much booty and cattle and brought the prince of Duma to Muhammad ﷺ at Madina. The Messenger spoke to him of Islam, and he became a Muslim and an ally of Muhammad ﷺ.

Some of those who had gone out full of enthusiasm to fight the enemy were disappointed for they had not fought a single battle. Had they marched a thousand miles or more in the heat for nothing? They did not fully grasp the importance of the treaties Muhammadﷺ had made with the border princes whose lands acted as buffer states between him and the Romans. They felt that if they did not fight and defeat the enemy then they had accomplished nothing. Muhammadﷺ tried to avoid armed conflict as much as possible and spared himself no effort towards this aim. He wanted to win people over to Islam and not to fight them. He fought only when it was inevitable, when the tribes decided to come and fight him or threatened freedom of religion on Arab land. He had to demonstrate to them that their idols were fake gods which did not give them victory in war or security in peace. However the Arabs were disgruntled, all they could see was that they had spent twenty days at the border doing nothing while Muhammadﷺ talked to the border princes instead of fighting them. They did not realize that to make the mind understand can be a greater victory than to compel the body.

Then they returned to Madina to discover another aspect of the matter. They saw how those who had stayed behind in fear of the Romans and the heat regretted it. They had thought Muhammadﷺ and those who volunteered would surely perish, if not by killing heat then by Roman swords. Then they saw Muhammadﷺ and the Muslims returning safe and sound with treaties of friendship covering the northern border.

The real battle had not been with the Romans but with themselves. It was a test of faith and courage and those who had gone out to meet the Romans had passed the test.

33.6 The Hypocrites' Mosque

Some of the hypocrites had built a mosque for a dark purpose of their own. They built it to alter the words of the Qur'an and place nonsensical words in it in order to shake people's faith. To hide their evil design, they asked the Prophet to come and pray with them. Muhammadﷺ was going to Tabuk and asked them to wait until his return, but when he returned these holy verses were sent down concerning the mosque:

And those who built a mosque
for mischief, denial and separation between those who believe,
and watching for the arrival of him
who has fought Allah and His Messenger before.
They will swear, 'We sought only the good.'

And Allah witnesses that they are liars.
Do not ever pray in it.
A mosque founded on piety from the first day
is more worthy of your prayers in it.
There are men in it who love to purify themselves,
and Allah loves those who purify themselves. (9:107-108)

In the verses above, reference is made to another mosque built before this by people sincere in their faith. They had asked Muhammad✲ to pray in it and he had done so. Reference is also made to a monk called Abu 'Amr who had fought Muhammad✲ before.

The mosque was burnt and the hypocrites were scattered. No one would help or support them except their chief, 'Abdullah ibn Ubayy ibn Salul. Two months later, 'Abdullah ibn Ubayy ibn Salul fell ill and died, so their last support was gone and they became inconsequential.

CHAPTER THIRTY-FOUR

34.1 'Urwa ibn Mas'ud

After the march to Tabuk and the retreat of the Romans before Muhammad☺, the Arabs who had not entered into Islam began to reconsider the matter. Here was an Arab like them, of noble birth and character, who called to a religion more sound and true than anything they had known. So why not forsake the stone and wooden idols and march under the banner of Allah, the One, the Invincible? Many tribes now hurried to the Messenger, but some still clung to their tribal idols and tribal isolation. That year delegation after delegation came to the Prophet to profess Islam so that historians call it the Year of Delegations. It was the tenth year after the Hijra (Emigration).

The city of Al-Ta'if had strong forts and rich lands. Thaqif, the city's tribe, had an idol called Al-Lat which they cherished. Muhammad☺ had besieged them after the battle of Hunayn in which they had participated, then broke the siege, giving them time to think.

One of their great men, 'Urwa ibn Mas'ud, who had acted as an intermediary between the Prophet and Quraysh at Hudaybiya, had been in Yemen when the Prophet had besieged Al-Ta'if. After his return, he went to Muhammad☺ and pledged him allegiance and asked him to let him speak to Thaqif, but Muhammad☺ feared he would not be able to cope with them. 'They will kill you,' he said.

But 'Urwa insisted, saying, 'I am dearer to them than the apple of their eye.' He kept after the Prophet until Muhammad☺ gave him permission. So he went to his people and spoke to them of Islam. They listened and then asked him to give them time to think it over. The next day 'Urwa woke up with the dawn and chanted the call to prayer. Fanaticism for their idol drove them to shoot arrows at him from every direction. 'Urwa fell down. His family gathered around him, and before his death, he said to them, 'This is a great thing that Allah has brought my way. It is martyrdom. Now I shall die like the martyrs who fought with the Prophet at Badr.' Then he asked his family to bury him with the martyrs of Badr. And his request was attended to.

34.2 Al-Ta'if Enters into Islam

When the people of Al-Ta'if killed one of their own nobles because he proclaimed what he believed in, the tribes around them who had entered into Islam would have nothing to do with them. If one of them went out singly he did not return, and even in a group they were not safe. Soon they realized that they would have to come to an understanding with their neighbours. They chose an emissary to go and speak to Muhammad☀ since these tribes and in effect the whole peninsula were now under his rule. But the man chosen feared he would be treated in the same way by the tribes, so he would not go until five others from different tribes went with him, so that each would have a tribe to avenge him should he get killed. They came recalcitrant and wary of the Muslims. One of them carried out negotiations between them and the Prophet.

Curiously they professed their willingness to enter into Islam provided that their idol was left to them and that they did not have to pray.

The Prophet refused their request. He said, 'There is no good in religion when there is no prayer.' He used to tell his Companions, 'He who wants to speak to his Lord, let him pray: he who wants his Lord to speak to him, let him read the Qur'an.'

At the end they agreed to pray and break their idol, but requested that they should be spared doing it themselves. To this Muhammad☀ acquiesced. He sent Abu Sufyan and Al-Mughira ibn Shu'ba, who were liked and respected by the people of Thaqif, to break it. They broke it with the women of Al-Ta'if wailing around them, then Al-Mughira, by the Prophet's permission and in agreement with Abu Sufyan, took the money in the idol's temple and paid a debt with it that 'Urwa ibn Mas'ud had left behind. With this all of the Hijaz became Muslim.

The delegation of Al-Ta'if remained with Muhammad☀ the whole month of Ramadan and fasted with him. Muhammad☀ initiated one of them in Islam so that he could teach people when he returned home. He charged him to be brief in prayer and to think of the old man and the child praying behind him, to make religion easy and not difficult for them. To each Muhammad☀ gave of religion according to his readiness to understand.

When Muhammad☀ prayed with his Companions, he prayed for hours sometimes, and when he prayed alone, he prayed for long, long watches of the night. Nothing gave him more spiritual content than calling upon his Lord.

34.3 The Pilgrimage and 'Ali's Announcement

The year went round and it was time for the pilgrimage to Makka, but delegation after delegation continued to come, giving Muhammadﷺ no respite, so he asked Abu Bakr to lead the pilgrims to Makka instead of him.

After Abu Bakr had left with the pilgrims, the holy verses came down saying that no polytheist should enter the House of Allah after that year. Polytheists were given four months to return to their lands in peace after which they were never to return to the Sacred Precincts. Should they wish to retain amicable relations with the Muslims, they were to forsake their idols and enter into Islam, otherwise they should expect war from Allah and His Prophet. Those with whom the Muslims had pacts were to be treated according to the terms until their dates of expiry.

Muhammadﷺ sent 'Ali ibn Abi Talib after Abu Bakr with the newly revealed decrees. 'Ali read the newly-revealed verses of Surat Al-Tawba to the people which contained these decrees, then said, 'No denier shall enter paradise; and no polytheist shall make the pilgrimage to the House of Allah after this day. No naked person shall go around the Ancient House. Those who have covenants with the Messenger of Allah, their covenants shall be observed until their time of expiry.'

Thus after twenty-three years of struggle and sacrifice, after long and dark centuries of idolatry, the first house built for the worship of Allah once more became exclusively dedicated to pure worship of Him.

Islam had now spread throughout the peninsula, north and south, east and west. When it went to the Yemen, the Prophet sent one of his Companions to initiate its people in religion and said to him, 'Make things easy and do not complicate them. Give tidings of cheer and do not repel. You will be over people of the Book who will ask you what is the key to paradise. Say, "It is the testimony that Allah is One and that He has no partner.'

34.4 The Messenger's Last Pilgrimage

The year went round and it was once more time for the pilgrimage to Makka. Muhammadﷺ decided to make the pilgrimage himself that year in order to teach people its rites, for they learned more easily by example. As soon as news spread that the Prophet was going on pilgrimage to Makka, thousands began to flock towards Madina to go with him from all parts of the peninsula. A multitude of tents were erected for them around Madina for nearly one hundred thousand came in answer to this call. All came to worship in humility and brotherhood behind a leader they loved and trusted.

That year, contrary to all preceding travels and pilgrimages, the Prophet asked all his wives to accompany him. He wanted to make sure that they all performed the pilgrimage to Makka, which is a duty that the Muslim owes his Lord once in a lifetime. Muhammadﷺ seemed to know that this would be the last time they would perform the pilgrimage with him. All his words to the pilgrims as well as his actions denote that he was saying his farewells to his people and to this world.

34.5 The Rites of Pilgrimage

When the pilgrims reached Dhu'l-Hulayfa, they began to purify themselves in preparation for entry into the Sacred Precincts. Then marching towards Makka they began to call, 'I come in answer to Thee, my Lord, I come in answer to Thee. Thou hast no partner, my Lord, I come in answer to Thee.' These words chanted by one hundred thousand men echoed through the valleys and mountains of Arabia until they reached Makka.

As the Muslims passed by each mosque in village or oasis they stopped to pray. The Prophet said to them, 'Those of you who have no offering to sacrifice and prefer to make this a visit and not a pilgrimage may do so. Those who have brought an offering may not.'

The Qur'an had stated the basic conditions for the pilgrimage in the following words:

The pilgrimage is in certain appointed months.
For he who undertakes to make the pilgrimage in them;
there shall be no copulation,
no transgression and no arguments on the pilgrimage.
The good you do Allah knows about.
And take provisions with you, the best provision is piety.
And fear Me, you of best intellects. (2:197)

People were to devote themselves completely to their Lord during the pilgrimage.

On the day of gathering on the plain of Arafat at the culmination of the pilgrimage's rites, the Prophet spoke to the assembled mass of people.

34.6 The Prophet's Farewell Speech

'Listen to my words, for I may not meet you again after this year in such circumstances. Sacred to you is the blood of others, sacred to you is the money of others until the day you meet your Lord, as sacred as this day and month. You shall meet your Lord and He will question you about your deeds. There, I have proclaimed this to you. He of you who has been entrusted with a trust, let him deliver it to its owner. All usury is forbidden. You may have your initial capital back, you do not wrong and you are not wronged.

'The devil has despaired of being worshipped in your land ever again, but if he is obeyed, he will accept the mean of your deeds, so fear for your religion from him.' After further admonition, among them urging men to be good to women, for they were under their care, the Prophet continued, 'Understand my words, for I am delivering a message to you and I shall leave among you what, if you adhere to it, will never let you go wrong. the Book of Allah and the Way of His Messenger. Listen to my words and grasp their meaning. Realize that each Muslim is a brother to other Muslims. Muslims are brethren. No man shall take from his brother, except what his brother gives him willingly. So do not wrong each other.' He ended by saying, 'My Lord, have I delivered the message?'

The Messenger spoke in a loud, clear voice. Nevertheless he feared lest people would not hear well - there were so many, so he let Rabi'a ibn Umayya repeat it after him to the people part by part exactly as he had said it. Then he asked them questions to make sure that they had grasped what he had said. In the end when he said, 'My Lord, have I delivered the message?' thousands upon thousands of voices answered from all directions, 'Yes, you have.'

34.7 The Last Revelation

The Prophet prayed the noon and afternoon prayers and rode his camel up to the rocks. There he read these newly-revealed verses to the people:

> **Today I have completed your religion for you,**
> **completed bestowing My blessing upon you,**
> **and approved Islam as a religion for you. (5:3)**

On hearing these words Abu Bakr burst into tears. This was an unmistakable sign to him. Perhaps all the time the Messenger was repeating to them the basic precepts of Islam, precepts he had taught them twenty-three years earlier, Abu Bakr could feel that this was the end. Muhammadﷺ was saying farewell to this world and the people to whom he had been entrusted with the Message and that was the reason he was repeating things he had taught them so many years ago. Such behaviour would not escape Abu Bakr who knew him so well. But these verses from the Qur'an made his fears turn into an awful certainty. If religion was complete, if the message had been delivered, what need had the Messenger to remain in the land of his sojourn? He realized that Muhammadﷺ would soon be taken from them. He was dearer than life or child to Abu Bakr, but the will of Allah is ever executed.

Muhammadﷺ's words were paving the way for those who would come after him, and securing the gains Islam had given the Arab nation. Abu Bakr noted all this and followed Muhammadﷺ with an anxious eye and mournful heart.

When a few months later Muhammadﷺ passed away, the whole nation was in convulsion, friend and foe alike were thrown into confusion, all except Abu Bakr. With a hand of steel, he steadied the faltering, rectified the erring, and carried the banner of the nation entrusted to him high over distant lands and foreign climes.

Continuing the rites of pilgrimage, the Prophet spent the night at Muzdalifa, then in the morning moved on to Al-Hashr al-Haram (amountain) from where he returned to Mina where he threw the symbolic stones at the devil. When he returned to his tent, he sacrificed sixty-three offerings, one for each year of his life. Then he shaved his head and ended the rites of pilgrimage.

This was the last time he made the pilgrimage, the last time he visited the Ancient House. After twenty-three years of constant struggle, of patience and indomitable courage, he was soon to attain rest and peace, and the true promise that he was promised.

34.8 False Prophets

Now the whole peninsula was at peace under the rule of the Messenger. . Its tribes and clans were at last united in a coherent whole. In the rule of Muhammadﷺ they found an impartial justice, and secure freedom that they had never attained before alone or under Persian or Roman rule. He asked for no temporal power or territory; all he asked was that they realize that Allah is One. Once they grasped this concept he let them rule themselves in their own lands in peace, provided it was according to the justice, brotherhood, and benevolence that Islam decreed.

Some people from the tribes were still unable to grasp the greatness of what had happened to the Arabs, and still thought in terms of temporal power and influence. They resented that a man from Quraysh should have power over them. Why not a man from their own tribe? Then they too would have the pride and glory of a prophet to boast of before all the Arabs. They could not defeat Muhammadﷺ by the force of arms nor could they defeat him by their decadent superstitions and idol worship, for Muhammadﷺ had put an end to the worship of idols once and forever. So they began to produce prophets of their own. These would-be prophets did not dare attack Muhammadﷺ or the Qur'an, but simply said that they also received messages from heaven. Most of them, so long as Muhammadﷺ was alive, kept their pretensions secret. Muhammadﷺ paid little attention to these prophets and concentrated all his efforts on assembling an army to counteract Roman troop movements.

One of these pretenders was a little ugly creature called Musaylima, so ugly that his tribe would not take him- with them to meet the Prophet in the Year of the Delegations. This Musaylima sent Muhammadﷺ a message saying that half the land belonged to Quraysh and half of it belonged to his tribe, but that Quraysh were unfair. Muhammadﷺ wrote in reply, 'The land belongs to Allah. He makes heir to it whom He will of His righteous slaves, and peace unto those who follow guidance.' Another such prophet appeared in Yemen and was killed by his own people after his behaviour proved him to be a liar.

34.9 Preparations Against Rome

The Roman and Persian empires were the two mighty neighbours of the Arabs. The Arab kingdoms on the borders of Roman territory paid homage to the Romans; the Arabs kingdoms on the border of the Persian territory paid homage to the Persian empire. The Persian empire, as mentioned earlier, was rent by internal strife, but the Roman empire was a formidable enemy and a real danger to Arab freedom. Arab rulers in the Roman dominions were Roman vassals.

As soon a Muhammadﷺ returned from the Pilgrimage of Farewell, he began to prepare a great army to meet the Romans. The army was to go to the northern border and contained many of the great men of Islam, among them Muhammadﷺ's two ministers, 'Umar ibn al-Khattab and Abu Bakr. But the honorary position of leadership was given to a very young man, Usama, son of Zayd ibn Haritha, Muhammadﷺ's client, who had been killed fighting the Romans at the Battle of Mu'ta. Zayd was a brave leader of men and it was an Arab custom that the son should follow in the footsteps of the father and should seek revenge for his death. But there were two obstacles in this case: the fast was that Usama was very young, barely twenty, and the second that his father had been only a client, while there were many of noble birth and much experience in this army.

As always Muhammadﷺ made new customs. If Zayd was brave enough to lead the army against the Romans, then his son should have the honour of leading this army, even if, it contained men of experience and nobility. Zayd had grown up in Muhammadﷺ's house and when he was killed fighting at Mula, Muhammadﷺ had grieved deeply for him. Usama, Zayd's son, had often sat on Muhammadﷺ's knee. Now when he had barely passed the threshold of boyhood, he was given this command of great moment. It was to honour the name of his father and to wipe out from the Arab mind once and for all the idea of the superiority of masters over clients.

He commanded Usama to take the enemy by surprise at early dawn. Then when Allah granted him victory, he was to return immediately and not to penetrate too deeply into Roman territory or remain too long in it.

CHAPTER THIRTY-FIVE

35.1 Mercy in the Qur'anic Sense

If one were asked to name the dominant characteristic of the Messenger of Allah, one would not hesitate to say mercy. It is a character trait that permeates all his words, all his actions. The Holy Qur'an tells him:

And We have not sent you except out of mercy to mankind.

This is the essence of the Message to Muhammadﷺ. Every action, every word was to lead people to be merciful to each other. He used to say, 'I was sent a teacher, 'and this is what he taught.

'Allah has mercy upon the merciful.'

'You do not truly believe until you desire for your brother (the word in Arabic is used in the sense of your fellow men) what you desire for yourself. '

'He who relieves a believer of one of the cares of this world, Allah will relieve of one of the cares of the Day of Judgement. He who relieves a man in financial difficulties, Allah will make things easy for him in this world and the eternal. He who shields a Muslim (covers his secrets, weakness, or want), Allah will shield in this world and the eternal. Allah continues to aid His slave so long as this slave continues to aid his brother.'

Mercy in the Qur'anic senses is a very great thing. It is not merely compassion or sympathy, but real and active concern. We are told that the mercy of Allah encompasses everything. Hence every good that comes to man is an aspect of His mercy. Help, guidance, care, and forgiveness are all different factors of mercy. It is out of His mercy that man is guided out of darkness into light. Muhammadﷺ came with mercy from heaven to bring that dark age out of its evil corruptions and superstitions into the light of justice and truth, which are also aspects of Allah's mercy. The holy verses point out that the Qur'an was sent down ,on a blessed day' 'out of your Lord's mercy.'

The Messenger used to say, *'I was sent to complete good character, I was sent to complete gracious character, I was sent to complete righteous character.'*

Again goodness, graciousness, and righteousness are all aspects of mercy. He says 'to complete' because the prophets before him had begun to teach men - it was his job to complete what they had begun.

35.2 Kindness to Animals

In that age when men were often cruel to each other, let alone to animals, Muhammadﷺ taught his Companions that one should be kind to all living things, animal or plant, since they are all part of Allah's creation. He taught that a woman would enter Jahannam (Hell) because she had locked up a cat without giving it anything to eat.

He nursed a sick rooster back to health. He was kind to a cat who liked to sleep in his house every night and used to rise and open the door for it himself. Once when 'A'isha was riding a camel who would not obey, she beat it, so he said to her, admonishing, 'Gently, 'A'isha, gently.'

Once a rough and uncouth Arab came to the Messenger and said, 'Muhammadﷺ, give me of what Allah has given you.' So the Messenger gave him the money that was on him, then asked if he had given enough. The man answered in a rude manner that it was not enough, nor was it adequate. The Companions wanted to shove the man away or beat him, but the Messenger said, 'No, no, leave him to me.' He took him to his house and gave him more, then asked if this was enough. The man, well pleased, answered that it was enough and began to thank Allah and His Messenger. The Messenger asked him to go out to the Companions and to tell them that he was satisfied, for they may have resented his former behaviour. The man did so.

When the Messenger met his Companions later he explained that to them by means of an allegory. He said that there was once a man who had a recalcitrant camel that had run away from him. People kept trying to bring it back to him by pulling or beating it, but he asked them not to interfere between him and his camel. Then he took some bush and kept giving it to the camel little by little until the camel came back to him again. He concluded the story by saying that had they beat or rough-handled the man, it would not have helped him towards faith, but if he left content he had a better chance of coming closer to faith.

One day while he was teaching a group of people a little bird kept hovering over his head. He stopped and asked, 'Who has deprived this poor bird of its chick?' A little boy in the group said, 'It was I, Messenger of Allah.' Whereupon the Messenger instructed him to return the chick immediately.

35.3 A Kindness to the Old and Young

He was very kind and understanding with little children in an age when people thought the whip was the best way to bring them up. He used to joke with them, put the little ones on his knee and kiss them. He loved his two grandsons, Hasan and Husayn, with deep paternal devotion. When they were very young, they used to climb over his back while he was. praying, and he would either carry them and continue to pray or put them down gently and continue his prayers.

One day he passed by the house of his servant, Anas ibn Malik, and found Anas' little brother looking miserable and depressed. When he asked what the matter was, he was informed that the little boy had been in this mood ever since his little bird died. When the little boy came back again, Muhammadﷺ said, 'Abu 'Umayr, what did the little bird do?' whereupon the boy burst out laughing and snapped out of his misery.

(The phrasing of the Prophet's question in Arabic has a very subtle humour. It begins by a solemn address and ends in an anticlimax. Thus the Messenger taught him to accept life and death.)

Just as he was kind and understanding to the young, he was most kind and reverential to the old. The holy verses say,

And bend your wing humbly down to them, out of mercy,
and say, "My Lord, have mercy upon them,
as they have brought me up when little." (17:24)

In an age when women were considered inferior (by Romans and Arabs), and that it was beneath a man's dignity to love them, the Messenger insisted again and again that each man should be good to his womenfolk.

In the very last talk he gave, his farewell speech, he charged men to be just and kind in dealing with women.

To the treatment of servants and slaves he gave particular care.

The treatment of orphans has very powerful and merciful legislation in the Qur'an, but in addition to this the Messenger used to say, 'He who brings up an orphan has earned his place in Paradise.' Orphans are not only to be treated kindly, but to be educated, guided, and treated as one would like one's own children to be treated should one pass away.

35.4 Kindness to Enemies

To be kind to the weak is a characteristic found in most human beings, it is in harmony with human nature, but to be kind to one's enemies is a trait few men possess. The Messenger possessed this characteristic to a surprising degree. He was deeply concerned when people denied his message, not because it had any reflection on him, but because they were injuring themselves and jeopardising their immortal souls by rejecting the word of Allah. A great many people denied, and in consequence he was often sad and thoughtful, mourning for their future. The Qur'an gently admonished him more than once for his compassion and over concern for the erring. The Holy verses say:

Perchance you will destroy yourself of grief lest they do not believe. Should We wish it, We could send down a token from heaven that would keep their necks bent in submission. (26:3:41)

It is Allah alone who can grant the gift of faith; nevertheless the Messenger felt very sorry for those who were deprived of this gift. They called him a liar, a sorcerer, a madman, while he mourned out of pity for them.

When the Muslims were given permission to fight those who had persecuted them for their religion, and the Messenger saw his men hard-pressed, one to three or four, and being killed by the polytheists at the battle of Uhud, people urged him to curse the enemy, but he answered, 'I was not sent to curse.' Instead he said (with his face wounded and his men dying on the battlefield), 'My Lord, forgive my people for they do not know.'

When Thumama ibn Athal of Yamama entered into Islam, he swore that he would not send one grain of wheat to Makka unless the Messenger ordered it. The Makkans lived by trade, their land could produce no wheat. The wheat of Yamama was a vital article of food for them, so they wrote to the Messenger to bid Thumama sell wheat to them.

It was these same Makkans who had plotted for years against the Messenger and compelled him and his followers to leave Makka; it was these same Makkans who had made an economic and social boycott against him and his tribe for three years, so that he had to live in the mountains in semi- starvation, putting stones in his waistband to quell the pains of hunger. At last, after Islam spread and the Muslims had power in Madina, Muhammadﷺ was in a position to return to the Makkans some of their own treatment, but what did he do? He wrote to Thumama asking him to sell his wheat to them.

When the tribe of Banu Kilab, Christian Bedouins who lived on the borders of Madina, were making preparations to raid the city, the

Messenger sent people to them to call them to Islam and teach them that raids were against Divine decree. These emissaries were warriors as well as teachers for the tribes respected the word of no man who could not carry a sword as well as a book.

Before they left the Messenger gave them the instructions he gave all such armed forces. He charged them to beware of using treachery or betrayal, adding to be careful not to kill women, children, old men, the sick, lame or blind, not to pull down houses, or burn palms or fruit-bearing trees, and not to injure the people's means of subsistence in any way. Thus mercy rules, even in war.

One aspect of mercy is tolerance. Muhammad⁕ was most tolerant to all people and made every effort to instil this quality in his followers. He charged them to be particularly good to the People of the Book (Jews and Christians) and never to try and lure a man away from his religion.

35.5 Tolerance

In an age when persecution for the sake of religion was common in the world all around him, we find the Messenger giving the Christian monks of St. Catherine in Sinai a promise of protection and exemption from taxes. A Christian woman may marry a Muslim and retain her faith if she so desires. Islam has to come willingly from the heart or not at all.

The enemies of Islam tried more than once to assassinate the Messenger. It was only fair that such assassins be killed, but when they were caught and brought before him, the Messenger made them promise not to make the attempt again, then set them free.

He taught 'A'isha to pray, 'My Lord, Thou art the Pardoning, Thou lovest those who pardon, so pardon me.' For to pardon is an aspect of His mercy.

The holy verses say,

'The mercy of Allah is close by the gracious. (7:56
and also:

When those who believe Our words come to you, say,
"Peace be upon you. Your Lord has undertaken mercy upon Himself.
If any of you does wrong in ignorance,
then repents after it and reforms,
He is the Merciful, the Forgiving. (6:54)

CHAPTER THIRTY-SIX

36.1 Muhammad☙ Falls Ill

Muhammad☙ fell ill. He had never been seriously ill before, for he lived a life that discouraged illness. He ate sparingly of food, of a simple nature, mostly dry bread, a few dates or a little milk. Occasionally he ate honey which he liked. He never overate and always advised people to undereat rather than overeat. He washed five times a day for prayer and wore simple clothes.

The Muslims were bewildered. They had never seen Muhammad☙ ill before or giving in to a physical need. Consequently Usama's army did not move, but waited on the outskirts of the city to be reassured that all was well.

On the first day of his illness when he was still able to move about, Muhammad☙ went to visit the graves, taking only his servant, Abu Muwayhiba, with him.

36.2 The Visit to the Graves

He said to him, 'Abu Muwayhiba, I was ordered to pray for forgiveness for these people.' When he approached the graves, he said, 'Peace unto you, people of the graves, and joy for what you are in, and what people are in, for temptations like dark patches of the night come one after the other.'

Abu Muwayhiba relates that the Prophet said to him as they walked towards the graves, 'I was given the keys of the treasures of this world and living eternally in it and paradise after it, or the meeting with my Lord and Paradise now.'

'Bless you, Messenger of Allah,' said Abu Muwayhiba, 'choose the keys of the treasure of this world, then Paradise afterwards.'

'No, Abu Muwayhiba, I have chosen the meeting with my Lord and Paradise,' said Muhammad☙.

He did not keep the Prophet's conversation with him secret, but related it to others, but no one seems to have considered Abu Muwayhiba's words.

The next day Muhammad☙ went from house to house to visit his relations. Then he went to his wives' houses to visit them. Passing by 'A'isha's house, he found her suffering from a headache.

'Woe, my head,' she said.

And Muhammadﷺ laughed and answered, 'Me too, woe my head.' Then he called all his wives to the house of Maymuna and asked their permission to be nursed in the house of 'A'isha. They all agreed, so he went to 'A'isha's house helped by Al -'Abbas and 'Ali ibn Abi Talib, for his illness was beginning to take its toll.

For several days Muhammadﷺ suffered from fever. When it subsided, he would go to pray with his friends. When it increased, he remained at home.

He heard that some were grumbling about his giving command of the army to Usama. He had fever, so he called his wives and asked them to pour water over him from seven different wells. The fever went down, he dressed and went out to the people.

36.3 The Last Speech

After thanking Allah and praying for the dead of Uhud, he said, 'Let the mission of Usama go through. You are criticising his command as you have criticised his father's command before him. When he is worthy of it as his father was worthy of it.'

He was quiet for a moment, then spoke again. 'A slave of Allah who was asked to choose between this world and the eternal has chosen the eternal with Allah,' he said.

He did not speak for a moment after it and all listened, waiting for the rest of his words. They thought he was giving them counsel and examples as he used to do. They did not realize he was bidding them farewell, all except Abu Bakr. Abu Bakr, his closest and dearest friend, could not bear the situation and burst into tears, saying, 'Nay, let us ransom you with ourselves, our wives and children.'

Muhammadﷺ had much to tell them, and feared that Abu Bakr's emotion might move others so that they would not be able to grasp with cool brains what he had to say. So he made a gesture to him with his hand, charging him to be silent. Then he began to revise the basic precepts of Islam, pointing out the temptations and pitfalls before the few hours left to him on earth expired. Towards the end he asked to have all the doors leading onto the mosque from the adjacent houses closed, except the one from Abu Bakr's house. Then he said, 'I know of no man who was a better companion to me than Abu Bakr. If I were to choose a friend among men (meaning that the Friend is Allah) I would choose Abu Bakr in companionship, faith, and brotherhood until Allah brings us together in His realm.'

Then he turned to the people and said, 'Emigrants, be good to the Supporters, for they were close to me - the refuge I sought. So extol the good in them and overlook their faults.'

The next day Muhammadﷺ was too tired to lead prayers and asked that Abu Bakr should lead prayers instead. 'A'isha, the daughter of Abu Bakr, said, 'Messenger of Allah, Abu Bakr is a sensitive man. He cries when he reads the Qur'an.' She meant that in such a situation he would cry and no one would hear anything, but Muhammadﷺ insisted.

36.4 Abu Bakr Leads Prayers

One day Abu Bakr was absent, so 'Umar ibn Al-Khattab led prayers instead. Muhammadﷺ, whose house was near the mosque, heard him and said, 'Where is Abu Bakr? Nay, Allah and the Muslims will resent this.'

Muhammadﷺ led his people to what was good for them by example and suggestion and not by command. He knew how noble and true Abu Bakr was, and that he was the only man who could deal with the perilous circumstances that the nascent Muslim nation would have to face after his death. He was not deceived by Abu Bakr's gentle exterior and meek, conciliatory ways. He knew that behind that gentle exterior there was a will of steel, a deep brooding mind, and infinite faith. But Muhammadﷺ would not command them directly to let Abu Bakr be the Khalif after him (the Qur'an decrees that the affairs of Muslims are settled by consultation among themselves) but suggested it to them in different ways - by letting him lead prayers, by letting him head the pilgrims to Makka, and by praising him as the best companion he ever had.

36.5 Fatima, the Prophet's Daughter, Visits Him

Fatima, Muhammadﷺ's only living child, used to visit him every day during his illness. He always rose to greet her and gave her the most comfortable place. 'A'isha saw her crying beside him, then she saw her laugh immediately afterwards. When she was alone with her, she asked her what had made her cry, then what had made her laugh immediately afterwards, and she said, 'I am not to betray the confidence of the Messenger of Allah.'

After Muhammadﷺ had passed away, she explained to 'A'isha. She had cried because he told her he would be collected to Allah in this illness, then she laughed when he told her she would be the first of his family to join him. Six months later Fatima had also passed away.

Muhammadﷺ suffered patiently during this fever. Seeing him in this condition, Fatima cried, 'Oh, grief, my father.'

'No, there shall be no more grief for your father from now on,' he answered. He meant that once he left this world of cares and sorrow he would never suffer again.

36.6 The Writ

One day during this illness when his Companions had gathered around him, as if afraid for them, Muhammadﷺ said, 'Give me pen and ink and I shall write for you what would make you never go astray.'

Some of them hurried to do so, but others, among them 'Umar, said that the Prophet was very ill and that the Book of Allah sufficed.

When Muhammadﷺ saw their dissension, he said, 'Leave me now, it is not meet that people dispute in the presence of their prophet.'

After he passed away some expressed their regret at this lost opportunity, while 'Umar remained sure that this was right since the Holy Book mentioned everything. He was referring to the verse:

And we have neglected nothing in the Book. (6:38)

36.7 Disposing of Last Possessions

When Muhammadﷺ fell ill, all he had with him were seven dinars, and he asked his family to give them away. They were so preoccupied nursing him that they forgot all about them. One day when the fever had abated, he asked what they had done with the seven dinars. 'A'isha said that she still had them. He asked her to bring them to him, then holding the seven dinars in his hand, he said, 'What would Muhammadﷺ do if he met His Lord and this was with him?' Then he gave them away.

36.8 The Last Prayer

On the last day, Muhammadﷺ had slept a quiet sleep. The fever had abated to the extent that he was allowed to go out to take leave of his Companions for the last time. He went out to attend the dawn prayers, leaning on 'Ali ibn Abi Talib and Al-Fadl ibn Al-'Abbas. When people saw he was better, their hearts leapt for joy for they loved him dearly. They made way and could hardly keep their places, but he made a sign to them to attend to their prayers. Abu Bakr, who was leading the prayers, sensed how suddenly the people were overjoyed and how they made way and realized it could be for no one but Muhammad. He was about to leave his place and allow Muhammad to lead the prayer, but Muhammad put his hand on his arm to detain him and quietly sat beside him to pray.

When prayers were terminated, he spoke to the people, 'The fire is stirred high and temptations come like dark patches of the night. I have not allowed you except what the Qur'an allows, and I have not forbidden you except what the Qur'an forbids.' He also said, 'After me you will differ much. Whatever agrees with the Qur'an is from me; whatever differs from the Qur'an is not from me.'

The Muslims gathered around their Messenger, all so happy to see him better, and Usama son of Zayd came and asked permission for the army to start out on its mission. Abu Bakr asked permission to go to his home on the outskirts of the city, and all the people returned to their homes optimistic and in good spirits. But their happiness did not last long, for the Prophet's revival was only long enough to allow him to see his Companions before he left. He began to feel weaker and weaker every moment and knew that he had only a few hours to live. When the fever was high, he put his hand in a bowl of cool water and wiped his forehead. He said, 'My Lord, help me bear the pangs of death.' And his last words were in answer to a question unheard by those around him. They were, 'Nay, the Eternal Companion in Paradise.'

36.9 The Messenger Passes Away

Muhammad, who only a few hours before was so alive, so perspicacious, was gone. People heard women crying and wailing, but they were stunned. This could not be. Only a few hours before he was among them, admonishing them, telling them not to forget. Could he be gone forever. Impossible! A spirit so strong cannot, does not, die. They stood bewildered, not knowing what to think.

36.10 'Umar's Reaction

'Umar ibn Al-Khattab stood brandishing his sword, saying he would kill anyone who told him that Muhammad was dead. He said to the bewildered crowd that the Prophet had gone to speak to his Lord and would soon be back to punish those who said he was dead. 'Umar ibn Al-Khattab was a most powerful personality, a formidable man, courageous and indomitable, just and severe. But this great man had found in Muhammadﷺ an even greater spirit, greater vision, greater justice tempered by mercy, and greater will-power and perseverance for the sake of truth. For seventeen years 'Umar had bowed to him in love and esteem, for nothing else could control the dauntless 'Umar; seventeen years he had fought under his banner and struggled by his side to uphold the word of Allah. Now he could not face the fact that Muhammadﷺ was dead - the leader like no other, the king like no other, the friend like no other. 'Umar, this brave man who had faced so many adversaries, overcome so many hardships, could not face this one fact because it was a matter of the heart. He had loved Muhammadﷺ dearly and, as he did everything else, passionately. Now he was ready to kill any man who told him Muhammadﷺ was no more. As a shield to his heart against this terrible reality, 'Umar had invented the idea that Muhammadﷺ would consult his Lord and then return to them. Many of the men believed him for they felt the same, but the women inside Muhammadﷺ's house continued to cry and moan.

According to material fact, 'Umar was mistaken, but according to higher truth he was not far wrong. The spirit does not die. Muhammadﷺ was more alive, more happy, and more free than he ever was in this world of cares, but to mortal men living in this world of cares he was gone, separated forever by impassable barriers.

36.11 Abu Bakr Takes Matters into His Hands

Hearing the appalling grief, Abu Bakr hurried back from his house in Al- Sunh. 'Umar was talking to the people, saying that only hypocrites said that the Messenger of Allah was dead. He did not stop to listen but hurried to his daughter's house where Muhammadﷺ lay. He asked permission to enter, but all were so woe begone there was no one to give him permission or refuse it. He went to Muhammadﷺ and uncovered his face. Bending over him, he kissed him, saying, 'How good you were alive, and how good you look, even in death.' Then he covered his beloved face again and went out to the people.

From that moment the great and terrible responsibility of carrying the banner of Islam fell upon the slim but steely shoulders of Abu Bakr, unofficially at first, then soon officially as the first khalif. He heard 'Umar talking and said, 'Be quiet for a moment, 'Umar, and listen.' But 'Umar would not be quiet or listen. So Abu Bakr began to address the people who flocked around him like bewildered lambs. After praising Allah and giving thanks to Him, Abu Bakr said, 'He who worshipped Muhammadﷺ, Muhammadﷺ is dead. He who worships Allah, Allah is alive, He does not die.' Then he read to them these verses from the Qur'an:

Muhammadﷺ is only a messenger whom other messengers have preceded. Should he die or get killed, would you turn on your heels? He who turns on his heels shall not harm Allah in the least, and Allah will reward the thankful. (3:144)

Upon hearing these words from the Qur'an, 'Umar fell unconscious for at last he realized that Muhammadﷺ had gone. People stood listening dumb as stone, for 'Umar's words had given them a flicker of hope. Now these verses from the Book of Truth left no doubt that he was no more. The greatest of leaders, the greatest of messengers, the most noble spirit that ever walked the earth was lost to them until the Day of Judgment.

Abu Bakr continued to read the words of the Qur'an that bring solace while they bring the terrible truth, for at that moment only the Qur'an, the word of Allah that Muhammadﷺ had taught them to love and understand could be tolerated by those bereaved hearts. The Qur'an alone could bring peace and a promise of a meeting in a world where death does not separate, where age does not make the eye grow dim with tears, and where loss does not clutch at the heart with pain.

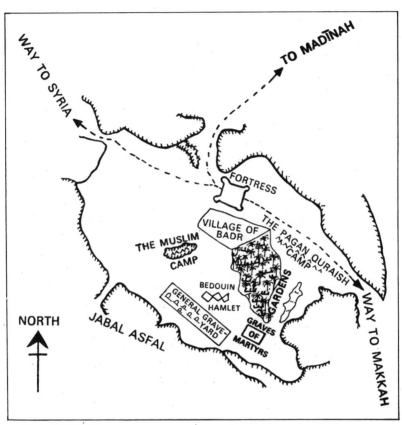

The Battlefield of Badr

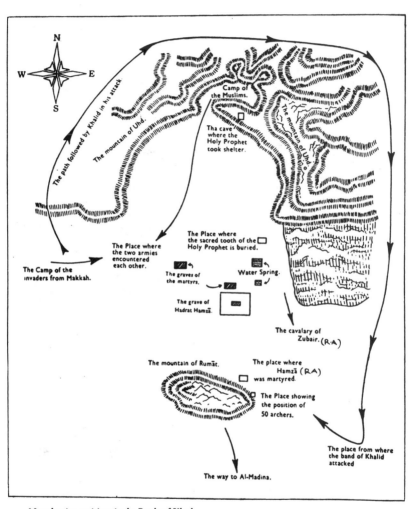

Map showing positions in the Battle of Uhud

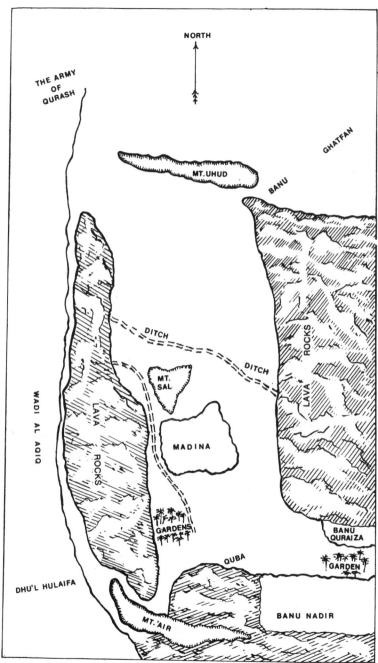

NORTH

THE ARMY
OF
QURASH

GHATFAN

MT. UHUD

BANU

WADI AL AQIQ

DITCH

DITCH

MT.
SAL

LAVA

ROCKS

LAVA

ROCKS

MADINA

GARDENS

BANU
QURAIZA

DHU'L HULAIFA

QUBA

GARDEN

MT. 'AIR

BANU NADIR

Map of The Battle of Ditch (Khandaq)